SO-ADH-082

donated by
THE WOMAN'S CLUB
OF CLEVELAND

IN MEMORIUM
OF

BILL B.
BRATTON

Austin Memorial Library

The Southern
Heirloom Garden

635.9 WEL   140510
Welch, William C.
   The southern heirloom
garden

APR 06 1998   OCT 24 2000

AUG 11 1999
DEC 15 1999

                FEB 15 2001

    MAR 16 2000

             APR 21 2001

MAY 08 2000

MAY 10 2000 DEC 10 2001
          MAY 15 2002

AUSTIN MEMORIAL LIBRARY
220 S _____
CLEVELAND, TEXAS 77327

ALSO BY WILLIAM C. WELCH

———————

Perennial Garden Color

Antique Roses for the South

A Southern Gardener's Notebook (co-author)

The Southern Heirloom Garden

William C. Welch and Greg Grant

Foreword by

THOMAS CHRISTOPHER

Introduction by

PEGGY CORNETT NEWCOMB
DIRECTOR, CENTER FOR HISTORIC PLANTS, MONTICELLO

With Contributions by

NANCY VOLKMAN, HILARY SOMERVILLE IRVIN, JAMES R. COTHRAN,
RICHARD WESTMACOTT, RUDY J. FAVRETI, AND FLORA ANN BYNUM

Taylor Publishing Company
Dallas, Texas

Copyright © 1995 William C. Welch and Greg Grant

All rights reserved.

No part of this book may be reproduced in any form—including photocopies or electronic media—without
written permission from the publisher.

Published by Taylor Publishing Company
1550 West Mockingbird Lane
Dallas, Texas 75235

Photographs on pages ii, vi, viii, and xii by William C. Welch
Designed by David Timmons

Library of Congress Cataloging-in-Publication Data

Welch, William C. (William Carlisle), 1939–
    The southern heirloom garden / William C. Welch and Greg Grant ;
  foreword by Thomas Christopher ; introduction by Peggy Cornett Newcomb ;
  with contributions by Nancy Volkman … [et al.].
        p.   cm.
    Includes bibliographical references (p. 183) and index.
    ISBN 0-87833-877-2
    1. Gardens—Southern States—History. 2. Gardens—Southern States—Styles—History.
  3. Landscape plants—Heirloom varieties—Southern States. 4. Heirloom varieties (Plants)—
  Southern States.
I. Grant, Greg. II. Title.
SB466.U65S695 1995
635.9'0975—dc20   94-49724
                                                                                      CIP

Printed in the United States of America

10 9 8 7 6 5 4 3 2 1

To all the gardeners who keep faith with the past—
and create a beautiful present.

To my girlfriends: Grandmother Emanis (Marquette
Oliver), Grandmother Ruth (Ruth Mena), Mrs. Daly
(Marie Daly), and Miss Mozelle (Mozelle Johnston).
GREG GRANT

To my dear aunts Edna, Estelle, and Bernice and to my
mother, Grandmother Dook.
WILLIAM C. WELCH

Contents

Foreword

THOMAS CHRISTOPHER

Bill Welch and Greg Grant provided my introduction to Southern gardening, and I couldn't have had better. I arrived in Central Texas in 1985, a Yankee horticulturist with no understanding of gardening in an area where a plant's tolerance for summer heat was far more important than its tolerance for winter cold, and where okra is regarded not as a vice but as a cherished inheritance. I learned a lot about such heirlooms, though, when I met Bill and Greg at a meeting of antique rose collectors—"old rose rustlers" as they are called in Texas.

Bill (Dr. Welch I called him then) immediately took me in hand, advising me on how I might better cultivate my own new garden, and taking me on drives and tramps through remote little towns like North Zulch and Industry, introducing me not only to roses I had never seen before (who in the North could even imagine the glory of a full-blown tea rose?) but also a host of other plants—perennials, annuals, shrubs, and trees—that were rooted deep into the Southern landscape and the Southern experience.

Were there any plants Bill didn't recognize? I'm sure there were, for he has been exploring and studying all the time I have known him, and he always has something new growing in his garden. His willingness to listen is characteristic of the man: Bill never sets out to impress, but his quiet scholarship is all the more impressive for that reason. And I found equally appealing the mixture of scholarship and horticultural horse sense displayed by one of Bill's students, Greg Grant, when he delivered a lecture on traditional cottage gardens

that first year. Though a graduate student at the time, Greg (like Bill) had fresh calluses on his hands. Pervading all Greg said was his affection for the quirks and personalities of the gardeners and gardens he showed us in his slides—this was Greg's childhood, his family, and his friends he was sharing.

The two of them seemed able to talk their way into any backroad garden, nearly always emerging with a "start" of some choice plant that had been a part of the local landscape for generations. Both Greg and Bill travel widely, and between the two of them, they have assembled the greatest network of green-thumbed grandmothers in the South—Bill and Greg know who the real experts on Southern garden heritage are.

My move South proved temporary, and within four years I was back North, a genuine Connecticut Yankee this time. But during my time in Texas I had learned a whole new kind of horticulture. American gardening is coming into its own at last, and the South is leading the way. It is leading because while creating new kinds of gardens it keeps faith with its past. Elsewhere in the United States gardeners may plant by whim, trying to convert their backyard into photocopies of the latest fashionable landscape. In Connecticut, for example, I have watched as neighbors imported English perennials wholesale in an attempt to turn our rocky hillsides into counterfeits of Gertrude Jekyll's England. Usually, it doesn't work, and when it does it just looks wrong.

In the South, the better gardeners know all about English gardens—for Southern gardeners have kept the plants and skills that came in with the

Oglethorpes, Percivals, and Pinckneys. But Southern gardeners have mixed that inheritance with the traditions of a half dozen other nations and peoples to create gardens unique to their region. I have found Southern gardeners always ready to try new plants and techniques—but only as an addition to the living tradition that stretches back over 350 years.

In their past Southerners have found the best guide to their future. That's the most important lesson I brought back north with me. That's why I still go back to Texas every year now, to find out what's new—and old—with Bill and Greg.

Introduction

PEGGY CORNETT NEWCOMB

Director, Center for Historic Plants, Monticello

The Southern Heirloom Garden is the collaborative effort of Dr. William C. Welch and Greg Grant—two plant enthusiasts writing on a subject they love above all others. Accomplished gardeners in their own right, Welch and Grant have joined their talents and expertise in the past on a variety of horticultural pursuits, from rose rustling to garden design. Here, they combine their intimate knowledge of plants with a historical focus to create a readable, informative, and truly genuine work.

The unifying theme is implicit in its title: *Southern*. This is a distinctly Southern history written by Southerners. And yet its appeal is wide-ranging. The first half paints a historical perspective with broad strokes, paying particular attention to the impact of many different cultures on the South. Contributed essays by Nancy Volkman, Hilary Somerville Irvin, Rudy J. Favretti, Richard Westmacott, Flora Ann Bynum, and James R. Cothran relate the regional diversity and ethnic influences upon gardening that survive to this day.

The book's second half applies this regional approach to the individual plants themselves. A mere mention of their choices—poet's laurel, sweet myrtle, pomegranate, banana shrub, cape jasmine, jujube, camellia, chinaberry—evokes the South in sight, fragrance, and flavor. Our authors tell the rich stories of the magnolia fig, of T.V. Munson and the muscadines, of crinums developed in Florida, and many more. This focus makes *The Southern Heirloom Garden* all the more important. It is the authors' use of regional documentation that is especially valuable for the student of Southern gardening during the late nineteenth century. Nursery catalogues of familiar Southern enterprises—namely Thomas Affleck's Southern Nurseries in Washington, Mississippi and Berkman's Fruitlands Nurseries in Augusta, Georgia—are reinforced by many lesser known companies. Welch and Grant carefully link a variety of catalogue citations from numerous Texas and Alabama firms, including Langdon, Mission Valley, The Austin, Pearfield, and Waldheim nurseries, to reveal the movement and popularity of plants throughout the trade, and subsequently, within the Southern garden.

Finally, this book will be read and savored not only for what it reveals of the past, but also for what it says of the present. By documenting the regional lore and historical fact and trivia behind once commonly cultivated Southern plants, the authors expose the very essence of these horticultural treasures. In so doing, they connect the efforts of Rosedown Plantation's Martha Turnball, Texas gardener Emily West de Zavala, and the beloved Southern garden writer Elizabeth Lawrence, with today's Cleo Barnwell, Sadie Gwin Blackburn, Francis Parker, J.C. Raulston, Felder Rushing, Florence Griffin, and all other ardent gardeners who "pass along" the memory behind the plants they love.

Preface

Immigrants and Native Americans: Both played their part in building our nation and both have contributed greatly to the beauty of our Southern gardens. The immigrants contributed diversity, and with it the fruits and flowers of many different cultural, economic, and religious traditions. Each immigrant brought from a distant homeland a mental picture of what a garden ought to be. Of course, new gardens were often simpler due to frontier conditions and priorities for food and shelter. But gardens also served new arrivals as links to the life they left behind. For each group brought treasured seeds and cuttings—remembrances of homes and family that were sometimes oceans away.

We sometimes overlook the traditions and contributions of Native Americans, who had lived in relative harmony with the natural environment long before colonists arrived. The impact of Native Americans on our land was important both for the physical changes they made, and for their philosophy of respect for the land. Native Americans domesticated many of the plants that are still central to the Southern garden, and in many ways created the outlines along which the Southern landscape developed.

It is the wealth of our Southern gardening heritage—a wealth both stimulating and challenging to today's garden designers and makers—that inspired this book. *The Southern Heirloom Garden* is a celebration of cultures and plants, a look at how these came together to create memorable gardens, whether they be small swept plots or large formal landscapes. We wrote this book in hope that by examining our gardening heritage we will be better equipped to create distinctive and useful new gardens and landscapes that truly reflect all of our region and its peoples.

This book has two parts: the first part explores Native American, Spanish, African-American, French, German, and English contributions to our gardens. These essays are provided by authorities well known for their scholarship and knowledge of specific cultural contributions to our Southern gardens. Some of these authorities I have known and worked with for many years, while others I met for the first time when I began searching for the best authorities on each aspect of Southern garden history.

Nancy Volkman, who writes of Native American landscape contributions, is Associate Professor in the Department of Landscape Architecture at Texas A&M University. She is the co-author of *Landscapes in History, Design and Planning in the Western Tradition*. Hilary Somerville Irvin, writing of French influences, is Senior Architectural Historian for the Vieux Carré Commission, City of New Orleans. She is responsible for historic consultation and writing as well as special projects and public relations activities for the district. Writing here about African-American gardening, Richard Westmacott is a professor in the School of Environmental Design at the University of Georgia. He is the author of *African-American Gardens and Yards in the Rural South*, published by University of Tennessee Press. Rudy J. Favretti, FASLA, who writes of the English landscape influence, is Professor Emeritus of Landscape Architecture at the University of Connecticut. He is a practicing restoration landscape architect, with commissions including Mount Vernon, Monticello, Bacon's Castle, and many others. His authorship includes *Landscapes and Gardens for Historic Buildings*, which he coauthored with his wife, Joy Putman Favretti. Flora Ann Bynum, who contributes the essay on German-Moravian influences, is Chair of the Landscape Restoration Committee, Old Salem Inc. in Winston-Salem, and is a founding member and Secretary-Treasurer of the Southern Garden History Society. She also serves as Chair of the Biannual Conference on Restoring Southern Gardens and Landscapes.

The work of these contributors was an inspiration to Greg and me as we prepared our own essays on the German and Spanish influences. Greg and I want to sincerely thank each of those individuals for the interest and enthusiasm they have brought to the project.

Although this section does not attempt to address all of the cultural contributors to our Southern landscapes and gardens, it does include a fair representation. The development of the *parterre* in Southern gardens I found to be a useful device in this regard—it has emerged as a genuinely cross-cultural concept. As an expression of geometry in the garden, it has been important to all our contributing cultures. As such, it is also important as we attempt to relate today's homes to their gardens and natural environments. The concept of the *parterre* is a fascinating subject contributed to this section by James R. Cothran, ASLA, from Atlanta, Georgia, where he is a practicing landscape architect. He has a special interest and expertise in restoring Southern gardens and is the author of *Gardens of Historic Charleston*.

Also included in the first part of *The Southern Heirloom Garden* is an essay on restoring Southern gardens. Historic garden restoration is a field in which the South may reasonably claim to lead. For we have a number of garden restorations that have set the benchmark for authenticity and excellence: Mount Vernon, Old Salem, Colonial Williamsburg, and others. Landscape architects, horticulturists, and other professionals associated with these and numerous other Southern gardens enjoy sharing information with fellow members of the Southern Garden History Society, which is headquartered in Winston-Salem, North Carolina. We sincerely appreciate the assistance and support of many of our fellow members and friends associated with the SGHS.

The second part of the book addresses the plants our ancestors used to build and enrich their gardens. Our only regret is that time and space prevented including all of the plants we and you encounter as we review the literature and examine the gardens, cemeteries, and abandoned sites that add such richness to our countryside and communities. We think of these plants as heirlooms, or living antiques, because they are tangible symbols of success for generations of Southern gardeners. Many have been lovingly handed down from generation to generation within and among the families that contribute cultural diversity and richness to our gardens. The fact that these plants have been time-tested in our Southern climate and soils over a long period makes their use in today's gardens a compelling choice. In addition to being adapted and easy to grow, many of these plants add fragrance, color, and historical importance to our gardens. We hope that the information accumulated here will help document their expanded use for restored gardens as well as encourage their rightful place in modern gardens. Homeowners will appreciate their ability to survive and flourish for long periods with less maintenance than many of the modern hybrids.

Since obtaining the plants we describe is sometimes a challenge, a source list is included. Interest in heirloom plants is definitely increasing, and we are encouraged to see availability improving for many of our favorites. Don't overlook propagating interesting plants from your own area. Many can be rooted or divided with little difficulty. Propagation information is included for most of the plants.

As we become more and more a nation of gardeners, the successful traditions and plants of our ancestors offer a unique opportunity from which to reflect and build our future. The most meaningful gardens of our past are those that reflected the lifestyle of their times and the individual style and tastes of their owners. We hope that you will find as much pleasure in remembering your own gardening heritage as we have in collecting and presenting the material included in this book. Our most sincere wish is to enrich your personal gardening experience.

Below is only a partial list of individuals to whom we are deeply indebted. Such a list is never adequate. We especially appreciate guidance and assistance from Florence Griffin of Atlanta; the Cherokee Garden Library at the Atlanta History Center, Flora Ann Bynum, Old Salem, North Carolina; Holly McGuire, our editor and liaison at Taylor Publishing Company in Dallas; and Thomas Christopher, for his capable editorial assistance and guidance as we prepared this text. Patience and support from our families and friends and coworkers provides much of the inspiration necessary for a project such as this. I especially want to thank my colleagues in Extension Horticulture at Texas A&M University and the Texas Agricultural Extension Service for their encouragement and support.

—*WCW*

Contributions

Jeff Abt
William D. Adams
Linda Askey
Max E. Austin
Gwen Barclay
Cleo Barnwell
Robert Basye
Sadie Gwin Blackburn
Joe Bradberry
Flora Ann Bynum
Thomas Christopher
Nell Crandall
Mrs. Autry Daly
Hugh Dargan
Mary Palmer Dargan
Jack Davis
Maureen Reed Detweiler
Tom Dickerson
Nancy Dyer
Joyce Ewald
Annie Lee Finch
Barry Fugatt
Edgar G. Givhan II
Jackie Grant
Florence Griffin

Glenn L. Haltom
Elizabeth Head
Madalene Hill
John and Marilee Hooper
Catherine M. Howett
William Lanier Hunt
Marge Hurt
Mozelle Johnston
Celia Jones
Nan Kelly
Ruth Knopf
Ruthie Lacey
Dan Lineberger
Lone Star Growers
Lynn Lowrey
Shingo Manard
Hazel McCoy
Mary Coit McMains
Ruth Grant Mena
Roger Meyer
Ethan A. Natalson, M.D.
Peggy C. Newcomb
Neil G. Odenwald
Scott Ogden
Marquette Emanis Oliver
Brennis Burgher O'Neal

Ben G. Page, Jr.
Libby Page
Frances Parker
Dr. Jerry Parsons
Mary Anne Pickens
Harley and Jayme Ponder
Tom Pope
Earl Puls
Pamela Ashworth Puryear
Lucas Reyes
Jack E. Rice
Donna Robilyer
Mattie Rosprim
Felder Rushing
Bob Ruth
Margaret Sharpe
Bernice Menke Smith
Neil Sperry
George R. Stritikus
Jane Symmes
Joe Tocquigny
Suzanne L. Turner
Dixie Watkins III
Maxie Wells
Dr. John H. Wiersema

Restoring Southern Gardens

 ardening is one of the oldest, and richest, of our Southern folk arts. Our pioneer ancestors began planting for pleasure as well as profit almost as soon as they stepped off the incoming ships. Actually, many elements of our Southern gardens originated even before the arrival of white and black immigrants. For a strong horticultural tradition was passed down to us by local Native Americans.

Above: French hydrangea (*Hydrangea macrophylla macrophylla*) (*Greg Grant*)

Archaeology work in progress at Monticello. (*Courtesy of Peggy Newcomb and the Thomas Jefferson Memorial Foundation.*)

So gardens are a central part of our Southern cultural heritage. Yet until recently, they were largely overlooked as historical artifacts. Generations of scholarship have been given to the preservation and restoration of Southern architecture, furniture, and other household objects. But only recently have we begun to give a similar kind of attention to the landscape outside the house.

That gardens are coming to the attention of scholars is largely due to the cutting-edge research at sites such as Mount Vernon, Monticello, and Old Salem, North Carolina. The re-emergence of original landscapes in those places is making us aware of the treasures to be won by applying techniques of historical research to our Southern landscape. At last scholars are recognizing the prominent role that gardens should play in the interpretation of regional and national history.

Viewing the landscape as an artifact helps put these concepts into perspective. Most certainly, not every old garden is worthy of restoration or a practical subject for this process, but conservation along with careful interpretation should be the goal at many more of our nation's gardens. Through careful research, professionals and volunteers can avoid merely creating "pretty pictures" and provide accurate, meaningful information for presentation to visitors and scholars interested in gaining insight into the lifestyles of our ancestors. In addition, today's gardeners can find valuable lessons in restorations, as we see how others before us solved their daily challenges.

There is also much to guard against while conducting garden restorations. Well-meaning decision makers are often misled, for example, by the natural desire to create a beautiful setting for a period structure. Other obstacles to accurate and meaningful garden restoration include current needs for convenience and practicality, as well as egocentrism, fashion, and personal preferences.

Some of the tools used by the leading professionals in the field of landscape restoration include archaeology, archival research, oral history, analysis of old plans and letters, as well as comparisons with other gardens of a similar time and place. The study of nursery catalogs and gardening periodicals of the period can be very helpful. Libraries in many Southern towns and cities include at least some collections of these sorts of materials. Out-

standing examples of historical gardening information in the South are located at the Cherokee Garden Library in Atlanta, which is the official repository for the Southern Garden History Society, the Southeastern Architectural Archives of Tulane University in New Orleans, and the Center for American History (the Barker Library) at the University of Texas at Austin.

If we view our historical gardens as artifacts, it becomes apparent that plants are the primary pieces. Among the facts we seek about plants are their first dates of introduction, when they became commonly available to gardeners of the region, and when they first appeared on the specific site we are studying. For some plants this may be relatively simple, but for others it can be very challenging. Roses, for instance, are well documented in both art and history, so that an abundance of information exists concerning their dates of introduction, breeder's name, and other relevant facts. Yet even in this case, the researcher meets with many difficulties, since over the years rose names have changed and nurserymen have sent out legions of mislabelled plants to further confuse the nomenclature. Most gardeners, meanwhile, have relied on common names, and these typically vary from region to region, providing additional opportunities for inaccuracy. The effect of all this confusion is that the identification of

The Pleasure Garden at Mount Vernon features period roses, annuals, and perennials accented by fruit trees. (*William C. Welch*)

Dwarf yaupon is a native plant used here to outline perimeters of a *parterre* garden at Rosedawn Plantation. (*Greg Grant*).

authentic period plants is something of a detective story.

Gardens such as Monticello that are offering plants and seeds true to the original species and period of emphasis in the garden are to be applauded and emulated. It is important to remember that although some plants may remain true to their type from seed, most must be propagated vegetatively by means of cuttings, grafting, or tissue culture to ensure their genetic authenticity. Of course, this ability plants have to reproduce true to type is one of their most attractive qualities to the antique collector. Period furniture or architecture is irreproducible; period plants may be cloned to yield an endless supply of absolutely authentic antiques.

Since various levels or types of garden restorations exist, it may be helpful to define and briefly discuss their characteristics.

Preservation is the least intrusive treatment of a site and mainly involves stabilization and maintenance. Challenges to the effective preservation of a site include the well-intentioned urge to clean and clear the area before it has been fully evaluated.

Rehabilitating: Making changes to address current needs such as parking, signs, and control of intrusive vegetation are considered rehabilitating a site.

Restoration should be the goal for many impor-

tant landscapes, and requires careful documentation. Restoration implies the use of archival research, including letters, plans, oral history, and interviews with neighbors. Aerial or infrared photography and archaeology are other tools that may be useful. Many critical decisions will be necessary. Among these is the selection of a time period for the garden. Although there may be situations where a very short time frame is appropriate, most successful garden restorations embrace a longer period.

Re-creation: Most sites lack sufficient documentation for a restoration. For these situations a re-creation can be a viable choice. To be most meaningful, a re-creation should reflect landscape design and plant material appropriate to the time frame chosen. Nursery catalogs and other documentation (especially materials used) for garden restorations of similar periods and locations are invaluable for establishing an authentic re-creation.

Maintenance is integral to all levels of landscape restoration. It may not be possible to utilize original pruning, mowing, and other maintenance practices for restored or re-created gardens, but maintenance should be evaluated constantly and carefully as decisions regarding design and plant materials are made.

Eclectic gardens: Many gardens designed today for

Southern heirloom plants are featured at "Cricket Court," an eclectic garden of Bill and Diane Welch in Winedale, Texas. (*William* C. *Welch*)

restored or new architecture could be classified in this category. In many instances, practicalities, expense, or owner preference may rule out a restoration or re-creation. Eclectic gardens are modern gardens, but they can still be sensitive to existing architecture. Ideally, eclectic gardens meet the needs of their current owners while reflecting upon our gardening heritage both in design and plant choices.

Though not the authentic type of historical garden, still the eclectic garden can be among the most successful of such efforts since it is likely to reflect the needs and wishes of those using the spaces. It is important, too, to remember that gardening has never been a static process. Through the ages, gardening ideas and plant materials have been continuously modified. The more one studies garden history the more it becomes apparent that borrowing from one culture by another has been in practice as long as man has been building shelters and garden spaces. It is in this sharing spirit so prevalent among most gardeners that we pass along our design concepts as well as favorite ornamental and otherwise useful plants.

Antique roses accent fences and arches surrounding "Cricket Court." (*William C. Welch*)

Accessories for the Heirloom Garden

The acquisition of appropriate and authentic garden accessories can add significantly to the interpretation and appreciation of a period landscape. Garden art, furniture, and maintenance tools help to complete the picture and add richness to the experiences of visitors.

Unfortunately, the current interest in our gardening heritage has made authentic accessories considerably less affordable. There is a brisk market now in such garden treasures as good statuary, furniture, edging materials, urns, and even once-common items like clay pots. This has driven prices upward. However, the demand for such artifacts has stimulated their reproduction in vast quantities. This is both good and bad. Where modern artisans have carefully reproduced classic garden objects, the result can be satisfying; many of the reproductions that are issued under the sanction of museums and garden or preservation societies are of especially fine quality. At the same time, other manufacturers are churning out floods of poor quality items.

An attractive bench accents the Hayward-Washington garden in Charleston, South Carolina. (*William C. Welch*)

This, of course, is very similar to the situation that existed when the historic landscapes were new: there were good furnishings and bad furnishings then, too. (Accessories will be discussed in more detail in the sections on cultural contributions to our Southern gardens.)

Referring to living animals and birds as "accessories" may be stretching the concept, but anyone who has visited a garden adorned with authentic, period livestock has been impressed with the impact of its presence. Gardeners interested in the concept of preservation of earlier species may end up by finding that this pursuit extends far beyond heirloom plants. An example might be having an appropriate breed of sheep to graze the turf in a fenced lawn area of a farmstead—if this type of maintenance was practiced during the period to which the garden is being restored. Pigeons, chickens, ducks, and other birds and fowl can add life and color to the landscape setting while helping to present an accurate picture of the lifestyle of the period. Don Shadow is actively developing "Shadows of the Past," a combination wholesale nursery and heirloom display garden/farm, in Winchester, Tennessee, which will offer a most interesting example of incorporating heirloom fowl and animals in a garden setting. Shadow Nursery has long been known for its extensive collection of heirloom and unusual woody landscape plants.

Our gardening ancestors also realized the practicality and beauty of wild bird species and encouraged their presence in the garden by providing them food and shelter. Like other garden accessories, vintage bird houses can add interest, beauty, and color to the landscape.

Whether it's the addition of one treasured and unique garden accessory or a full-scale restoration, exploring our gardening past can be an enriching experience.   —WCW

With the Three Sisters:

Native American Contributions to the Southern Landscape

NANCY VOLKMAN

In understanding our present use of the landscape we often have debts that are not widely recognized. Such is certainly the case when we consider the patterns and techniques of land use that occur in the Southeast. Most people would consider that the locations of towns and roads or the types of crops grown on farms are solely the results of European and, later, American influences. But there is a much older pattern, although largely veiled by subsequent layers of land use, that has definitely influenced

---

Above: Four-o'clock *(Mirabilis jalapa)*(*Greg Grant*)

the landscape that we see and use daily. This is the landscape pattern created over centuries by the Native American peoples, who were the first to populate the southeastern portion of the present United States.

Unfortunately it is not easy today to understand completely the type and nature of all the influences that Native American landscape alterations may have had on the modern scene. There are several reasons why this is so difficult.

First, dramatic cultural differences may make it hard for modern observers of European descent to see and appreciate those influences that do exist. In particular there is a basic philosophical difference in the way the natural world is perceived. The cultural tradition inherited from Europe sees man as master of Nature; whereas Indians traditionally viewed all creation as part of the circle of life, of which they themselves were just one small segment. In addition, Euroamericans of past generations tended to consider Indians to be a cultureless people, and thus presented an unbalanced account of their activities. Thirdly, enmity toward Native Americans by early Euroamerican settlers may have, in some cases, led to masking of their influences, lest the European be seen as having succumbed to aboriginal influences. Despite these factors, the consequences of Native American land use decisions can be documented in three important areas: in agriculture; in site and urban planning, including trail locations, which still follow, in many cases, the patterns of Indian trails; and in wild plant use.

Scientists currently believe that Native Americans first arrived in the southeastern region at least ten thousand years ago and that these first arrivals were distant descendants of peoples who had crossed the Bering Sea ice bridge from Asia at least fifteen hundred years earlier. Few remains, other than stone implements, from these early cultures referred to as the Eastern Archaic Tradition persist in the archaeological record. One factor is certain, that during the Archaic period the climate and therefore the landscape of the

Native American Contributions at a Glance

- **Roads and paths connecting communities, trade areas, and waterways.**
- **Locations of Indian villages often became cities in colonial times.**
- **Early farming of beans, squash, and corn.**
- **Use of gathered plants for food, dyeing, medicine, and ceremonial purposes.**
- **An intimate understanding of environmental processes learned over many generations.**

Southeast was quite different than that of the present historic period.

The Archaic period was followed by a number of distinct prehistoric cultural phases, the last of which is known as the Mississippian, because it was centered on that river and its tributaries. Mississippian culture, best known for its earthen mounds that bear some similarity to the stone-clad pyramids of central Mexico, formed the foundation culture from which many southeastern peoples of the historic period emerged. At the time when Europeans first came in contact with these native peoples of the southeast, the Indians numbered perhaps as many as five million. Groups such as the Creek, Choctaw, Chickasaw, and Cherokee are well known by name, but there were also equally important but less well-known groups, such as the Caddo, Houma, Alabama, and the Timucua, as well as numerous smaller communities. Among the common cultural characteristics of most of these people—likely the result of Mississippian influence—were their agricultural activities and the use of mounds for burial and to elevate structures.

Native Agriculture

Contrary to the television- and movie-generated image of Native Americans as strictly nomadic hunters and gatherers, most groups actually consisted of settled or semisettled farmers who relied upon the hunting of wild plants and animals only as a supplement to the food that they grew. This was especially true in the Southeast, where the native peoples for the most part lived on lands well suited to agriculture and in a region with a long growing season.

Throughout North America the principal crops grown by Native Americans were remarkably consistent. Although they are known to have cultivated more than one hundred and fifty domestic plants, three were paramount—corn (*Zea mays*), beans

(*Phaseolus* spp.), and squash (*Curcurbita* spp.). So important was this trio that the Iroquois Confederacy of upstate New York referred to them poetically as the "Three Sisters." This combination of crops is a particularly nutritious one, although we will never know if native farmers were fully aware of its benefits. When eaten in combination, these three vegetables provide a balanced diet, since corn is an excellent source of carbohydrates while beans and squash furnish vegetable protein. In addition, when beans and corn are consumed together, lysine, which increases the protein extractable from beans, is produced.

Several types of corn were typically grown in the Southeast, with each maturing at a slightly different time. This helped ensure that, regardless of early freezes, there would be a sufficient store of this essential crop. Squashes grown included cushaw squash, pepo squash, pumpkin, and bottle gourd. Beans, such as scarlet runner, lima, and kidney, were mainstays of the native diet.

The farming of these three crops in North America is believed to have originated in central Mexico almost ten thousand years ago, when indigenous peoples began to domesticate a wild ancestor of Indian corn. By the seventh century B.C., they also cultivated domestic forms of beans and squash. From Mexico this triad of crops appears to have been diffused northward, reaching the central Mississippi River region by about 2000 B.C. From there it likely spread eastward and north, although southeastern peoples may have acquired these crops by other means. Recent research has suggested that domestic hybrids could have been developed from locally occurring wild types. In any event, by at least one thousand years ago these three crops were grown all across North America and were prevalent in the Southeast.

Though beans, corn, and squash were central to the Native American diet, they were not the only crops grown by peoples of the Southeast. There were also a number of regionally grown crops that were quite important diet supplements. In what is now Florida, Indians are known to have used and likely cultivated a native root—the arrowroot (*Zamia* spp.)—which they used

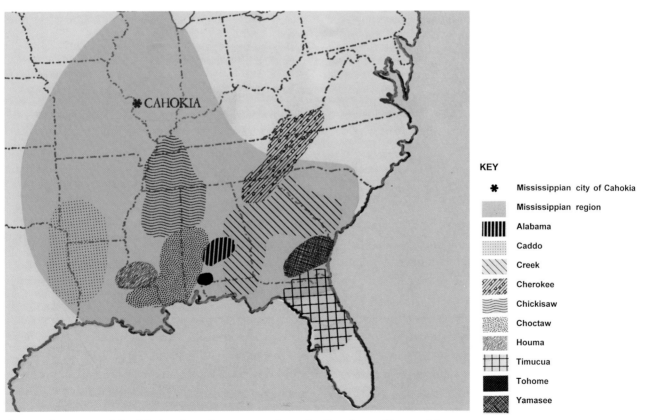

Occupation areas of the Native American groups from the Southeast discussed here are shown as they occurred at the time of European contact. (*Redrawn from data in Coe, Show, and Benson, 1986 and Waldman, 1985*)

to make bread. Sunflowers (*Helianthus annuus*) were grown for seed to augment those gathered from the wild. Giant ragweed (*Ambrosia trifida*), pokeweed (*Phytolacca americana*), and pigweed (*Amaranthus* spp.) may have been cultivated as greens. Several plants cultivated or collected as starches and for their oil included maygrass (*Phalaris caroliniana*), and chenopod (*Chenopodium berlandieri*). Of course, after European contact, Native Americans adopted many Euroamerican crops, such as peach (*Prunus persica*), watermelon (*Citrullus vulgaris*), and wheat (*Triticum* spp.) in their gardens. Tobacco (*Nicotiana rustica* and *N. tobacum*), an important non-dietary crop, was also cultivated and became one of a host of Native American plants that has been carried around the world. Some well-known dishes first concocted by Native Americans from these crops, including succotash and hoe-cakes, have become part of the modern American diet.

Of course, Indian crops were not grown in the huge, monocultural fields that now dominate American agriculture. Rather, they were grown in relatively small plots and cultivated by traditional cropping techniques. Manuring appears to have been used to a small extent, probably in the cultivation of a select group of plants. The native peoples of the Southeast practiced field rotation, either changing crops with each planting or allowing some land to lie idle for a season. Seed was often sown in raised mounds, which were used to control both soil moisture and temperature, as well as to allow easier weed and nutrient control. In a very efficient use of space and resources, corn and beans were often planted in the same holes so the corn stalks became convenient, free bean poles. The ravages of animals were checked by fencing some fields, and native farmers built elevated watch towers from which lookouts could scatter birds by making noise and flapping various materials. These techniques allowed efficient use of the land, generally without exhausting it for future plantings.

Agricultural labor was customarily provided by women, who cultivated both small house-garden plots and larger fields at the edge of villages. They also had responsibility for harvesting crops and processing them for storage. Children often assisted with the most repetitive chores, such as weeding and hoeing. Among some groups, such as the Choctaw, men did participate in planting and harvesting, but in many tribes the male

contribution was limited to land clearing.

A very important part of native agriculture was the selection of land for fields. In this they demonstrated a very sound understanding of local natural processes, an understanding acquired over centuries of trial and error. Native peoples are not known to have used fertilizers to any large extent, and so the selection of an appropriate site was essential to ensure soil fertility. They achieved this in two ways. Many groups practiced a shifting form of agriculture in which they cleared land, usually with fire or by girdling trees, and then farmed it for only a short time before moving on to a new tract. This practice was common in the coastal plain, because its soils were naturally somewhat less fertile. The second way of ensuring fertility was to farm on lowlands that were regularly reinvigorated by nutrient-laden floodwaters. This practice was also common among the peoples of the flat coastal plain, where brief inundations were common in the spring and fall. Inland, Indians found somewhat similar conditions in valleys, where over the centuries floods had deposited rich sandy loam soils. Here too farmers could rely on fertilization by natural flooding.

Native Site Planning

Site planning refers to the use and alteration of any small tract of land to serve human purposes. All peoples alter the natural landscape, to varying degrees, for their own benefit. The native peoples of the Southeast certainly made many adaptations of the land to suit their purposes; they cleared land for farms, they built towns, they made roads, and they extracted minerals and other raw materials. Most of these activities left some visible impact on the landscape and in a variety of ways influenced later Euroamerican land-use decisions.

Some of the most important and lasting planned features of the Native American landscape were roads and paths. Native American trails ranged widely and likely connected all of the continent, although most trails were created for local traffic. Commonly these trails were no more than narrow footpaths, especially in wooded areas such as the Southeast, and they typically connected to waterways that were part of the larger transportation system. These trails might be marked by stones set on end, but most often the way

The most complete visual record of Native American agriculture in the sixteenth century comes from this engraving, "The Towne of Secota," by Theodore de Bry, which illustrated Thomas Harriot's *A Briefe and True Report of the New Found Land of Virginia* (1590). This village in Virginia was ringed with extensive fields for growing corn and smaller areas for crops such as tobacco, squash, and sunflowers. (*Library of Congress*)

was indicated only by a path worn through use.

Larger paths formed part of interconnected routes that are known to have linked the eastern woodlands with the Great Plains. Two major east-to-west routes were the southern trail from northern Florida to the present area of Natchitoches, Louisiana and a route from coastal Georgia to the Mississippian capital at Cahokia in Illinois. Other major routes ran north to south. The most important and famous of these was the Great Warrior Path, which ran from Florida north into Pennsylvania. One branch of this trail headed east into Virginia and was known as the Virginia Warriors' Path. As its name suggests, one of the Warriors' Path's major purposes was for travel associated with war, but it was equally important for trade, including the trade in plants and plant products. Other important north-to-south trails were the Natchez Trace and the Occaneechi Path. So vital were trails in Native Ameri-

can land exploitation that they were among the most prominent features of traditional Indian maps. Later these routes became equally important to European settlers. Portions of the Florida to Natchitoches trail eventually formed part of a Spanish colonial route known as El Camino Real, while the Occaneechi Path is now part of the right-of-way for modern U.S. Highway 40.

Just as European settlers used Indian trails, so too did they usurp village and farmland locations, often after native communities were emptied by epidemics of European diseases. Many early colonial towns were built on or adjacent to existing native villages, thus utilizing the advanced site selection skills of indigenous peoples. The most well-known example of such a process occurred at the Aztec captial of Tenochtitlan, which was transformed into Spanish Mexico City. There many Spanish urban facilities, such as the zócalo (market plaza) and cathedral, occupied Aztec sites of similar function. Other important North American cities have also grown up on Indian sites. The city of Savannah, Georgia, was founded on the same bluff above the Savannah River as a Yamacraw Indian village. In the Southwest, some of the more picturesque urban settings, such as Santa Fe, were probably originally native pueblos. Elsewhere, as at Taos, dual cities—one Indian, one Euroamerican—came to share the same dramatic landscape.

Since many of the native peoples of the Southeast lived in settled communities, the siting and design of their towns was a very important part of their overall land use. Each group had, of course, a distinctive approach to town design, but some general characteristics did occur throughout much of the Southeast. Communities were not uniform in size, but rather formed hierarchies with the larger towns being political and social capitals. These capitals often had larger, distinctively designed buildings for meetings sometimes elevated on flat-topped mounds of earth. Town layout followed two general patterns—that of a centralized, somewhat circular form or that of a linear form, usually laid out along streams. Cherokee towns visited by early European visitors were described as following this latter pattern. Although towns were often located in woodland areas, it was just as common for them to be built in areas described as prairies, that is, large natural grasslands.

While native Southeastern towns should be considered permanent settlements, this does not mean that they were continually occupied. It was a common practice to abandon a town for a time and then return to it at a later date. This may have been due to the depletion of a regional natural resource such as the soil or wildlife, but in some cases it was also associated with warfare. Among some peoples the selection of a new leader also led to the relocation of the town.

Many Native American towns of the Southeast followed patterns originated by the Mississippian people. Their towns were built in a fairly regular pattern centered on a grouping of community buildings and open areas. The residential areas were then established in small clusters often with dwellings arranged to form a square with a plaza in the middle. In 1789, when William Bartram visited several Creek villages, he found that they had been constructed in this form with the house compounds set amidst small cultivated plots. Each house compound might be occupied by more than one family, but when a family held more than one building each was used for a different purpose, with cooking, reception, and sleeping functions allocated to different structures.

Native Use of Wild Plants

For the gathering of food and other wild materials, Native Americans relied on both hunting and plant collection. Hunting was a wide-ranging activity, for tribal hunting areas covered thousands of square miles. While most hunting strategies relied on intelligence and skill, they also involved manipulation of the landscape. An intimate knowledge of the landscape and how it related to animal behavior was essential, of course, if hunters were to locate the desired prey efficiently. But native peoples also modified the landscape to aid the hunt. Hunters commonly set fires to stampede animals, and this often dramatically changed regional landscapes. For example, some scientists have speculated that the isolated prairie pockets originally found in northern Alabama may have been generated through hunters' repeated burning or clearing of these areas.

The use of wild plants was also vital in the economy of the Southeastern Native Americans. In fact, with our present limited knowledge from ethnobotanical sources, it is not always clear whether certain crops were actually cultivated in a formal manner or merely collected from wild sources, or if wild sources were managed but not actually planted in a form of quasi-agriculture. In this last method, the crop area management would be limited to keeping out competing woody plants.

Gathered plants served as fuel, food, medicine, as dye-stuffs, and for ceremonial uses including smoking. The plants used for fuel were primarily trees, and much of what the Indians took was probably dead wood collected in the forest. In heavily populated areas near major towns, actual wood cutting would have occurred and perhaps led to local deforestation. An extreme example of this, based upon archaeological information, occurred at the large Mississippian community of Cahokia. There scientists estimate that all standing woody vegetation had been cleared for a radius of three miles around the city. During the historic period, after Native Americans acquired European livestock, par-

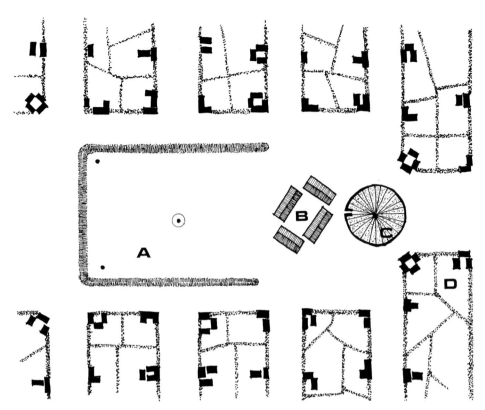

William Bartram's plan of an unnamed Upper Creek village (redrawn from Bartram, 1853). Within each family plot (D) are several structures, each serving a different purpose, whether for dwelling, cooking, or storage. Also within plots, "each inhabitant in the town incloses a garden spot adjoining his house, where he plants corn, rice, squashes, etc., which, by early planting and close attention, affords an earlier supply [of produce]. . . ." (40-41). The Chunky Yard (A) is a playing field, while the Square (B) and Rotunda (C) are public meeting areas.

ticularly swine, forest depletion and extension of grasslands became common throughout the Southeast, due to the rooting and grazing habits of these animals. Of course, trees were also harvested to use as materials for buildings and equipment. For example, native craftsmen often burned the centers of tulip tree (*Liriodendron tulipfera*) trunks to make canoes.

The range of wild plants collected for food was extensive and included all parts of plants: fruits, twigs and branches, nuts, roots, and tubers, and leaves. The entire forest provided fruits to supplement farm crops. Persimmons (*Diospyros virgiana*), wild grapes (*Vitis rotundifolia* and *V. cinerea*), maypop (*Passiflora incarnata*), rose hips (*Rosa* spp.), and a variety of berries (*Vaccinium*, *Rubus*, and *Sambucus* spp.) were all widely collected. Popular nuts included those of several hickories (*Carya tomentosa* and *C. aquatica*, for example), pecans, and acorns from white oaks, those without the bitter taste produced by high tannin levels, as in overcup oak (*Quercus lyrata*) and live oak (*Q. virginiana*).

Branches and twigs formed many useful products. Twigs of alternate-leaved dogwood (*Cornus alterniflora*) were made into pipestems, branches from witchhazel

(*Hamamelis virginiana*) furnished flexible bows, and thick branches of sheep laurel (*Kalmia angustifolia*) could be made into spoons. Roots and tubers were collected for use as both food and dyes. Greenbriar (*Smilax* spp.) was ground to make starch for breads. Jerusalem artichokes (*Helianthus tuberosa*), which contained high levels of fructose, were cooked in a variety of ways. Leaves such as those of pokeberry (*Phytolacca americana*) were eaten as greens just as they are today. This is just a sample of the beneficial uses Native Americans made of foodstuffs provided by the natural supermarket of the Southeastern forests and grasslands.

An equally extensive list of plants made up the native pharmacopoeia. Some very important medical materials include Indian pink (*Spigelia marlandia*), Virginia snake root (*Aristolochia serpentaria*), yarrow (*Achillea* spp.), wild onion (*Allium canadense*), dogbane (*Apocyum cannabinum*), beebalm (*Monarda fistulosa*), New Jersey tea (*Ceanothus americus*), blue flag iris (*Iris versicolor*), and witchhazel (*Hamamelis* spp.). The exact application of these plants varied regionally, but each was considered an important remedy for at least one condition or disease. Yarrow was used to stop coughing and bleeding in the throat, wild onion and beebalm were applied topically as treatment for bee stings, infusions of New Jersey tea were ingested to cure stomach afflictions, and witchhazel bark was ground to produce an ointment for piles and external tumors. Some native remedies were adopted during colonial times by Europeans. Indian pink root, for example, was used by colonists and Indians alike to purge parasitic worms from children. The English experimented with Virginia snake root, used by Native Americans as a diaphoretic, to cure plague.

Naturally occurring plants were also an important source of color for garments, basketry, ornaments, and body decorations, including hair dyes. Smooth sumac (*Rhus glabra*) leaves and bark produced a yellow dye, as did the leaves of milkweeds (*Asclepias* spp.) and onion skins. Yarrow produced a deep cream, black walnuts (*Juglans nigra*) a deep brown, and sassafras (*Sassafras albidum*) twigs and leaves a tan dye. A celery-green color could be extracted from the leaves of bindweed (*Convovulus* spp.). Vibrant red-oranges came from madder (*Rubia tinctorium*) and pokeberries.

Plants played an important part in ceremonial life as well. The best known use is that of a number of plants, especially tobacco, smoked in ceremonial pipes, often referred to in modern usage as "peace pipes." Ginseng (*Panax quinquefolium*), widely used as a herb, also was included in religious ceremonies for, like Asians, Native Americans found special meaning in these roots that often took on human form. Eastern red cedar (*Juniperus virginiana*) was burned as an incense in purification rituals.

It is interesting to note that very little is known about Native American ornamental plant use. Plant themes and patterns were often used in the decoration of clothing and household utensils, but there is no indication that the ornamental garden, so common in Europe and Asia, was part of the native landscape. This may seem surprising given the Native American affinity for nature, but it is a pattern that is common in other parts of the world where people live in close proximity to wild landscapes. When the entire landscape appears as a lush garden, then there is no need to capture it in a small patch next to one's house. The garden as an artificial world of nature is a fabrication of people who have become separated from the natural world. As such, it had little appeal for the Southeast's first inhabitants.

The North America that Europeans "discovered" in 1492 and conquered over the next centuries was not an empty canvas. Rather, it had already been transformed from a natural landscape into an intricate cultural landscape, with overlays from thousands of years' occupation by Native Americans. In many instances, Indian landscape modifications were relatively simple and nonintrusive, such as buffalo-hunting practices in which kills were often large but rare occurrences. Locally, though, activities such as collecting wood for fuel or farming may have altered the landscape in notable and permanent ways.

In general, Native American lifeways demonstrated a thorough and intimate understanding of environmental process learned over many generations. It is ironic that so much of this sound environmentally based knowledge was not only put aside by European settlers, but actually disparaged as superstitious or nonscientific. In our now more environmentally sensitive era, the positive benefits of simple practices are being recognized once again. Although much native wisdom remains with us in the routes we travel and the foods we eat, we can only regret how much landscape knowledge and practice of great value has been lost.

Bibliography

Bartram, William. "Observations on the Creek and Cherokee Indians, 1789" in *Transactions of the American Ethnological Society* Vol. 3, Part 1, 1853.

Coe, Michael, Dean Snow, and Elizabeth Benson. *Atlas of Ancient America.* New York: Facts on File, 1986.

Erichsen-Brown, Charlotte. *Medicinal and Other Uses of North American Plants.* New York: Dover Publications, 1989.

Fagan, Brian M. *The Great Journey: The Peopling of Ancient America.* New York: Thames and Hudson, 1987.

Harriot, Thomas. *A Briefe and True Report of the New Found Land of Virginia.* 1590. New York: Dover Publications, 1972.

Hulbert, Archer Butler. *Historic Highways of America, Volume 2: Indian Thoroughfares.* 1905. New York: AMS Press, 1971.

Hurt, R. Douglas. *Indian Agriculture in America: Prehistory to the Present.* Lawrence, Kansas: University of Kansas Press, 1987.

Kindscher, Kelly. *Medicinal Wild Plants of the Prairie: An Ethnobotanical Guide*. Lawrence, Kansas: University of Kansas Press, 1992.

McCary, Ben C. *Indians in Seventeenth-Century Virginia*. Charlottesville: University of Virginia Press, 1957.

Meyer, William E. "Indian Trails of the Southeast." *Forty-second Annual Report of the Bureau of American Ethnology to the Secretary of the Smithsonian Institution, 1924–1925*. Washington, D.C.: U.S. Government Printing Office, 1928.

Office of Indian Affairs. *Notes on the Primitive Agriculture of the Indians*. 1921. Unpublished manuscript, Ayers Collection, Newberry Library.

Scarry, C. Margaret, ed. *Foraging and Farming in the Eastern Woodlands*. Gainesville, Florida: University Press of Florida, 1993.

Waldman, Carl. *Atlas of the North American Indian*. New York: Facts on File, 1985.

Wood, Peter H., Gregory A. Waselkov, and M. Thomas Hatley, eds. *Powhatan's Mantle*. Lincoln, Nebraska: University of Nebraska Press, 1989.

Arches and Arches of Roses:

The Spanish Influence

WILLIAM C. WELCH

Gardeners may feel fortunate that it was Spanish ships which first found the way from Europe to the southern part of North America. For Spain is a country with an old and especially rich horticultural tradition. The conquistadors who spread Spanish colonies throughout the Americas are remembered today chiefly for their ruthless courage—historians rarely choose to

Above: 'Général Jacqueminot' (*Greg Grant*)

remember the gentler arts the Spanish brought with them. Yet the Spanish were expert gardeners and had a history of adapting freely from other cultures. Moreover, because they travelled so widely, establishing colonies in all of our Gulf Coast states, their influence on American colonial gardening was unusually pervasive and remains strong in the South to this day.

However, it is important to remember, as Herman J. Viola ststes in his introduction to *Seeds of Change* (1991), that when Columbus discovered America in 1492, what he "really discovered was…another old world, one long populated by numerous and diverse peoples with cultures as distinct, vibrant, and worthy as any to be found in Europe…. [W]hat Columbus did in 1492 was to link two old worlds, thereby creating one new world." In fact, some modern authors treat Columbus' landing not as a beginning but as a disastrous end to Native American culture.

The Spanish Influence in Mexico

Texas was claimed as a part of Northern Mexico when the Spanish domination of the American mainland began with Hernando Cortez's defeat of the Aztecs in 1521. From central Mexico the Spanish influence spread north and westward through Texas, into New Mexico, Arizona, and California, and to the east through Florida. The motives for this steady expansion of territory were various, and included a desire to Christianize the native peoples, discover minerals, agricultural land and other raw materials, as well as to protect established settlements from raids by more distant native groups. The relative importance of each of these

Spanish Contributions at a Glance

- **Open plazas often found in our towns and cities.**
- **Land planning, such as land grants, presidios, missions, villas, or pueblos.**
- **Four-part garden plans that focused on a central water feature.**
- **Structures built for shade.**
- **Symmetrical plans (formal) often contrasted with asymmetrical (informal) plantings.**
- **Intensely developed and utilized small garden spaces.**
- **Boldly contrasting colors for garden materials with earth-tone backgrounds. Use of many fragrant and colorful plants. Addition of many garden plants now considered mainstays in our gardens.**
- **Use of water as a garden feature. Often this is functional as well as ornamental (as with wells).**
- **Use of walls to enclose garden spaces.**
- **Ornamental tiles used for wall and pool adornment.**

motives can be debated; recent critics, however, make a strong case that the major objective was to enrich the Spanish crown and the colonists.

Nevertheless, it is undeniable that faith played a crucial role in the colonization process, for priests were regularly at the forefront. This was true from the beginning. Soon after Cortez's conquest of Mexico, the Spanish government sent twelve missionaries to the New World to work among the native peoples. Among these twelve was Toribio de Motolinia, who recorded his five years of observations and experiences in Mexico (a period lasting from 1536 to 1541) in a book: the *History of the Indians of New Spain*. This furnishes an invaluable insight into the culture of the Aztecs and other Indians who lived in an area roughly between Veracruz and what we now know as Mexico City. With regard to the Indians' use of plants, he noted:

The Indians celebrate the feasts of the Lord, of Our Lady and the principal Patron Saints of the town with much rejoicing and solemnity. They decorate their churches very tastefully with what ornaments they are able to get, and their lack of tapestry they make up for with tree branches, flowers, reed mace and sedge. These they spread on the ground, together with leaves of mint which has thrived incredibly in this land. Where a procession is to pass they erect numerous triumphal arches made of roses and adorned with trimmings and garlands of the same flowers. The wreaths of flowers they fashion are very attractive. This is the reason why in this land everybody is bent on having rose-gardens. It has happened that, if they have no roses, they sent ten or

Mission Desierto de los Leones, near Mexico City, built in 1606 by the Carmelites. (Actually known as the Carmelitas Descalzos, the "Barefoot Carmelites.") (*William C. Welch*)

twelve leagues for them to the towns of the warm climate where roses are nearly always in bloom and have a very sweet odor.

In addition to revealing a degree of gardening sophistication among the Indians of Mexico, this passage is provocative for rose historians, because of its reference to what seem to have been everblooming roses. Roses of this type are Asian in origin, and are not native to the Americas. It wasn't until the eighteenth century that such roses came to Europe from China—how then could they have been established in Mexico a couple of centuries earlier?

In another passage of his book Motolinia describes decorations for the Feast of Corpus Christi in 1538:

Down the two side lanes, which were twenty-five feet in width, passed all the people, and their number in this city and province is not small. The space for the procession was marked off by medium-sized arches, set about nine feet apart. There were by actual count one thousand and sixty-eight arches of this kind. Because this was something worthy of note and admiration three Spaniards and many others counted the arches. All the arches were covered with roses and flowers in dif-

ferent colors and shapes. It was figured that each arch had a carga and a half [a carga is approximately 4 ⅔ bushels]. Adding to these the roses that were in the chapels, on the triumphal arches, and on the sixty-six other small arches, together with those that the people had on their person and in their hands, the total amount of flowers was two thousand cargas. About a fifth part of the flowers seemed to be carnations. These came from Castile and have multiplied incredibly. The bushes are much larger than in Spain and they bear flowers all year round. . . .

Early Settlement in Florida, Louisiana, Alabama, and Texas

The oldest continuously populated community of European descent in the United States is St. Augustine, Florida, which was established in 1565 as an urban setting for a colony of more than 2500 people. The original plan for the town was military in character, since St. Augustine was established to provide refuge and protection during siege. Agriculture was a secondary function, and military considerations actually limited planting in the immediate vicinity of the town. Thus, the planners allowed few tall trees or other plant masses in St. Augustine.

Individual properties typically included 6700 square feet, and the defining element of these landscapes was the 5 ½-foot-tall whitewashed walls of vertical planks or tabby (a mixture of oyster shells, lime, and sea water) that were raised around the perimeter to enclose the areas as expansive courtyards. Planting was utilitarian: the tabby walls were often topped with prickly pear (*Opuntia*) to serve as a natural sort of razor wire. *Yucca foliosa*, whose spine-tipped leaves have earned it the common name of Spanish-dagger, was also used for fencing. Within the walled compounds were houses with windows to the South and solid walls to the North. The concept of zero lot lines was utilized throughout.

Arbors covered with grapes provided cooling shade within the courts, and archaeologists' excavations have uncovered wells in many of the original yards. Some of these featured shafts fashioned from shipping barrels, while in others coquina (a native stone) was used as a lining and to make walls around the wellhead. Figs, onions, melons, citrus, peaches, grapes, mulberries, lemons, sour orange, pomegranates, and sweet orange trees were commonly planted within the walled spaces.

Louisiana was under Spanish rule from 1769 to 1803, although little remains or is known of its direct influence on the gardens and plant materials of the area. It is thought that the extensive use of container plants in French Quarter courtyards may have its origins with the Spanish. The use of citrus trees, although enthusiastically adopted by French settlers, seems likely to have been a Spanish contribution originally. Early records refer to the planting of orange trees on the levees of New Orleans.

There are also, in the records of New Orleans' Spanish period, references to roof gardens. These were made possible by a safety measure adopted after the catastrophic fires of 1789 and 1792: to inhibit the spread of fires, the city authorities required thereafter that all walls be brick and the roofs be flat and tiled. Because flat roofs almost always leak in areas of high rainfall (such as New Orleans), however, the new building code proved unenforceable in the long run, and the roof gardens didn't persist. Nor did the Spanish colonial administration; it ended in 1803, and because the French

influence on local culture was overwhelming, evidences of Spanish gardening, though intriguing, are hard to trace.

New Orleans has always given due credit to its Spanish roots—far less well known is the role that Spanish colonists played in opening up Alabama. In fact, this state was also under Spanish control for a considerable period. It had been claimed by the French from 1702–1763, and then the English from 1763–1782, but for 31 years immediately thereafter (from 1782–1813) Alabama was ruled by a Spanish administration seated in Mobile.

According to research by Dr. Ed Givhan, a physician and historian from Montgomery, Alabama, the interior courtyards that are a traditional feature of older houses in Mobile were a relic of this period. Mobile remained a small town through the Spanish period— Dr. Givhan calculates that when the Spanish left in 1813, its total population was less than 1000. But one clue as to the persistence of Spanish influence is the fact that the city's population still remains 45 percent Roman Catholic, and this in a state that is approximately 96 percent Protestant.

Texas Mission Gardens

Spanish domination lasted longer in Texas than any other of our Southern states, and it is here that the finest examples of Spanish colonial-era architecture survive. These survivals are chiefly mission buildings that Spanish priests erected as centers for the Christianization of the natives; these have been carefully restored in San Antonio and other sites in South Texas.

Built of native stone, these South Texas missions represented a spectacular architectural achievement for the period, especially when one considers that they were built largely by Indian labor supervised only by priests. Unfortunately, although the missions also penetrated into East Texas, there they were built of wood and of these little remains.

From the garden historian's point of view, the mission restorations remain distinctly incomplete. To date, there has been very little research or restoration of the gardens that tradition says must have accompanied these structures.

Some tantalizing glimpses come from a preliminary study of Mission San Juan conducted by Dr.

The Bandera, Texas courtyard garden of Mr. and Mrs. Clyde Ikins, reflecting the Spanish influence, especially in its water feature. (*Greg Grant*)

Rosalind Z. Rock, Park Historian, for the San Antonio Missions National Historical Park in February, 1993. She found that intensive farming methods and use of irrigation ditches characterized the Spanish colonial farming there. This, incidentally, is in strong contrast to the more typical dry land farming practiced by later settlers in Texas. Crops of Mission San Juan included corn (maize), other grains (wheat, grown little until the 1790s, and feed grain), cotton, figs, grapes, watermelon, cantaloupe, beans (a pinto type and a chickpea type most common), sugar cane, and squashes (gourds, pumpkins).

The Spanish Garden

Even if it is impossible in most cases to reconstruct specific gardens that Spanish colonists planted in the American South, it is possible to outline the shape these gardens would have taken.

Spain during its imperial period fancied itself the political successor to ancient Rome, and as a result, the Spanish imitated everything Roman, including the ancient gardens. The Roman gardens had, in turn, inherited much of their horticultural tradition from the

Roof garden in Mexico City. (*William C. Welch*)

ancient Greeks, and like them tended to associate gardens with religious rites, focusing the landscapes on sacred groves, grottoes, and temples dedicated to specific deities. The ideal Greco-Roman garden merged building with the garden by utilizing a series of covered walks, peristyles, and porticos. Daily activities took place in these courtyards which were constructed on a central axis, usually originating with the main room in the house. The garden was actually viewed from this room through the peristyle.

Water was a major focus of these gardens, even though it often had to be brought in through elaborate canal systems and aqueducts at great effort and expense. Some of these aqueducts are still in place in Spain today. Fountains, bathing pools, and wells were considered necessities for luxurious living. Mosaics depicting fish and birds sometimes adorned these water features.

As Roman civilization spread through conquest to Spain, new varieties of trees, shrubs and herbs were brought from other Roman outposts in the Orient. Pot marigolds (calendulas), snapdragons, lilies, narcissus, white and blue hyacinths, violets, pansies, roses, poppies, many vegetables and aromatic herbs came to Spain in this way. The three most popular shrubs in Roman gardens were laurel (*Laurus nobilis*), myrtle (*Myrtis communis*), and acanthus (*Acanthus mollis*).

Favorite trees included plane trees (sycamores), oaks, cypresses, peaches, cherries, and other fruits. Garlands in which fruit, flowers, and foliage intermingled were favorite decorations of the Romans. Pliny the Elder, a Roman writer of the first century A.D. who lived in Spain for a few years, described these at length in his encyclopedia, the *Natural History*. Roses were a favorite flower both for garlands and in the garden, and the types grown probably included the dog rose and autumn damask.

Vines were another Roman favorite. Grapes, ivy, and other creeping plants were often utilized to decorate pergolas and porticos. Apples were native to Italy, but the more exotic apricots, pomegranates, lemons, and oranges were highly prized imports. Plums, almonds and figs were also favorites that were cultivated early on in Spain. Chamomile, mint, thyme, oregano, and rosemary were among the extensive variety of aromatic and medicinal plants that thrive in Spain and were common to gardens there.

After the fall of Rome and an ensuing period of barbarian kingdoms, civilization returned to Spain with the Arabs, who dominated the Southern part of the Iberian peninsula for two centuries. The Arabs fostered a brilliant flowering of Islamic art in their Spanish territories, and this influenced all the inhabitants of the peninsula and remains still much in evidence today. Interestingly, the Arabs served principally as synthesizers rather than initiators. Through their conquests in the East, they had been exposed to the art of Persia, Egypt, Syria, and India, and it was with elements taken from all those traditions that they enriched the culture of Spain.

As a desert people, the Arabs had a special affection for gardens, and developed them in a Middle Eastern style of an oasis. From Egypt and Babylon, the Arabs had learned the tricks of capturing distant water sources and carrying it through aqueducts to fountains and artificial waterways with which they ornamented their palace courts. Sheltered within high, cool walls, the Spanish Arabic gardens were made lush with fragrant and flowering plants. There was considerable emphasis on shaded areas, and commonly the gardens were arranged symmetrically, with four quarters divided by two crossing paths whose intersection was marked by a fountain. Though simple, this concept has proved remarkably durable and continued to dominate Spanish garden design right through the colonial period.

From a desire to enrich the subject territories, Arab overlords energetically promoted agriculture throughout southern Spain. By the year 1253, Hispanic-Muslim farmers had planted millions of fig, olive, and other fruit trees in the province of Seville. Along with these strictly utilitarian plants, the Arabs introduced a number of ornamentals, including yellow jasmine, narcissus variegated white, yellow and green (the poet's narcissus), violets, red and yellow dianthus, scented jonquils, trumpet-shaped narcissus, red roses, *Lilium candidum*, blue iris, poppies, bean flowers, and flowers of the pomegranate.

Other garden favorites were sweet basil, lavender, orange blossoms, carnations, sweet marjoram, oleander, quince, apple trees, blackberries, carob trees, banana trees, cypress, willows, fig, thyme, and mint. All of these plants remain as fixtures of Spanish gardens today, and our use of them in the American South is at least partly a legacy of Spanish colonization.

But the Arabs' enthusiasm for plants also traced to a very active interest in medicine. Arab doctors were famous throughout the medieval world, and since most medicines were of herbal origin, the Arab physicians were probably the best plantsmen of their time. Spain became a center for the teaching of botany and medicine, and this interest continued long after the last Arab rulers were expelled in 1492. So, for example, a Sevillian physician, Simon Tovar, who died in 1596, maintained a garden of medicinal and other exotic plants in Seville. Interestingly, among his plants was the tuberose

Mission Nuestra Señora de la Purísima Concepción in San Antonio. (*Greg Grant*)

Pomegranate (**William C. Welch**)

Sour orange (**Greg Grant**)

(*Polianthes tuberosa*), a native of Mexico that is often grown in gardens in Texas and the Gulf South today. This is concrete evidence that not all the movement in garden traditions was from the mother country to the colonies, but that instead the process was one of cross-pollination.

From an American gardener's point of view, the debt to Spain, and so to Arab and Roman colleagues, is considerable. From the introductions of Spanish colonists come some of our most treasured Southern heirloom plants. Most of the plants cited above are familiar standbys; to the list we should add such familiar vegetables as asparagus, beet, cabbage, carrot, celery, cress, cucumber, eggplant, endive, lettuce, mustard, radish, spinach, okra, and turnip. Florentine irises, white lilies, and certain roses were also contributions from Spain to the New World.

Spanish Land Planning

LAND GRANTS

Certainly the most important effect that Spanish colonization has had on our modern landscape was that country's approach to land use and planning. The Spanish government maintained a consistent approach to this throughout the colonial period. The conquered territories, which were possessions of the crown, were parcelled out in large tracts—Royal or Spanish Land Grants—to individuals who performed valuable services for the crown.

Although sometimes thought of as a form of slavery because they included the grant of the population

as well as the land itself, these grants were actually more feudal in nature. Moreover in Texas, Spanish land grants were usually limited to land rights. The grantee was expected to bring in Europeans, Americans, or "mestizos" (children of European men and Indian women) to populate the land and work it as tenant farmers and ranchers.

PRESIDIOS

Presidios were military in nature and have been commonly treated as forts by historians. But on a broader scale, presidios were actually seats of government that included political as well as military offices. Usually sited on top of a hill, and next to a river or highway, presidios were built with an inward orientation. That is, the buildings faced a central plaza that was used for military drills or storage of agricultural commodities and livestock. The plaza was left unpaved and barren, although it might offer the relief of a few shade trees. Within the presidios the governor's residence often included a small courtyard garden. Although there is little documentation for presidio gardens, Spanish tradition suggests that they would have an Arabic flavor—a quartered arrangement with a central water feature. Near the presidio agricultural plots were laid out as long and narrow strips along streams.

MISSIONS

Some mention has already been made of mission gardens and architecture, but these institutions were also interesting as examples of urban planning.

Though not all alike, missions were typically arranged around a large, open central courtyard. The architectural anchor was a church, but living quarters and work rooms typically also surrounded the open court. The central open area served many purposes, and at various times might provide an overflow for church activities, or as a space for crafts and crop storage, or even as an outdoor classroom.

Villas or Pueblos

In addition to presidios and missions a third type of settlement was common during the Spanish colonial period. This was the villa or pueblo, which was a center of commerce and a residence for European settlers.

Plans for villas were detailed in the Spanish planning guidelines known as the Law of the Indies, which was established in 1512. These guidelines stated that all villas should center upon a plaza or open area. The only other open area specified was for the cemetery, or campos santos. The major objective of the 1512 law was to induce Indians to live in an orderly way and to adopt the same Christian way of life of Spanish citizens.

In 1546 under the rule of Charles V, the Council of the Indies refined the laws to further promote bringing the Indians into planned communities rather than allowing them to live in scattered mountain and wilderness communities. Under Philip II in 1573 urban planning design and guidelines were again refined, and in this new incarnation showed the influence of the ancient Roman architect and planner Vitruvius.

Today, after 350 years, the Spanish style of town planning still influences communities throughout the area of former colonization. Although the Spanish edicts were not always implemented in a humane manner, the objective was admirable: to preserve the new community members and integrate them into Spanish culture. The legacy of these urban landscapes is their sense of order and the open plazas that provide a more comfortable scale for human use in an otherwise hostile environment.

An Early Hispano-Texan Garden

A definitive description of an early Texas garden is provided by Adina de Zavala in an article published on September 2, 1934, in the *San Antonio Express*, and on December 16, 1934, in *The Dallas Morning News*. In this article the author related her memories of conversations with her grandmother, Emily West de Zavala, and of visits to the garden she had created in the early 1830s.

The de Zavala Plantation was located at Lynchburg on the San Jacinto River near the present site of the San Jacinto Monument. Lorenzo de Zavala, Emily's husband, was an early Mexican and Texan statesman and the first vice president of the Republic of Texas. Adina (the granddaughter's) recollections included the names of many roses that grew in her grandmother's garden, for roses were Emily de Zavala's favorite flower. In addition, Adina's article described borders of violets and masses of dianthus and verbenas.

Pictures of the home and garden indicate a large columned front porch of the typical East Texas house surrounded by an attractive wooden picket fence. Roses, perennials, annuals, and herbs filled the inside of the garden. Occasional hedges and borders of roses added a touch of formality to what could be described as an early Texas cottage garden. The de Zavala home and garden surely ranked among the finest of early Texas.

Bibliography

de Casa Valdes, Marquesa. *Spanish Gardens*. Trans. Antique Collectors' Club, 1987.

de Montolinia, Toribio. *History of the Indians of New Spain*. Trans. Richmond, Virginia: Academy of American Franciscan History and the William Byrd Press, 1951.

Viola, Herman, and Carolyn Margolis. *Seeds of Change: 500 Years Since Columbus*. Washington, D.C.: Smithsonian Institution Press, 1991.

'Old Blush'—the first discovered everblooming rose.
(Greg Grant)

Through the Allées:

The French Influence

HILARY SOMERVILLE IRVIN

Almost upon their arrival in the lower Mississippi valley in the eighteenth century, French settlers turned to landscape design in their effort to civilize the wilderness. Their European knowledge and precepts, however, did not always fit with the locale's flat terrain, heavy rain, heat, and humidity. Therefore, as with architecture, in which a distinctive colonial style developed, a French colonial gardening tradition soon evolved in response to the local conditions. This tradition

Above: Cape jessamine (*Gardenia jasminoides*) (*Greg Grant*)

resulted from the fusion of the French colonists' cultural heritage and social aspirations, tempered by climatic and geographic conditions and limitations.

Isolating specific characteristics of the lower South's French landscape tradition, however, presents a challenge. France lost her North American colony in 1763, and few structures survive from before that date. In New Orleans, the devastating fires of 1788 and 1794 leveled most of the French colonial buildings, and many of the outlying eighteenth-century plantation houses have either been stripped of their grounds or demolished. Additionally, cultural influences freely intermingled in eighteenth- and nineteenth-century Louisiana, particularly during the Spanish colonial and early American periods. This makes it difficult to determine the ethnic origins of specific landscape features and styles. In southern Louisiana, however, and especially in New Orleans and the plantations along the Mississippi river and nearby bayous, French traditions continued especially strong. Throughout the nineteenth century, contemporaries noted a conservative retention of French customs, fashions, and manners in southern Louisiana.

Eighteenth- and nineteenth-century pictorial representations, plans, and written descriptions reveal a distinctive landscape tradition that can be identified with areas of primarily French settlement in southern Louisiana. Features of this tradition emerge as a formality of design defined by the use of *parterres* and *allées*; a striving for the visual unity of the dwelling house with its gardens, along with a separation between the pleasure and utilitarian areas; and a predominance in the ornamental areas of flowering, sweet-smelling plants, often cultivated in pots.

Formality of Plan

The French surveyors who laid out the Vieux Carré, or the original city of New Orleans, left room for gardens while plotting the traditional gridiron pattern of nar-

French Contributions at a Glance

- **Formality of plan**
- *Parterres*: **flower gardens having beds and paths arranged in patterns**
- *Allées*: **avenues or rows of trees**
- **Unity of dwelling house with gardens**
- **Division between pleasure and utilitarian areas**
- **Aromatic, colorful plants and containers in the ornamental areas**

row, deep building lots and narrow streets. In 1722, the French military engineer Adrien De Pauger explained that the lot configurations were proportioned so that "each and every one may have the houses on the street front and may still have some land in the rear to have a garden, which here is half of life" (Wilson, *Vieux Carré*). Eighteenth-century plans show rear gardens with flower or vegetable beds arranged in *parterres*, or flower gardens in which beds and paths are arranged in patterns. Such a formal arrangement for the open spaces of the French city's small-scaled structures contrasts with the naturally arranged front gardens of the English cottage garden tradition customary in Anglo-American areas of settlement. The Vieux Carré's rear gardens or courtyards not only appealed to the French settlers' European-derived taste, but they also were well suited to the shape of the narrow, deep lots. Most importantly, the raised beds combined with circulation areas paved in brick or flagstone provided drainage in this low-lying, subtropical locale. Furthermore, rear courtyards, walled in by neighboring structures, provided an intimate retreat in a densely packed urban area. Lastly, confining plant materials to rigidly arranged beds provided some order in a climate where growing conditions produce an almost uncontrollable lushness.

In the eighteenth century, some affluent French settlers designed estates and gardens which mimicked the grandeur of the France of Louis XIV and Louis XV, to express their status in the New World. Just above the Vieux Carré, the city's founder, Jean Baptiste Le Moyne Sieur de Bienville, created a fine estate, where an avenue of trees led up to the dwelling, behind which spread intricate *parterres*. French draftsman Gonichon's "Plan of New Orleans such as it was in the month of December 1731" outlines numerous elaborate gardens, especially near the city's center at the Place d'Armes. In the 1750s, the Chevalier de Pradel erected a plantation residence, facing the Mississippi River across from the Place d'Armes. In letters written to his family in France, de Pradel described a fan-shaped garden which he designed for the front of his estate, appropriately called *Monplaisir* ("My Pleasure"). A Frenchman designed de Pradel's house, and the furniture and garden seeds came from France. The governor of the Louisiana province rated Pradel's *Monplaisir* as not just a provincial chateau "but as that of a farmer-general in the environs of Paris" (Wilson, "Louisiana Drawings").

In the early nineteenth century, New Orleans grew and pushed out of the Vieux Carré into surrounding suburbs, areas that formerly had been plantation lands. Nineteenth-century plan book drawings (detailed watercolor plans and elevations used originally for advertising property for sale and now preserved with the Orleans Parish real estate records) outline dwellings oftentimes accompanied by formally arranged gardens and open spaces. In 1807, architect Jean Hyacinthe Laclotte, a native of Bordeaux, executed plans for the proposed residential development of a plantation located a few miles upriver from Vieux Carré. Laclotte's drawing for this "model" but never constructed villa included a sophisticated garden in the Empire style that was cut into an elaborate pattern of rectangles, squares, and circular forms (Schlesinger). A watercolor by Laclotte of the Edmund Macarty plantation house shows a less academic, stylized interpretation of a formal French garden. Interestingly, this house,

which before its demolition was located below the city on the site of the Battle of New Orleans, served as the headquarters of General Andrew Jackson.

Most of New Orleans's nineteenth-century gardens actually used the simplest geometric forms, frequently rows of long, rectangular *parterres* or flower beds, which followed the angular lines of the houses. Formality was also expressed through an ordered arrangement of trees, usually planted in rows of single species, as seen in an 1862 plan book drawing of an early nineteenth-century plantation house, which before its demolition overlooked the Mississippi River a few miles below the Vieux Carré.

Nineteenth-century observers regularly remarked on the persistence of formal garden design in southern Louisiana. In 1801, Englishman John Pintard traveling there commented on what he considered a provincialism in garden design. "But no great taste as yet prevails in the design of any garden," he wrote, "I have seen all that have any pretensions that way, being disposed in the old still formal style, the border and circles kept up with strips of board wh[ich] have a mean effect"(Sterling). In 1815, architect Benjamin Henry Latrobe also noted the formality of the "old-fashioned, but otherwise handsome garden and house" of Mr. Montgomery, the new owner of the above-mentioned

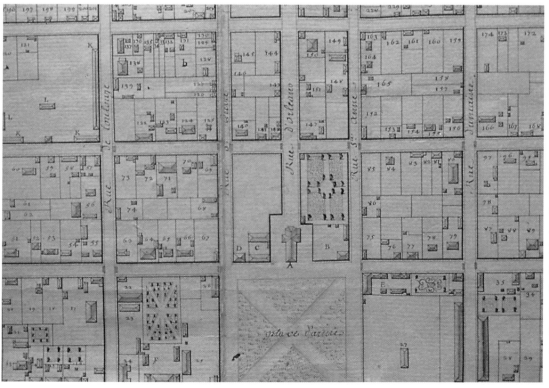

This detail from "Gonichon's Plan of New Orleans Such as it was in the Month of December 1731" outlines formal gardens near the public square. (*Paris—Archives Nationales, Section Outremer, courtesy of Koch and Wilson Architects*)

French-born architect Jean Hyacinth Laclotte's watercolor shows the Macarthy Plantation house and its formal French garden in 1815, at the time of the Battle of New Orleans. (*Courtesy of Koch and Wilson Architects*)

Macarty house. The garden was "laid out in square walks and flower beds in the old French style and is entirely enclosed by a thick hedge of orange trees, which have been suffered to run up fifteen or sixteen feet high on the flanks and rear, but which are shorn down to the hight [sic] of four or five feet along the road." The garden had walks, Latrobe wrote, which were bordered by large myrtles shaped in the form of "large haycocks" (Latrobe).

Although by 1850 English natural landscape design had taken hold throughout much of the United States, most antebellum gardens in southern Louisiana ignored the romantic movement. In 1849, Alexander Gordon attributed the persistence of formal gardens in New Orleans to the city's Creole population. "This leads me to remark, in general," Gordon wrote, that "the French style in the ornamental department of gardening is the most frequently adopted, particularly among the Creole population of the city." Even when New Orleans's Jackson Square (formerly the Place d'Armes) was refurbished around 1850, it was replanted with low, small-scaled vegetation. The French mode of landscape design did eventually pass out of fashion in New Orleans, but not until late in the nineteenth century. Still, by 1885, the *New Orleans Historical Sketchbook* noted that "the old and rigid style of angular precise beds has

passed away, and even where the space is small there are gratifying attempts at landscape gardening."

This formality of plan, frequently identified by contemporaries as French garden design, stands out as the foremost characteristic of the landscape tradition in eighteenth- and nineteenth-century southern Louisiana. A simple, conservative retention of outmoded fashions, however, does not satisfactorily explain the long-lasting popularity of the formal garden plan. At first, in the eighteenth century, European-inspired formality successfully imposed order on Louisiana's wild landscape. Space constraints, lot configurations, and drainage needs later affected the choice to use simple *parterres*. Gardens in the English mode require large expanses of well-drained land. Southern Louisiana's flat terrain, akin to France's landscape, adapts well to a formal scheme.

Unity and Separation

The Renaissance-Baroque concept of order brought to Louisiana by the eighteenth-century French colonists insisted that the house should be treated as a single unit with its gardens; and yet also called for division between the pleasure and utilitarian areas. A naively executed drawing made in 1730 by François Benjamin Dumont de Montigny illustrates the form this concept could take when translated into reality. Dumont graphically outlined the components of his modest Vieux Carré estate: a fence separated the street-fronting principal house from the "first" rear garden with its trellised vines, behind which a "sort of pond" set off a large, formally arranged garden, where both edibles and nonedibles were probably grown.

In Vieux Carré properties where space allowed, areas adjacent to houses seem to have been arranged formally and used as open-air reception rooms or for viewing and strolling. Ornamental plantings were arranged in a regular manner suited to these decorous activities. An extensive illustration of this sort of treatment survives at the mansion of Samuel Hermann, a German immigrant, built in the Vieux Carré in the 1830s. Located at 820 St. Louis Street, this residence, the Hermann-Grima Historic House, is today a museum open to the public. It includes a well-restored courtyard that retains its original flagstone paving and long, rectangular *parterres*. Although this court served in the nineteenth century as a means of communication between the main dwelling and the utilitarian outbuildings that lay at the rear of the large, multiple-lot property, it was arranged in an aesthetic manner, as an extension of the main house. Samuel Hermann had an advantage in the relatively expansive size of the property; owners of smaller properties could not relegate household tasks and functions to unseen areas.

Plantation houses likewise followed the formula of a house visually connected with the gardens but screened from agricultural operations. New Englander Joseph Holt Ingraham visited Louisiana in the 1830s and published his vivid impressions in *The Southwest by a Yankee* (1835). His description of a plantation located an hour's carriage ride above New Orleans captured the southern Louisiana landscape:

> An hour's ride . . . brought us in front of a charming residence situated at the head of a broad, gravelled avenue, bordered by lemon and orange trees, forming in the heat of summer, by arching naturally overhead, a cool and shady promenade.

This avenue, or *allée*, led up to the main house, and at this point, branched to both sides of the house into narrower walks, which were lined with evergreen and flowering shrubs. Looking back from the piazza, or verandah, the main avenue swept back to a vista of the river through the *allées*, a "paradise of althea, orange, lemons, and olive trees." As in the landscapes of Louis XIV's France, order and unity are created on this Louisiana plantation by the *allées* that grandly led to the manor house, encompassed the dwelling, and then pointed back toward the fertile, alluvial-fed land that produced south Louisiana's new aristocracy. The open

Formality is expressed through an ordered arrangement of trees on the grounds of this early nineteenth-century plantation house in New Orleans, shown here in an 1862 watercolor. (Plan book 6A, Folio 105, Notarial Archives of New Orleans, courtesy of Koch and Wilson Architects)

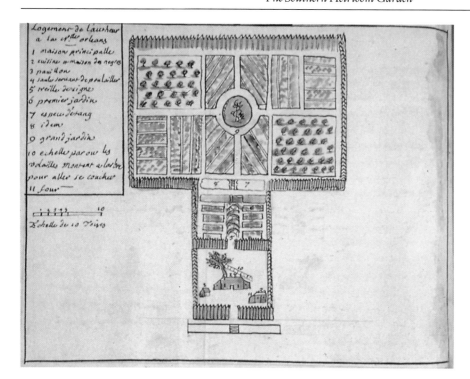

Dumont de Montigny's circa 1730 drawing of his modest Vieux Carré estates illustrates the concept of separation between pleasure and working areas. (*Courtesy of Newberry Library, Chicago*)

vista with its sweep of the horizon suggested the owner's prosperity and well-being, as did the ornamental gardens that lay near the main house. Many remnants of such *allées*, which appeared in the earliest years of French settlement, remain, oftentimes leading to an hauntingly empty site. For something like the original experience, however, the visitor need only stop at Evergreen Plantation, which is located on the west bank of the river near Vacherie. There the *allées* draw strollers into a well-preserved landscape of Louisiana's agricultural past—an intact arrangement of main house, grounds, domestic dependencies, and slave cabin rows.

Between 1857 and 1861, architect-artist Marie Adrien Persac, a Lyons, France, native who lived in New Orleans, executed a series of gouache-on-paper views of plantations located along the Mississippi River and bayous. These gouaches finely detail the relationship of the main house and grounds with ancillary structures and document well the separation of main house and ornamental grounds from utilitarian features, a separation achieved through a careful arrangement of fencing. Persac's attractive images, however, present several difficulties for anyone interpreting the form and arrangement of the ornamental gardens. First, because Persac painted only from the frontal perspective, gardens that typically lay next to or behind the main house are seldom visible. Secondly, Persac treated all the landscape in a romantic vein; one of his favorite devices

was to view a scene in reflection, as mirrored in the water of bayou or river. This technique reduces the recognizable vegetation to randomly planted ornamental trees.

Persac's views of two St. Martin Parish plantations, however, reveal a decided formality in landscaping. The trees on the grounds of "St. John Plantation" line up in a linear fashion to flank the main house; and "View from the Front of Albania" clearly shows in the foreground an ordered space, divided into square *parterres*, filled with small-scaled plantings and interspersed fruit trees. Extant photographs display an ornate formal garden which in the nineteenth century was similarly located in front of San Francisco Plantation, constructed during the 1850s by Edmond Bozonier Marmillon on the east bank of the Mississippi River near Garyville. (For further information on Persac, see Barbara Sorelle Bacot's article in the November 1991 issue of *Antiques*.)

With the changes in lifestyle that have come in the last hundred years, Vieux Carré courtyards no longer function as they did originally. Likewise, most of the extant plantation houses have lost their environments of grounds, outbuildings, and cane fields. Visual and written documentation, however, indicate that whenever possible, pleasure and working areas were separated, thus enabling a formal use of the ornamental grounds.

Plants and Containers in the Ornamental Areas

Writing about New Orleans in the 1830s, Joseph Ingraham noted that "in their love for flowers, the Creoles are truly and especially French, and the glimpses one has now and then, in passing through the streets, and by the ever-open doors of Creole residences of brilliant flowers and luxuriantly blooming exotics, are delightfully refreshing, and almost sufficient to tempt one to a petit larceny." In the country, this traveler similarly related:

> Around the semicircular flight of steps, ascending to the piazza of the dwelling, the columns of which were festooned with the garden jasmine and luxuriant multiflora, stood in large green vases, a variety of flowers, among which I observed the tiny florets of the diamond myrtle, sparkling like crystals of snow, scattered upon rich leaves, the dark foliaged Arabian jasmine silvered with its opulently leaved flowers redolent of the sweetest perfume, and the rose geranium, breathing gales of fragrance upon the air.

Fifty years later in 1887, Charles Dudley Warner wrote in *Harper's New Monthly Magazine* that in all areas of New Orleans, one ran across "now and then a flowery court or a pretty rose garden, occupied mainly by people of French or Spanish descent."

Written descriptions, garden manuals, and advertisements indicate the continued popularity of fragrant, floriferous plants in nineteenth-century southern Louisiana. The planting of fruit trees—orange, lemon, fig, pomegranate, Japanese plum, and pear—had begun with the earliest years of French settlement. Standing in groves or forming promenades, citrus trees were historically the most frequently cited providers of fragrance. Non-fruit-bearing trees or shrubs also were popular in the antebellum period, and these included sweet olive, althaea, myrtle, camellia, cape jasmine (gardenia), and roses, most of which bear fragrant blossoms. Both the written and artistic records suggest the prevalence of vines—climbing walls or trellises or spreading to form arbors. Sweet-scented jasmines, honeysuckles, and climbing roses such as Lady Banksia numbered among the popular vines. Other noted perennial, bulb, and tuber plants were rose geraniums (described as fragrant), ginger lilies, tuberoses, ranunculus (buttercups), jonquils, stock, hyacinths, and even tulips.

While not dramatic, seasonal changes do occur in southern Louisiana and can be marked by planting

The Hermann-Grima Historic House in New Orleans includes a well-restored courtyard that retains its original paving and long, rectangular *parterres.* **(Hilary Somerville Irvin)**

and blooming cycles. Between 1848 and 1869, a Lyonnaise French priest named Joseph Michel Paret served as priest of the Red Church near Destrehan. Paret painted a number of remarkably detailed watercolors of plantation scenes and kept a journal (published in France under the title *Mon Journal D'Amerique*, 1853). In letters home, Paret told of the pleasure and relaxation found in gardening and in watching plant and animal life throughout the seasons. Paret wrote about a winter's stroll in his "immense garden," where all the walks and beds were "straight as boards" and where recently planted jonquils, tulips, stock, hyacinth, and buttercups, along with endive, bordered the beds. Paret also described 488 square feet of trees he had just set out around his garden—orange, peach, plum, cherry, lilac, persimmon, magnolia, mulberry, rose, and althea. The colors and smells of Paret's matured garden must have been dramatic indeed.

Where did the settlers obtain all these species of nonindigenous plants? An intense interest in horticulture marked the early nineteenth century in England and North America alike. New varieties were brought to Europe from the orient, and from Europe into America. Many plants now associated with southern Louisiana actually came from China via France. During southern Louisiana's halcyon, antebellum years in the early nineteenth century, the variety of imported planting materials steadily increased. Ships arriving at the river port of New Orleans brought exotic horticultural specimens that soon appeared in local nurseries. Newspaper advertisements, such as the following from January 4, 1832, indicate the great variety of flowering and fragrant plants a Louisiana gardener might find locally:

FRUIT TREES, DWARF ORANGES, CAMELLIAS, ROSES.

The subscriber in addition to his already splendid collection of flowering shrubs, plants, etc. has just received from Tennessee in a short passage, a collection of fruit trees, Camelias, Japonicas, Dwarf Oranges, Roses . . . also a number of hardy flowering plants such as Snow Balls, Syringas, Lilacs, Chinese and French, Viburnums, Strawberry Tree, Sweet-scented Vitex, Blue Jasmin or Chinese Box, Thorn, Evergreen Privet, Honey Suckles, Double Dahlias with the new and most approved varieties of the Fig Tree, consisting of 10 varieties of those most cultivated in Italy and South of France. (*The Courier*)

The appearance of locally published gardening manuals reflected the keen interest in horticulture and played their part in further stimulating it. In 1838, J.F. Lelievre published Louisiana's first gardening book, *Nouvelle Jardinière de la Louisiane*. Having served as the official Gardener-Horticulturist for the French colonial government, and later becoming the proprietor of a bookstore and seed shop in the Vieux Carré, Lelievre encouraged his readers to experiment with plants not yet routinely cultivated in Louisiana. A large portion of his work was devoted to a nomenclature of flowers, which he described as "the most beautiful ornament of a garden . . . as much for the variety of their colors as from the sweetness of the smells which almost all emit." He listed the size, color, and flowering season for each flower, so that gardeners could arrange them pleasingly in *parterres*. Lelievre instructed his readers to place such flowers as geraniums and pinks and "exotic plants, especially those from tropical climates and areas" in pots, to be taken inside during winter to a temperate and bright spot, sometimes to a greenhouse." Placing plants in pots solved another environmental problem identified by Lelievre: that of excessive water produced by violent rains, followed by periods of short drought.

Evidence indicates that nineteenth-century south Louisianians ornamented their courtyards, gardens, and galleries with pots or vases filled with showy plants, as suggested by Lelievre. In addition to addressing problems of drainage and unpredictable winter temperatures, container gardening creates an effect of profuse bloom, even in small spaces such as in the Vieux Carré's paved courtyards. High-style vases, fashioned in iron, porcelain, or marble, were used, as well as simpler terra cotta pots and wooden boxes. Sometimes the vases were painted Paris green (a bluish green), or in an imitation of marble. Ingraham described "large green vases" and "handsome vases of marble and china-ware" filled with plants in plantation house galleries, and large vases filled with flowers and plants arranged around cisterns in the center of Creole courtyards. An inventory taken on November 30, 1831 of the furnishings of James Pitot's house in the Vieux Carré found in the flower garden: six iron flower pots, six terra cotta pots painted green and twenty-four wooden boxes, all with plants.

Gratification of sight and smell figured strongly in the nineteenth-century pleasure gardens of southern Louisiana, where climate facilitates year-round color display and fragrance. In the city, flowers provided sweet

Marie Adrien Persac's 1861 "View from the Front of Albania" shows an ordered space, divided into square *parterres* in front of this St. Martin Parish plantation. (*Courtesy of Louisiana State Museum*)

balm to soothe the senses in the congested, frequently foul-smelling Vieux Carré; in the country, an aromatic garden helped relieve the stresses of an isolated plantation life, while emitting an aura of opulence. This fascination with the aromatic, colorful plants favored in the nineteenth century continues today.

While certainly not peculiar to the South's areas of French settlement, formality in both ornamental design and spatial arrangement persisted in southern Louisiana, lasting through most of the nineteenth century and even into the twentieth century. Whereas the English Renaissance landscape tradition produced formal plantation environments in the early Anglo-American South, in Louisiana aspects of a later romantic movement intermingled with the formal tradition to give rise to a softer landscape. Still it was a rational, ordered one—the picturesque exoticism as seen in planter Valcour Aime's elaborate gardens of the 1840s seems an anomaly in southern Louisiana. Indeed, by the time romanticism gained ground in late Victorian Louisiana, Beaux Arts classicism, popularized by the 1893 Columbian Exposition in Chicago, was already stimulating a nationwide interest in French and Italian gardens. Alongside this renewed classicism, the colonial revival movement further contributed toward a return to formal landscape design.

Associated with the colonial revival movement in southern Louisiana was New Orleans architect Richard Koch (1889–1971). After studying in Paris between 1911 and 1912 at a Beaux Arts affiliate, the Atelier Bernier, Koch returned to New Orleans and launched an influential career in architecture and landscape design. Beginning in the 1920s, he became a prime mover in the early restoration of Vieux Carré properties, which had suffered neglect since the 1880s. In his landscape designs for houses in the Quarter, as well as in the country and other areas of southern Louisiana, Koch combined aspects of colonial French and Spanish landscapes with new elements he introduced from Moorish Spain. Retaining a simplicity of forms, raised beds, flagstone and brick paving, and traditional plant material, this architect also introduced fountains, an element that had not, historically, been a part of the southern Louisiana garden. These fountains, typically consisting of masonry bases with cast iron pedestals and pans, served as a focal point, either at the intersection of walks or against walls. Koch's creative designs, which relied heavily on traditional landscape design, served as the model and inspiration for the frequently copied "French Quarter courtyard style."

Bibliography

Bacot, Barbara Sorelle. "Marie Adrien Persac: Architect, Artist, and Engineer." *Antiques* (November 1991).

Gordon, Alexander. "Remarks on Gardening in Louisiana by Alexander Gordon, Botanical Collector, Baton Rouge, Louisiana." *Magazine of Horticulture and Botany*. V. 16, no. 6 (June 1849).

Ingraham, Joseph Holt. *The Southwest by a Yankee*. Vol. 1 New York: Harper & Bros., 1835.

Latrobe, Benjamin Henry. *Impressions Respecting New Orleans: Diary and Sketches*. Trans. by Samuel Wilson, Jr. New York: Columbia University Press, 1951.

Lelievre, J.F. *Nouvelle Jardinière de la Louisiane*. New Orleans: J.F. Lelievre, 1838.

New Orleans Press. *Historical Sketch Book and Guide to New Orlean and Environs*. New York: William H. Coleman, 1885.

Paret, Joseph Michel. *Mon Journal D'Amerique*. 1853. Saint Etienne, France: Un Étude Historique de Marcel Boyer, 1988.

Schlesinger, Dorothy G., et al. *New Orleans Architecture: Jefferson City*. Vol. VII. Gretna, Louisiana: Pelican Publishing Company, 1989.

Warner, Charles Dudley. "Sui Generis." *Harper's New Monthly Magazine*. Vol. LXXIV. New York, 1887.

Wilson, Samuel, Jr. "Bienville's New Orleans: A French Colonial Capital, 1718–1768." *The Architecture of Colonial Louisiana: Collected Essays*. Ed. by Jean M. Farnsworth and Ann M. Masson. Lafayette, Louisiana: Center for Louisiana Studies, 1987.

———. "The Drawings of Francois Benjamin Dumont de Montigny." *The Architecture of Colonial Louisiana: Collected Essays*. Ed. by Jean M. Farnsworth and Ann M. Masson. Lafayette, Louisiana: Center for Louisiana Studies, 1987.

———. "Louisiana Drawings of Alexandre De Batz." *The Architecture of Colonial Louisiana: Collected Essays*. Ed. by Jean M. Farnsworth and Ann M. Masson. Lafayette, Louisiana: Center for Louisiana Studies, 1987.

———. *The Vieux Carré Historic District Demonstration Study: The Vieux Carré, New Orleans, Its Plan, Its Growth, Its Architecture*. New Orleans: Bureau of Governmental Research, 1968.

Parterre Gardens of the Old South:

A Treasured Tradition

JAMES R. COTHRAN

The garden tradition of creating decorative geometric designs in box, rosemary, thyme, germander, marjoram, and other low-growing plants is a horticultural practice that dates back to ancient times. Originally conceived by the ancient Greeks and Romans, the tradition spread to northern Europe, where, during the Middle Ages, the simple geometric patterns of an earlier era evolved into decorative "knot gardens" consisting of intricate ribbonlike designs in fanciful shapes

Above: Dwarf myrtle (*Myrtus communis* 'Dwarf') (*Greg Grant*)

and heraldic symbols. Italian gardeners of the Renaissance further refined knot garden design, but the art was perfected by the French during the eighteenth century in what came to be known as "parterres."

The word, *parterre*, is derived from a double source, from the Latin verb *partire*, "to divide," and also the French term *par terre*, which means "on the ground." *Parterres* by tradition were laid out on flat or level ground and were intended to be viewed from an elevated terrace or high point from which their intricate patterns could be suitably enjoyed. *Parterre* gardens were distinguished from earlier knot designs in that *parterres* were laid out almost exclusively in box, were freer in form, and served as an integral part of a garden's overall design.

French garden designers Claude Mollet, Andre Le Nôtre, and Jean-Baptiste Le Blond were instrumental in transforming basic *parterre* patterns into dazzling designs incorporating gravel, flowers, grass, and box-bordered beds. Fine examples of French *parterre* designs were evident at Chantilly, Fontainebleau, the Tuileries, Vaux-le-Vicomte, and Versailles. *Parterres* were generally placed into four distinct categories, including: *parterres de broderie* (*parterres* of embroidery), consisting of embroidery-like designs incorporating scrollwork and arabesque figures executed in dwarf box kept low by clipping; *parterres de compartiment* (*parterres* of compartment), distinguished by a varied assortment of scroll-like designs, flower beds, and grass plots combined in

Parterres—Contributions at a Glance

- **The age-old garden practice of creating decorative geometric designs in box and low-growing herbs dates back to ancient times.**
- **Knot gardens were refined by Italian gardeners during the Renaissance and perfected by the French during the eighteenth century in what were to be known as "parterres."**
- ***Parterres* by tradition were laid out on level ground and were intended to be viewed from a higher elevation, from which their intricate patterns could be seen and enjoyed.**
- ***Parterre* gardens during the Colonial period were greatly influenced by European garden styles, but, as a rule, were much simpler in layout and design.**
- **Colonial gardeners' need for an abundant supply of hedging material stimulated interest in native shrubs such as yaupon holly, American holly, and cherry laurel.**
- **The geometric formality of *parterre* designs was ideally suited to the monumental architecture of the Greek Revival school that flourished in the Antebellum South.**
- ***Parterre* gardens of the Old South were located either in front of or beside the house, and were typically surrounded by a decorative picket fence.**

perfectly ordered and symmetrical arrangements; *parterres à l'anglaise* (*parterres* after the English manner), which combined the English love of turf and the French passion for pattern into designs consisting of large grassed areas, decorative flower beds, and edgings of box; and *parterres de pièces coupées* (cutwork *parterres*), which are, in fact, the oldest form of *parterre* designs. In *parterres* of cutwork, the pattern was typically laid out in box, with individual pieces of the design serving as flower beds. In general, paths that were incorporated in the design of *parterres* were not intended for use as walks but rather were a device to separate the various borders and beds that comprised a design.

In 1709, A.J. Dezallier d'Argenville, a French engraver and writer on art, published *The Theory and Practice of Gardening*, a monumental work covering all aspects of the design and planting of pleasure gardens. Included in his treatise is a chapter providing rules and procedures for laying out *parterres* accompanied by illustrations of various designs. It is interesting to note that d'Argenville makes little mention of flowering plants but instead elaborates on the use of trees, shrubs, and evergreens along with their practical and aesthetic use in design. He extols boxwood as one of the finest and most useful of evergreen shrubs, and describes it as being of two sorts—dwarf or edging box (*Buxus sempervirens suffruticosa*) and the box tree (*Buxus sempervirens arborescens*), which "advances much higher." *The Theory and Practice of*

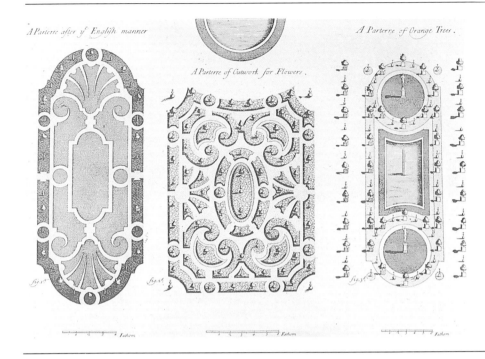

A Parterre after y *English manner*

A Parterre of Cutwork for Flowers .

A Parterre of Orange Trees .

Designs for garden *parterres* from Dezallier d'Argenville's *The Theory and Practice of Gardening.* (Courtesy of the Hunt Institute for Botanical Documentation, Carnegie Mellon University)

Gardening was translated into English by John James in 1712, and remained a tremendous influence on garden design through the middle of the eighteenth century, both in Europe and abroad.

Though d'Argenville identified just two forms of box, there are actually many varieties. Even so, it was the dwarf, or edging, box that was used almost exclusively in the laying out of formal *parterres*. Reasons for this preference include the ruggedness of dwarf box, its tolerance of shade, its slow growth, and its tolerance for shearing that made it an ideal material for intricate designs. Advice to gardeners on the care and culture of box was provided as early as the seventeenth century, when one authority noted that box used for borders should be cut "three times per annum, as April, June, and August: minding to cut their roots at the inside every second year." A later reference advises "clipping to prevent too much shade and to make easier the care and cultivation of the beds that are bordered."

The enormous prestige of French gardens and the popularity of d'Argenville's book helped to make the *parterre* a centerpiece of seventeenth- and early eighteenth-century English gardens as well. From England the *parterre* travelled to Virginia, where an early example survives in the palace garden re-created in Colonial Williamsburg. Developed under the direction of Lieutenant Governor Spotswood in 1710, this garden (really a series of gardens) includes a bowling green, deer park, terraces, canal, and formal *parterres* designed in the Dutch-English tradition. The *parterres* are located in what is generally termed the Ballroom Garden and North Garden beyond.

Actually, the Ballroom Garden consists entirely of a series of *parterres* in diamond-shaped designs. Individual beds created by the design are planted with groundcover and separated by brick-bordered walks made of crushed oyster shells. Large topiary pieces of yaupon holly, clipped in cylindrical shapes, complete the design.

The North Garden revolves around a central axis bordered by American beech trees. These in turn are flanked by large, rectangular-shaped *parterres* traditionally planted with tulips in spring and heirloom annuals and perennials in summer and fall. American beech are also used in the North Garden to create pleached arbors, which form cool, shaded retreats in summer. While the *parterres* that comprise the Palace Gardens were obviously influenced by English garden styles, their shapes and composition are simpler in design than those in fashion in Europe at the time. This trend was to characterize *parterre* gardens in the American colonies up until the time of the Revolution.

Other old Virginia gardens that contained formal *parterres* include: Tuckahoe (1698), Upper Brandon (1720), Westover (1737), and George Washington's beloved Mount Vernon (1743). Benjamin Henry Latrobe, the noted architect and engineer who left his mark on the design of the United States Capitol, com-

A view of the Ballroom Garden at Colonial Williamsburg showing *parterres* laid out in formal arrangements of squares, diamonds, and rectangles in designs reflecting the Dutch-English tradition. (*Courtesy of Colonial Williamsburg Foundation*)

ments on Mount Vernon in his *Journal* in 1796: "the farm of the president extends from the mill to the house. Good fences, clean grounds, and extensive cultivation strike the eye as something uncommon in this part of the world. . . . For the first time since I left Germany I saw here a *parterre* stripped and trimmed with infinite care in the form of a richly flourishing fleur-de-lis . . ." Records indicate that the *parterre* described by Latrobe was laid out with box in patterns similar to those of English gardens, that is, in shapes of "squares, circles, hearts, moons, lozenges, and double circles."

Another typical feature of early colonial *parterre* gardens was the substitution of native plants for traditional European hedging material. This was dictated largely by the difficulty colonists experienced in obtaining sufficient quantities of box. As an example of their resourcefulness, colonial gardeners soon discovered that yaupon holly (*Ilex vomitoria*) was a good hedging plant and could serve as a substitute for box. This is confirmed in the records of Dr. Alexander Garden (1728–1791) of Charleston, South Carolina, in which he observed that yaupon "makes a very good and most beautiful hedge and may be kept as short and neat as the Box." The use of yaupon for edging and topiary is evident today in many of the re-created gardens of Colonial Williamsburg. Other native plants frequently employed as clipped hedges in colonial gardens included

American holly (*Ilex opaca*), cherry laurel (*Prunus caroliniana*), and the wax myrtle (*Myrica cerifera*) from which bayberry candles were also made. Not only were native plants easy to obtain from the surrounding countryside, but they were generally more tolerant of local climates and soils than were imports from Europe.

Farther down the coast in South Carolina, large plantations were developed outside of Charleston along the Ashley and Cooper rivers. These large estates, which were developed by wealthy English gentlemen, frequently included elaborate gardens with *parterres* designed in the grand manner of England and France. Among the earliest of these plantation gardens was Crowfield, developed about 1730 by William Middleton in a style reminiscent of a fine eighteenth-century English country estate. Accounts of the garden indicate that it contained a large bowling green encircled by a double row of magnolias (*Magnolia grandiflora*) and catalpas (*Catalpa bignonioides*), a bosque of live oak trees (*Quercus virginiana*), a large water feature, and an elaborate *parterre* garden that served as the centerpiece of the design.

Another Carolina plantation developed shortly after Crowfield was Middleton Place, built by Henry Middleton in 1741. Like Crowfield, the gardens at Middleton Place were planted on a monumental scale, and in a plan reflecting the elegant symmetry of seventeenth- and early eighteenth-century European design. At the center of the Middleton Place gardens, and adjacent to the site where the plantation house stood, is a *parterre à l'anglaise*. To the north of this site lie the remnants of a series of individual garden features similar to those contained in illustrations of Dezallier d'Argenville's *The Theory and Practice of Gardening*. This similarity is surely no accident, for it can be safely assumed that this standard work was known and used by Henry Middleton in laying out his famous gardens. Visiting Middleton Place today, one can easily identify the influence d'Argenville had on the design:

There should always be a descent from the building to the garden of three steps at least, and from the head of these steps you have a general view of the garden. A parterre is the first thing which should present itself to sight. . . . The sides of a parterre should be furnished with such works as may improve and set it off . . . regards should be had to the situations of the place before you plant—whether the prospect that may be agreeable, for then the sides should be kept entirely open, making use of the quarters of grass and other flat works to make the best of the view. . . . After you have laid out the great walks and the chief lines and have disposed the parterres and works as is most suitable to the grounds, you may fur-nish the rest of the garden with many different designs, as tall groves, close walks, galleries, and halls of verdure, green arbors, labyrinths, bowling greens, canals, figures, etc.

Half a century after the establishment of Middleton Place, Captain Charles Ridgely began developing an equally fine series of *parterres* on his Hampton estate in Towson, Maryland, outside Baltimore. While the general layout and development of the gardens (begun in 1783) are based on a design prepared by William Russell Birch (a Philadelphia artist), it is generally believed that the formal *parterres* at Hampton, the true glory of the gardens, were executed around 1801 by William Booth. Booth was a well-respected nurseryman who laid out some of the finest early gardens in the area.

The formal geometric gardens at Hampton contain six *parterres* divided into two box gardens, one on each side of a grass walk connecting three terraces, or "falls" as they were known in the eighteenth century. The use of grass ramps instead of steps to make the transition from one terrace to another not only add an element of informality to the gardens but at the time of construction also served as a practical means of reducing costs.

So well conceived are the design and the engineering of Hampton's gardens, that, when viewed from

A formal *parterre* executed in common privet at Maison Chenal, a re-created Creole garden in Pointe Coupe Parish, Louisiana. (**William C. Welch**)

A plan of Hills and Dales, as the Ferrell Gardens are now called. LaGrange, Georgia. (*Courtesy of the Peachtree Garden Club, Atlanta*)

the cupola of the house, the terraces give the illusion of a continuous patterned garden laid out on flat or level terrain. Alice Morse Earle in *Old Time Gardens* provides the following description:

> The Ridgely estate, Hampton, in County Baltimore, Maryland, has a formal garden in which the perfection of box is a delight. . . . The high terrace which overlooks the garden and the shallow ones which break the southern slope and mark the boundaries of each parterre are fine examples of landscape art. . . By 1829 the garden was an object of beauty and much renown.

Farther south along the Mississippi many historic plantations at Natchez, St. Francisville, Baton Rouge, and New Orleans also exhibited elaborate formal gardens based on European styles and traditions. Strong ties with France up until the time of the Louisiana Purchase in 1803, greatly influenced the design of many of the old *parterre* gardens of the region, including those at Parlange and Valcour Aime plantations. Of the two, Parlange Plantation is the oldest. Located near New Roads, Pointe Coupe Parish, this property was developed in the mid-eighteenth century by Vincent de Ternant. According to family tradition, the gardens were designed by one of the finest French gardeners of the Jardin des Plantes in Paris in a formal manner with walks, borders, summer houses, ponds, and two tall,

octagonal pigeon houses (*pigeonnières*) as were customary on fine French estates. The house itself was surrounded by a *parterre* garden full of lilies, roses, banana trees, and hydrangeas.

Outside New Orleans along the historic River Road lay Valcour Aime, whose house and gardens date to the first half of the nineteenth century. Though only ruins remain today, Eliza Ripley, in the *Social Life of Old New Orleans* provides the following account of Valcour Aime's legendary gardens:

> The spacious grounds were considered the finest in Louisiana. There was a miniature river, meandering in and out and around the beautifully kept parterres, the banks of which were an unbroken mass of blooming violets. . . . Further on was—a mountain! Covered from base to top with blooming violets. A narrow, winding path led to the summit, from which a comprehensive view was obtained of the extensive gardens.

While many of the early gardens along the Mississippi contained *parterres* that were executed in box, it is believed that many were laid out using common privet (*Ligustrum vulgare*). This plant, though not highly prized as an ornamental today, has long been recognized for its use as hedge material because of its compact growth, deep green color, and small leaves that are not disfigured by clipping. While the leaves of the privet are not as small as those of the box, its roots, like those of boxwood, never extend far from the base of the plant, making it ideal for garden hedges.

As early as 1806, Bernard M'Mahon (1775–1810), a Philadelphia seedsman and one of America's first garden writers, remarked on the declining popularity of *parterres* in his book *The American Gardener's Calendar*. "Though parterres in general are now becoming rather unfashionable," he advised with apparent restraint, "a little of that kind of work might still be permitted for variety sake, though not immediately in front of the house as heretofore. A spacious lawn, bounded with rural shrubberies, is the most eligible situation for such…" A similar philosophy calling for greater informality in garden design was also espoused by Andrew Jackson Downing (1815–1852), America's first landscape gardener, in his influential *Treatise on Landscape Gardening*. Downing believed that the formal style of gardening, based on geometry and regular symmetry, should be replaced with the "beautiful and picturesque," characterized by simple and flowing lines expressed in irregular, spirited forms.

While these new American design philosophies associated with the informal style of gardening received widespread support and interest in the North, the South as a general rule, continued to adhere to the strict formality of geometric design referred to by M'Mahon and Downing as the "ancient style." Perhaps nowhere in the South was this more evident than in the magnificent *parterre* gardens that developed in Georgia in the antebellum era.

During the period from 1820 to 1861, there developed in Georgia, as well as throughout the South, a classical style of architecture known as Greek Revival. Based on the designs of classical Greek temples, these large, imposing structures were ideally suited to the geometric formality associated with *parterre* designs. *Parterre* gardens during the antebellum period were located either immediately in front or beside the house. As a general rule, they were surrounded on three sides by a picket fence with the fourth side being formed by the colonnaded facade of the mansion. Within these physical confines were developed decorative *parterres* that exhibited strong Italian and French designs. To keep the gardens in proper proportion and scale with the massive architecture of the house, plantings of magnolias, holly, tree box, crape myrtle, and flowering shrubs were often set out in individual *parterre* beds.

The Ferrell Gardens (now known as Hills and Dales) located in LaGrange, Georgia, represent one of the oldest and largest of Southern *parterre* gardens. Originally developed by Sarah Coleman Ferrell in 1841, the garden consisted of a series of boxwood *parterres* and descending terraces laid out in an Italian pattern of the Baroque period. While the layout is based on strong geometric forms, the design incorporates curving walks and irregular shaped box-bordered beds reflecting the subtle influence of a more up-to-date naturalistic style. It is interesting to note that the Italian garden style proved particularly adaptable to gardens of the antebellum South. The design that evolved in partnership with Italian noblemen's villas suited the equally grandiose plantation houses of the American South, and the Southern climate, like that of Italy, fostered the growth of evergreens but discouraged the maintenance of grass during the hot summer months.

The *parterre* gardens at Hills and Dales contained an elaborate *parterre* of embroidery, one of the few known in the South during antebellum times. The design was formed of scallops, scrolls, and the fleur-de-lys fashioned around a central floral motif. Individual beds in other parts of the garden include mottos executed in closely clipped dwarf box. Among these are Mrs. Ferrell's "God is Love" and "Fiat Justitia" (let justice be done) for Mrs. Ferrell's husband, who served as a circuit court judge. The gardens are connected by an elaborate system of swept earth paths, which add unity to the gardens and create a harmonious design.

Another example of a fine antebellum *parterre* garden is that of the Kolb-Newton House in Madison, Georgia—a picturesque piedmont town spared by General Sherman on his infamous march to the sea. The garden of the Kolb-Newton House, locally known as "Boxwood," contains not one but two *parterre* gardens. These lie at opposite ends of an imposing Italianate townhouse situated midblock between Academy Street and Old Post Road—an original link in a stagecoach route connecting Charleston with New Orleans.

Each of the *parterre* gardens at Boxwood are divided into four separate beds—two large squares and two rectangles—which are further subdivided into a variety of intricate and geometric designs, connected by a series of interlocking paths and walks. Beds within the gardens are planted with a variety of historic trees and shrubs, including magnolias, cedars, tree box, smoke tree, cherry laurel, flowering quince, and heritage roses, as well as many old-fashioned annuals, perennials, and flowering bulbs. The entire garden is enclosed and protected by a decorative picket fence.

Many of the South's finest *parterre* gardens fell into ruin or disrepair as a consequence of the overwhelming social and economic changes brought about by the Civil War. Of those that survived, the majority were either drastically altered or ruthlessly destroyed to make way for a new gardening style that evolved during the Victorian era when design and good taste were abandoned in pursuit of random plantings of new and exotic plants. While only a few of the original *parterre* gardens of the Old South have survived, their memories still remain as a treasured tradition in Southern garden history.

Bibliography

Banks, Elizabeth. *Creating Period Gardens.* The Preservation Press, 1991.

Downing, A.J. *A Treatise on the Theory and Practice of Land-scape Gardening adapted to North America.* 1841. Reprint.

Earle, Alice Morse. *Old-Time Gardens.* New York: Macmillan, 1901.

Hedrick, U.P. *A History of Horticulture in America to 1860. With an Addendum by Elisabeth Woodburn of Books Published between 1861 and 1920.* Portland, Oregon: Timber Press, 1988.

James, John. *The Theory and Practice of Gardening.* 1712.

The James River Garden Club. *Historic Gardens of Virginia.* Richmond, Virginia: The William Byrd Press, 1923.

Lewis, Albert Addison. *Boxwood Gardens, Old and New.* Richmond, Virginia: The William Byrd Press, 1924.

Lockwood, Alice, ed. *Gardens of Colony and State.* New York: Charles Scribner's Sons, for the Garden Club of America, 1934.

Loudon, J.C. *An Encyclopedia of Gardening.* London, England: 1827.

M'Mahon, Bernard. *The American Gardener's Calendar.* Philadelphia: 1806.

Shaffer, E.T.H. *Carolina Gardens.* Chapel Hill, North Carolina: University of North Carolina Press, 1939.

Wright, Richardson. *The Story of Gardening.* New York: Dodd, Mead and Company, 1934.

A Garden of Welcome:

The African-American Influence

Richard Westmacott

In any exploration of Southern gardens and their cultural roots, an enormous gap soon emerges. For until recently, almost no attention was given to the horticultural traditions of the region's African-American population, the South's largest single ethnic minority, and one of the dominant influences on the regional culture. Certainly this is true with respect to horticulture, for besides cultivating their own plots, African Americans supplied most of the gardeners who did the actual

Above: Bachelor's buttons (*Gomphrena globosa*) (*Greg Grant*)

planting and management of other Southerners' gardens. Their influence on the Southern garden has necessarily been profound, yet has been almost wholly neglected.

Filling this gap today is difficult, too. Literacy was intentionally denied the African slaves upon their arrival in the United States, so that there are no contemporary accounts of early African-American gardens written by African Americans. In addition, of course, the slaves faced a special challenge in that they gardened only at the whim of their masters—until after the Civil War, African Americans very rarely owned the ground they cultivated. And even later, after African Americans were freed and had access to at least rudimentary schooling, still their traditions were treated with condescension by society as a whole, so that there are relatively few descriptions of old-time African-American gardens even by outsiders.

All of this works together to make this a difficult subject to research. But with persistence, some sources of information can be found, and these piece together into a colorful and distinctive picture.

The first stop in re-creating African-American gardening traditions must be West Africa, for that was the original homeland for most of those who came to the South as slaves. Judging by the accounts of travelers of the early colonial period, there was very little ornamental gardening in West Africa at that time. That is, plants were rarely planted for purely decorative purposes in the space around homes. Trees might be planted or preserved for the shade they provided—a photograph taken in 1901 of the village of Lawra in the Gold Coast (now Ghana) shows a large shade tree growing up amidst the corn that fills the area around a house. However, there seems to have been no use of plants for ornamental purposes.

But if the West Africans were little interested in the ornamental use of plants, they were nevertheless expert gardeners who practiced a number of ingenious horticultural systems. One system that originated in the tropical parts of West Africa is often referred to as "vegeculture." This is a multilayered growing system that combined root crops, vines, and fruiting trees, and as a result helped protect the soil against intensive equatorial rains. Vegeculture is different from European-derived agricultural systems in that it emphasizes the planting of perennial crops, plants that can be harvested one at a time and used as needed, rather than harvested all at once for long-term storage (an efficient practice in the temperate zone, but a recipe for disaster in the tropics).

Hand tools were the standard in West African horticulture and agriculture, and draft animals rarely used, so that crops were grown in patches rather than rows. Especially in arid areas, the West African farmers did raise livestock, and one tribe of subsistence farmers, the Nabdam (Archer), developed a particularly efficient system of crop and livestock interaction. They enclosed family compounds with fences of laterite piers

African-American Contributions at a Glance

In the days following slavery:

- The role of the garden for survival and subsistence was crucial. The symbols of self-sufficiency and self-reliance—the garden, livestock pens, and other areas—are today a source of aesthetic satisfaction.
- Utilitarian yards were decorated with objects and plants—a gesture of graciousness in spite of a hard life.
- Spaces were kept swept with a brush broom.

Today:

- The flower yard is a gesture of welcome—always in front of the house—an invitation to stop and visit.
- The flower yard is highly decorated with plants and ornamental objects.
- Brightly colored flowers are chosen for impact. The choice of plants was limited by availability, and many plants were collected from the wild.
- Changes are common: displays are arranged and rearranged frequently.
- Yards show strong individuality of expression, and creative improvisation is an essential characteristic.

"Miss Cammie picking zinnias at Melrose Plantation" by the late folk artist Clementine Hunter. (*From the collection of Bert and Judy Boyce. Photo by Greg Grant.*)

and wooden rails, so that the animals might be enclosed around the house at night. Their manure was then harvested to nourish the surrounding gardens of tobacco, gourds, sweet potatoes, tomatoes, and peppers.

In the West Indies, there is evidence that some West African gardening and farming practices have survived, but the slaves brought to the United States had very little chance to practice traditional skills. This is not to say that plantation owners were blind to the skills of slaves from different regions of Africa. Littlefield showed that forty-three percent of the Africans brought to South Carolina in the eighteenth century came from regions where rice was an important crop, and he went on to suggest that the relationship between South Carolina and Gambia was "a purposeful one, related to the production of rice." However, the methods of cultivation used on the large coastal South Carolina plantations were very different from those of West Africa and many traditional skills were lost. Some traditional crafts such as basket weaving survived, modified of course to suit the raw materials available locally. But other crafts died out completely. The use of thatch for building, once used for roofing some slave cabins, died out during the nineteenth century (McDaniel). Not all slaves were permitted to have gardens. Those that did had little time to work them, although this varied from plantation to plantation and from region to region. In coastal regions, most plantations worked the slaves on the task system, whereby each slave was assigned a task. When completed, the slave's time was his own. In contrast, most up-country plantations used the gang system, often working the gangs of slaves from sun-up to sun-down, leaving little free time to work a garden. Frederick Law Olmsted, in *The Cotton Kingdom* (1860), described the slave cabins on a plantation near Charleston, South Carolina, as having a half-acre garden and yards for fowl and pigs. Eggs, it seems from some accounts, were used by slaves for barter.

Olmsted was one of the few visitors to the pre-Civil War South to describe slave gardens. In 1833, Fanny Kemble described each slave cabin on her husband's plantation on Butler Island, Georgia, as having "a small scrap of a garden," but she went on to say that it was "for most part untended or uncultivated." This entry in her diary was made in January, which is probably why the gardens were uncultivated. There is a serious lack of documented records of African-American gardens from either the period of enslavement or the decades following. During the period of the New Deal programs, Farm Security Administration photographers such as Jack Delano, Dorothea Lange, Marion Post Wolcott, Arthur Rothstein, and others compiled an extraordinarily descriptive portfolio of African-American life during the 1930s. Unfortunately, to make a record of the gardens and yards of African Americans was not part of these photographers' instruc-

A view in the village of Lawra, Ghana, 1901. (*Crown copyright. Photographic collection of the Foreign and Commonwealth Office Library, London*)

tions, and gardens appear only incidentally in the photographs. The transcriptions of interviews conducted with ex-slaves as part of the Federal Writer's Project also occasionally contain descriptions of yards and gardens. The writings of social scientists such as Arthur Raper, Charles Johnson, and Hortense Powdermaker also mention gardens occasionally but these accounts are neither complete or systematic. This lack of evidence makes the garden historian's work difficult. However, it is not only historical evidence that is lacking but also records of contemporary gardens and yards. It is only quite recently that vernacular gardens became a subject for scholarly study and certainly not the vernacular gardens of African Americans, which seem to have been regarded with disdain by many garden designers until quite recently. In fact, much of the recent interest in African-American yards has been inspired more by folk artists studying yard art than by gardeners studying gardens.

Because of the lack of historical evidence of the gardens and yards of African Americans, many of the traditions described in this essay are based on the memories of about fifty black gardeners, all of whom were over fifty years old, but who could describe their parents' gardens. These gardens were from three rural areas of the South: the Low Country in South Carolina, the Black Belt in Alabama, and the Southern Piedmont in Georgia. Some historically African-American

areas of the South therefore are not included here, notably the Mississippi Delta and the Gulf Coast, which surely offer their own contributions to gardening tradition.

When discussing the African-American contribution to gardening, it is difficult to separate the garden as a conscious creation of beauty and a place of leisure and contemplation from its utilitarian role as a source of food for the family and as a space for mundane tasks, such as cooking and washing, many of which are today carried out indoors. Until very recently, many black families in rural America had no running water in the house, and during the summer months all the cooking was done outside in the kitchen yard. This yard was usually located in the rear of the house, often shaded by a large tree and contained a series of work places, arranged to take advantage of the shade as it moved around the yard. Typically, however, there were two main centers for activities in the kitchen yard. The first was the wellhead and the second was the fire. Most tasks in a modern kitchen involve a constant to-and-fro between the sink and the stove. The same applied to the kitchen yard. Consider Mary Miller's memories of doing laundry in the yard.

Me and my brother had to get wood and put it under the pot and boil them clothes. Take them out of the pot, then you'd wash them, put them back in the pot, let them boil. Take them out of the pot, you had three pots, rinse them and put them on the line. You talk about a pretty white set of clothing on the line.

The photograph below shows Inez Faust's kitchen yard in Oglethorpe County, Georgia. Notice the cook/wash pots and the wellhead just to the left of the frame. As this photograph suggests, such kitchen yards were not highly decorated. A close examination of the kitchen yard in a photograph taken in 1914 in Southern Pines, North Carolina, does reveal plants and a vine decorating the porch and some shrubs under the chinaberry tree. But nevertheless, this yard was clearly shaped by functional considerations and the well at the end of the porch and the fire are the focal points of this scene. Note also that the yard's surface is bare earth. It would have been swept with a brush broom, usually made from dogwood, gallberry, or dog fennel branches bunched together. This practice, which became so characteristic of yards both black and white throughout the South, probably originated in the kitchen yard. Just as

Yard scene, Southern Pines, North Carolina, 1914. **(E.C. Eddy. Prints and Photographs Division, Library of Congress)**

one sweeps the hearth into the fire after cooking a meal in the chimney indoors, so one would sweep the area around the fire when clearing up after a meal in the yard. Any weeds that were growing in the vicinity would be cut with a hoe and swept into the fire.

Rural electrification and a pump on the well have long since brought running water into the house. Few kitchen yards still exist intact, though memories of them are still vivid for most elderly African Americans in the country. But the disappearance of this traditional landscape feature has not eliminated the swept yard. Instead, the practice of sweeping has been applied to other areas of the yard, including the flower yard. Although the swept yard clearly has African rather than European roots, it was adopted in the yards of the plantation houses throughout the South.

Originally, of course, the gardeners at the "Big House" were slaves. As such gardeners occupied an intermediate position in the slave hierarchy, ranking above the field hands but below the house slaves, and seem to have played an interesting role as cultural mediators. Historians (Genovese) have noted the part that the house slaves played in introducing the customs of the Big House to the slave quarters and vice versa; less well recognized is the role that gardeners seem to have played in introducing an African aesthetic and management practices to the planter and his family. Whatever the truth of this, however, it is a fact that the swept yard is one of many examples of African tradition that

Inez Faust's kitchen yard near Arnoldsville, Georgia, 1991. (Richard Westmacott)

Walter Cox's swept yard, Sandy Cross, Georgia, 1993. (*Richard Westmacott*)

found its way into all levels of Southern society.

Two other areas around the dwelling that were associated with the subsistence of the family were the vegetable garden and the livestock yard. In fact, many of the gardeners who took part in my study considered themselves to be farmers rather than gardeners. Even those who did define themselves as gardeners tended to cultivate plots far larger then were necessary to satisfy the needs of a single family. Some produce was sold, but most gardeners worked mainly to provide for their own extended family and for needy members of the community. A large productive garden is apparently seen as a sign of commitment to family and community.

The West African influence on African-American vegetable gardens is less visible than one might expect, and this has to do with the adoption of European-derived labor-saving techniques. Most of the gardeners interviewed for this study had at one time used a mule to work their land and mule barns were present on many homesteads. A few of the gardeners still have mules, but many others have acquired tractors. In any case, the influence of both draft animals and tractors had led to a complete absence of any traditional cropping methods used in equatorial Africa and European-style row cropping is practiced exclusively.

The role of the garden in providing for the sub-

sistence of rural families in the years after the Civil War and especially in the period following the devastation caused by the boll weevil was crucial, and the degree of self-sufficiency that many poor families in the rural South achieved during this period was remarkable. It continues to be a source of considerable pride among some families, although today it is regarded more as a challenge than absolute necessity. For these families some of the aesthetic satisfaction from gardening comes not from the flowers in the yard but from the satisfaction of seeing a good stand of collard greens on a cold January morning, hearing the roosters crowing in the fowl yard, feeling the smooth white skin of a hog's carcass after it has been scalded and shaved, or the wood smoke from a well-stocked smokehouse.

Aesthetic satisfaction therefore has as much to do with the symbols of self-reliance as with those features of the garden consciously designed for aesthetic pleasure. The aesthetic pleasure that James Colleton derived from the seasonal routine on his small farm is very apparent. "I ain't never been to heaven," he said, "but I'd rather have this here than anything I know… I can do anything I want to. All of it's mine. Nothing can be more enjoyable. Chickens crowing, get the eggs, eat the eggs, kill the chicken and eat the chickens and go on according to the year."

For James Colleton, owning the land was an es-

Mrs. Sylvester
Wright's yard in
Barnwell, South
Carolina, 1991.
(*Richard Westmacott*)

sential part of his enjoyment of it and so too is the work that it requires. The symbols of self-reliance, exemplified by the vegetable garden and the livestock yard, are associated strongly with hard work. Hard work is valued highly in this community, and much pleasure is derived from working, especially by those who own their own land. As Lucille Holly said, "All this is my own. I was raised with the work and I enjoy it. Used to truck farm and it would call for before-day and after-night a lot of times, but I was doing it for myself and I didn't mind it. It was mine."

The pleasure derived from working in the yard also applies to the flower yard. Janie Pinkney said, "I be in the yard practically every day doing a little something with a hoe or a rake or whatever. I enjoy doing that. I try to get my housework done and make it on outside. I go on over to my daughter's house and get in her yard and work there too." Most gardeners spoke of the enjoyment of watching things grow, and working with plants. In fact, several used the terms "watching" rather than "looking at" the flower yard, emphasizing that growth and change are essential processes in the garden, and great pleasure is derived from making the necessary adaptations to accommodate and to nurture this change.

Dynamic, changing traditions are characteristic of African-American culture. In part this reflects ne-

cessity. Many rural African-American families have barely enough income to pay for the necessities of life and, in these circumstances, often have had to improvise, to make do with whatever is at hand. The shelters and pens for livestock are usually put together from all sorts of found and recycled materials. To the outsider these structures may appear untidy, even ramshackle, but the ingenuity that has been employed in their construction is often considerable. Likewise in the flower yards, ordinary objects that might be discarded by a more affluent family are pressed into use for decorative purposes, often arranged in complex and delightful assemblies. They are, however, likely to be disassembled and reassembled frequently with the changing whims of the artist. What began as a necessity, though, ends up as a virtue. As art historian John Vlach has noted, improvisation is for African Americans the "touchstone of creativity" and that this creativity "is marked by constant and individuating change."

Vlach was not writing specifically about gardens, but about decorative arts generally. For instance, parallels can be drawn between the quilt design and the design of gardens. In quilting, there is a rigid discipline and a very precise pattern to be followed. So too in many gardens there are formal design motifs. Yet, perhaps because of their exclusion from the societal mainstream, African-American gardeners did not feel rig-

Ornamental bottle tree in a Texas yard. (Greg Grant)

idly bound by the norm. Vlach writes of African-American textiles and quilts that "in both cases there is a use of formal design motifs but not a submission to them. There is a playful assertion of creativity and innovation over the redundancies of disciplined order." This observation applies as much to African-American decorated yards as it does to quilts and textiles. Certainly formal motifs are used, a straight path to the front door, matched beds on each side, and patches of patterning appear and reappear through the yard. But formality continually submits to the growth requirements of plants, which spill out of bounds and ramble over artificially conceived boundaries.

Formal design motifs may also not be so apparent in African-American decorated yards because plants are not used to reinforce the structural composition of a garden. African-American gardeners did not, typically, regard these as "plant materials" as they are so often called by professional landscape designers. Afri-

can Americans rarely use plants for structural purposes, for hedges, to enclose a lawn, to create a background, for edging or groundcover, or for foundation plantings. Rather, plants are appreciated and admired as individuals and are usually set out and displayed as individuals, with space separating them from their neighbors. They are usually chosen for their flowers, but because each plant is seen as an individual, there is rarely a conscious arrangement of color. Most gardeners said that they preferred a mix of bright colors. It is significant that the evergreen shrubs best suited for use as structural "materials" are rarely seen in traditional African-American gardens. The one exception is privet, which is popular probably because it volunteers so enthusiastically. Privet is sometimes used as a hedge, but more often each plant is clipped separately and sometimes differently, giving each its own identity. Usually these shapes were quite abstract—mounds, cones, and other shapes and figurative topiary are rarely seen.

Few of the gardeners in my study visited nurseries. Most remembered quite nostalgically the times when the only plants they could acquire were from neighbors or by collecting them from the wild. Mary Miller recalled planting her yard:

And you can believe it or not, but all these trees and flowers and things you see around here, I set 'em around with my little boys. We would go in the woods and collect dogwood trees. When the smallest one come from school, we'd hitch up the wagon and take off in the woods and we would collect as much trees as I could set out while they gone to school the morrow. Sometimes it would be after night getting back up out of the woods… and we don't have no light on the wagon. But we'd make it home, unload them trees, and take out that wagon, feed the mule, and come on in the house. And next morning they go on into school, I get out in the yard and set them out.

An analysis of the plants growing in the yards studied shows that reliable, colorful plants of kinds that are easily propagated by cuttings, division, or seed are those most popular among African-American gardeners. So to some extent, the old tradition of self-reliance still prevails. But over the last ten years, colorful, container-grown plants have become easily available at local discount stores, and this is having an impact.

A "garden of welcome" in Louisiana. (Greg Grant)

Such plants are usually purchased singly and are often kept growing in a container. This also applies to house plants, which are usually arranged on plant stands or grouped under the shade of a tree or on the porch for the summer months. Plants growing in containers can of course be arranged and rearranged; one is continually surprised and delighted by unusual and unexpected combinations created by many of these gardeners.

The arrangement of plants and other ornaments in the flower yard is seen by most gardeners as a welcoming display. They are almost without exception in front of the house, in full view of the road. Privacy is emphatically not a criterion in their design. In fact, the opposite is true. Usually the flower yard contains a shaded seating area, preferably under a tree or, if there is no tree, on the porch. These shady spots have a view of the road, and passersby are welcomed with a wave and a shout. The yard and its decorations are an invitation to stop and visit. It is a place to receive visitors, a place to sit and talk—it is not a place to pass through.

Today, some of the old traditions are passing away. Sweeping the yard, for example, is a practice that is gradually disappearing, although many older rural families still do it. This, in turn, is changing garden design, for management by lawn mower dictates a very different kind of yard than one maintained with a chopping hoe and brush broom. It is comparatively easy to hoe and sweep between plants, but it is much easier to mow if plants are grouped in beds or rows, and the influence of this fact was seen in several of the yards studied. Edging practices are also changing. Whereas bottle and fieldstone edges were commonly used in swept yards, they do not make a satisfactory edge between mowed grass and a flower bed. As a result, bottle edging is rarely seen today.

Despite all the changes brought by modern times, still the gardens of the rural South that I studied showed a strong continuity. This is remarkable when one considers how distant the gardens were one from another, and that until recently, there was little mobility among the Southern African-American rural population. Nor was there any other obvious means of communication—rural African Americans rarely, if ever, read gardening magazines. Yet, although many of the practices were identical, each yard displayed an individuality that I came to expect and a creativity that was astonishing.

Bibliography

Archer, Ian. "Nabdam Compounds, Northern Ghana." *Shelter in Africa*. Paul Oliver, ed. London: Barrie and Jenkins, 1971.

Genovese, Eugene D. *Roll Jordan Roll: The World the Slave Made*. New York: Pantheon, 1972.

Kemble, Frances Anne. *Journal of a Residence on a Georgia Plantation* (1838–1839). Athens, Georgia: University of Georgia Press, 1984.

Littlefield, Dan C. *Rice and Slaves*. Baton Rouge, Louisiana: Louisiana State University Press, 1981.

McDaniel, George W. *Hearth and Home: Preserving a People's Culture*. Philadelphia: Temple University Press, 1982.

Oliver, Paul. *Shelter and Society*. New York: Praeger, 1969.

Oliver, Paul, ed. *Shelter in Africa*. London: Barrie and Jenkins, 1971.

Olmsted, Frederick Law. *The Cotton Kingdom: A Selection*. (1860) David F. Hawke, ed. Indianapolis, Indiana: Bobbs-Merrill, 1971.

Quimby, I.M.G. and S.T. Swank, eds. *Perspective on Folk Art*. Winterthur, Delaware: Winterthur Museum.

Vlach, John Michael. *Afro-American Tradition in the Decorative Arts*. Cleveland, Ohio: Cleveland Museum of Art, 1979.

Garden by Nature:

The English Influence

RUDY J. FAVRETTI

English gardens have had a greater influence on the American landscape than those of any other country because they have affected many diverse areas—residences, cemeteries, parks among them. It is also the English tradition, more than any other, that has determined the way we design gardens and entire landscapes in the twentieth century.

Above: **Daylily** (*Hemerocallis fulva*) (Greg Grant)

English Gardens at a Glance

- **The first settlers brought to this country the grid-plan garden with a central walk and secondary side walks and garden plots as intervening spaces.**

- **In the late eighteenth century, the new style of English gardens, the so-called natural style, came into practice in this country. Straight lines were banished and the design of the gardens followed the contours of the land.**

- **The natural style affected the layout of residential grounds in this country.**

- **Starting in the 1830s, it also influenced the design of the rural cemetery in America. The design of American parks was also influenced by the natural landscape style.**

- **In the twentieth century, Gertrude Jekyll's principles of color and planting design continue to affect greatly the design of American gardens.**

The types of gardens that the earliest settlers brought to this country in their mind's eye were of the "ancient style," to use an old phrase. This means that the gardens were laid out on a grid plan with the walk system marking the grid. The intervening spaces were the garden plots.

Usually the central walk was wider than the others, and it was often on axis with the main hall of the house. In other words, the central hall of the dwelling was extended, visually and physically, by the central garden path. Along the paths were narrow beds where flowers, herbs, shrubs, and small fruits were grown. These served as a "curtain" to shield the vegetables and common plants, grown in the center of the plots, from view. In this way, the garden was both practical and ornamental.

In the South there are several excellent examples of this garden type. Perhaps the best documented historically is the garden planted by Lady Jean Skipwith at Prestwould Plantation near Clarksville, Virginia, which was planned sometime around the year 1796. However, there are later examples of this garden type, such as Rachel Jackson's nineteenth-century garden at the Hermitage near Nashville, Tennessee. One of the oldest examples is the Bacon's Castle garden near Surrey, Virginia, which dates from the late seventeenth century: six garden plots within the grid plan.

All of these examples represent gardens of people with means. Common folk of this same period planned simpler gardens, usually a square or rectangular garden, and the walks between the raised beds were merely trodden soil rather than the rich man's turf, gravel, or harder paving materials. These simple gardens were not necessarily integrated with the house plan as were the plantation gardens mentioned above. Good examples of this type of garden may be seen at the Tully House in Atlanta, or at Old Salem.

In the early eighteenth century in England a new garden style emerged. It was called the "natural style" because instead of being grid-form, the plan was shaped to fit natural land forms. Walks through the landscape followed the curves of its contours; trees, shrubs, and other plantings were designed in an informal and picturesque manner; streams were dammed to form curvilinear lakes or ponds; and the whole landscape lost the straight and formal lines that were so dominant in the "ancient style." Such things as long avenues of trees, for example, gave way to informal groves.

From the mid- to late eighteenth century, this new garden style took hold in the American colonies and the new nation. Thomas Jefferson's Monticello was laid out in the natural style, with its grove, curving walks, and the picturesque plantings that enframe the distant views. George Washington's Mount Vernon ultimately developed into a natural-style landscape, though it retained two of the original, more formal, walled gardens. In the Deep South, Melrose, in Natchez, provides another good example.

Bernard M'Mahon's *The American Gardener's Calendar*, published in Philadelphia in 1806, was the first North American book to include a discussion of the two styles of gardens mentioned above. Later, Andrew Jackson Downing published his *Treatise on the Theory and Practice of Landscape Gardening* (1848), and

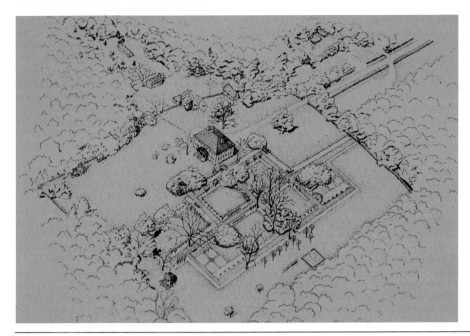

An aerial sketch of the re-created garden at Prestwould Plantation near Clarksville, Virginia, following the ancient style plan commissioned by Lady Jean Skipwith in 1796. (*Sketch drawn by Will Rieley, Charlottesville, Virginia*)

the entire book of 532 pages is devoted to laying out gardens in the natural style. Downing included long lists of plants appropriate to picturesque gardens, and because it was written at a time of very active plant collecting, the book recommends many species newly introduced into this country from the Orient and other exotic regions. Downing's book was used as a guide for laying out gardens for over a century, and many other authors copied his ideas or varied them slightly in their own published works.

Many authorities agree that the concept of today's residential landscape in the United States—which consists of a front yard, a rear yard or living space that is more private, and a service area—was invented by Downing and set forth in his various works. The informal manner in which he recommended designing these spaces was derived from the English natural style.

In 1829 Dr. Jacob Bigelow of Boston came up with an idea for designing a new cemetery in a totally different way. Instead of laying it out with graves row-on-

Gardens laid out in the ancient style but following a German custom of making the rows on the diagonal. These gardens are at Old Salem, Winston-Salem, North Carolina. (*Rudy Favretti*)

The gardens at Stourhead (1748) in England, laid out in the natural style. It is on this type of design that the layout of American parks was based. (*Rudy Favretti*)

row in a grid pattern, as had been done in the past, he and his committee drew plans reflecting the natural landscape style. Roads and paths followed the contours of the hilly site; low, wet areas were made into lakes and ponds; rows of graves also followed the contours of the land; and the whole site was enriched with informal tree groves and shrub plantings. This new, rural cemetery was named Mount Auburn, and it became the prototype for the rural cemetery movement in America. From the early 1830s until the late nineteenth century, most larger cities, north and south, planned rural cemeteries on their outskirts.

These cemeteries became places for Sunday outings. People would visit them to decorate their loved ones' graves, but would use this duty as an occasion to eat a picnic lunch and to walk about enjoying the plantings and winding paths, as well as the views from carefully contrived overlooks. This type of recreation became so popular that those in charge of the rural cemeteries had to publish and post regulations reminding everyone of the facility's main purpose.

Eventually, in the mid-1850s, the great park movement began. While Central Park in New York is credited with being the first public park in the United States, at least seven other parks were planned at the same time. As with rural cemeteries, public parks were planned following the same ideas as the natural landscape of English origin described above. In other words, the natural aspects of the site were carefully studied and

identified and then accentuated in the finished plan.

The great park designer, Frederick Law Olmsted, took his inspiration from the large estates that he saw on a trip to England, as well as a public park called Birkenhead, near Liverpool, where working class people came during their few hours of leisure to enjoy the out-of-doors and to take in the fresh air. Olmsted designed parks and estates in every state in the South, as did his firm after his death. (He also wrote books on his observations in the South following his travels there: *A Jour-*

A bird's-eye view sketch of Thomas Jefferson's mountain-top garden at Monticello, Charlottesville, Virginia, laid out in the natural style following the dictates of the site. (*Sketch by Lucia Stanton, Research Department, Monticello*)

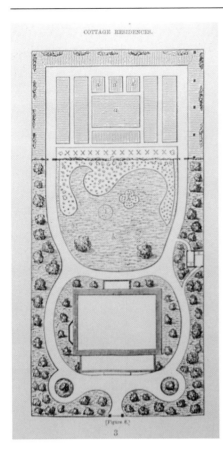

COTTAGE RESIDENCES.

[Figure 8.]

3

An Andrew Jackson Downing layout for the average person's yard. Note that there is a front yard, a backyard, and the serviceable vegetable and fruit garden in the rear. (*From Andrew Jackson Downing's Cottage Residences, 1856, fourth edition*)

ney Through Texas, or a Saddle Trip on the Western Frontier in 1857 and *The Cotton Kingdom: A Traveller's Observations on Cotton and Slavery in the American Slave States* in 1861. Both works contain extensive observations on both the domestic and natural landscape.)

Today, the concept of the natural-style landscape is as strong, if not stronger, than it was at its inception almost three hundred years ago. Indeed, many of the ideas that govern the design and planting of both private gardens and public landscapes today originated with the great English garden designer Gertrude Jekyll. Her rules concerning the manipulation of color and texture in plantings; her use of massed plants, with masses repeated to create a sense of flow; and her calculated varying of plant heights are ideas that are just as influential today as when she began writing about them in the 1890s. Her many books, as well as the gardens she designed, served as inspiration for many American garden writers as well.

Most estate gardens developed between 1900 and 1940 in the South followed the writing of Jekyll when

it came to their design. These gardens often followed a pastel color scheme, such as blue, yellow, and white, with plants in "drifts." The designs paid great attention to height, texture, and repetition. A fine Southern example is the garden at Reynolda House, Winston-Salem, North Carolina.

English influences, since they reached us largely through writings and the works of practitioners, greatly affected residential grounds as well as public spaces throughout the South. The long list of projects performed by the Olmsted firm, for example, contains numerous Southern examples at estates, parks, college campuses, and more in practically all the major cities of the South. Also, the extant plans of earlier Southern estates and residences correlate to the writings and teachings of M'Mahon, Downing, and Jekyll.

Bibliography

Betts, Edwin Morris. *Thomas Jefferson's Garden Book*. Memoirs, vol. 22. Philadelphia: The American Philosophical Society, 1944.

Downing, Andrew Jackson. *Landscape Gardening and Rural Architecture*. New York: G.P. Putnam and Co., 1853.

Favretti, Rudy J., and Joy P. Favretti. *Landscapes and Gardens for Historic Buildings*. 2nd ed. Nashville, Tennessee: American Association for State and Local History, 1991.

Hobhouse, Penelope. *Gardening through the Ages*. New York: Simon and Schuster, 1992.

Leighton, Ann. *American Gardens of the Eighteenth Century*. Boston: Houghton Mifflin, 1970.

———. *American Gardens of the Nineteenth Century*. "For Comfort and Affluence." Amherst: The University of Massachusetts Press, 1987.

M'Mahon, Bernard. *The American Gardener's Calendar*. Philadelphia, Pennsylvania, 1806.

Massingham, Betty. *Miss Jekyll*. London: Country Life Ltd., 1966.

Newton, Norman T., *Design of the Land*. Cambridge, Massachusetts: Harvard University Press, 1965.

Reps, John W. *The Making of Urban America*. Princeton, New Jersey: Princeton University Press, 1965.

Weidenmann, Jacob. *Beautifying Country Homes*. New York: Orange and Judd, 1870.

"A Garden in a Wilderness"

The German Influence on the Texas Landscape

Greg Grant

With the exception of Missouri, no other Southern state received such a massive influx of German immigrants as did Texas.[*] Ship after ship arrived into the ports of Galveston, Indianola, and New Orleans filled with Germans seeking

[*] In addition to Missouri, other Southern states that received substantial numbers of German immigrants were Louisiana, Georgia, Tennessee, and North Carolina.

Above: *Petunia* x *hybrida (Greg Grant)*

their "new Germany." In 1846 about 8,000 arrived in Galveston alone. In his 1857 book, *A Journey through Texas,* Frederick Law Olmsted estimated that there were 35,000 Germans in Texas at the time. And because the immigrants tended to settle together, the German influence was often far more pronounced, or even overwhelming, locally. So, at one point the populations of San Antonio, Houston, and Galveston were estimated to be one-third German.

The major influx of German immigrants into Texas occurred around the mid- and late nineteenth century. That was an era during which many Germans felt discontented with the political climate of their homeland, its division into many petty principalities, the compulsory military service of the German states, and the crowded conditions they were subjected to there. Many saw America—and more specifically, Texas—as a golden opportunity to start anew, a place of limitless potential.

So it was that in 1842 a group of noblemen in Germany formed the Society for the Protection of German Immigrants in Texas. The purpose of this organization was to purchase land and promote German settlement in Texas, and it published as its objectives the following:

[T]o improve the lot of the working class who are without employment, thus controlling their increasing poverty; to unite the immigrants by giving them protection through this Association in order to ease their burden by mutual assistance; to maintain contacts between Germany and the immigrants, and to develop maritime trade by establishing business connections; to find a market for German crafts in these settlements, and to provide a market in Germany for the products of these colonies.

(quoted in "A Guide for German Immigrants,"

German Contributions at a Glance

- **Neat, clean, orderly, industrious.**
- **Good gardeners and keen horticulturists.**
- **Scientific interest in plants, production, botany, and new plant material.**
- **Heavy emphasis on fruit and vegetable culture, many early market farmers.**
- **Love of flowers; houses frequently adorned with ornamentals.**
- **Placed high value on trees for shade, ornament, and lining streets.**
- **Frequently used summerhouses in their gardens.**
- **Yards and cemeteries often swept.**
- **High degree of craftsmanship in stone, wood, and iron.**

by Otto W. Tetzlaff, in Wilson, *Texas and Germany: Crosscurrents*)

The Society promised transportation, food, land, homes, schools, and churches to those who agreed to settle the foreign land. And while the aims and promises were admirable and not impractical, this venture did not long survive. Cheated in its land purchases, the Society soon depleted its treasury, and finally disbanded in 1847. But before this happened, it had already dispatched a reported ninety-three ships containing 10,695 immigrants to Texas (Bene). Many other Germans followed as well, not realizing the stark realities they would face. For the fact is that most of the German immigrants who came to Texas did experience hunger, poor living conditions, and a number of deadly diseases.

German settlement in Texas centered most heavily around two regions. The town of Industry in east-central Texas was the first focus of immigration, with the first German settlers arriving in 1838. Immigrants soon began spreading to other towns: Cat Springs, Frelsburg, Shelby, Oldenburg, New Ulm, and Roundtop. By 1845, German settlement had begun in the Hill Country of west-central Texas, too, with German settlers arriving that year in New Braunfels, and then in Fredericksburg the following year, 1846. Subsequently the immigrant wave spread north and west to Sisterdale, Boerne, and Comfort.

Because the motivation was political as well as economic, the Germans immigrants who came to Texas were a mixed lot. The bulk were hard-working peasants, but with a number of highly educated intellectuals, too. Many of the new arrivals settled onto farms; in fact, according to the United States census of 1900, the large majority of the farming nationwide was being carried out by Germans at that time. Yet many others

Traditionally, German people are fine gardeners, as can be seen in Germany today. (*Greg Grant*)

of the nineteenth-century German immigrants were skilled laborers, too. Whatever their profession, however, the Germans tended to share an enthusiasm for education and the arts—they cherished knowledge, accomplishment, and cultural entertainment, including singing, dancing, sports, art, and gardening.

As new arrivals, the Germans gardened to feed themselves. Besides what they could grow, the immigrants harvested a great many foods from the wild, including wild grapes, plums, blackberries, and anything else deemed edible. For as one German settler put it, "We ate what we liked and we ate what we didn't like."

Like most early settlers, the German grew such edible crops as sweet potatoes, Irish potatoes, corn, cabbage, etc. It doesn't appear that the Germans were responsible for introducing any new types of vegetables to Texas, but they can be credited with new uses for existing crops. It was the German influence that led to an increased consumption of white or "German" potatoes, and the use of cabbage for kraut, tobacco for cigars, and wheat for "light bread" and flour tortillas.

At least in their own estimation, the German immigrants were generally better gardeners than their Anglo neighbors. In 1845 Prince Carl of Solms-Braunfels, the first Commissioner-General of the Society for the Protection of German Immigrants in Texas, pointed out, "All of the garden vegetables grow abun-

dantly if one takes the pains to plant them. The American is usually too lazy to prepare a garden. Rather than go to such trouble, he prefers to live on salted meat, bacon, corn, and coffee and to deny himself any greenery either for nourishment or for beautifying the home. However, the German settlements are distinguished by their beautiful gardens, vegetables, and flowers."

Apparently, Germans were among the first settlers in Texas to adorn their surroundings with flowers and ornamental plantings. Travelling across Texas in 1854, Frederick Law Olmsted described his accommodations for a night he spent in the German community of New Braunfels: "A little room it proved, with blue walls again, and oak furniture; two beds, one of them would be for each of us—the first time we had been offered the luxury of sleeping alone in Texas; two large windows with curtains, and evergreen roses trained over them on the outside—not a pane of glass missing or broken—the first sleeping-room we have had in Texas where this was the case."

The love of flowers and an ornamental garden setting were part of the three gardens of Adolphus Sterne (1801–1852), one of the first German immigrants to Texas. Born in Cologne on the Rhine, he came to New Orleans at sixteen and in 1826 moved to Nacogdoches, where he remained the rest of his life. In 1923, his son, C.A. Sterne, described the lush gardens:

My father's house stood in Nacogdoches on the Lanana Creek, near where the Bonita and Lanana meet, with about 30 acres surrounding it. . . . My father took great pride and interest in his gardens and orchard. There were three gardens on the place. The one on the north was devoted to flowers, with a great variety of roses and rare shrubs and plants, which he had brought from Louisiana, and which had been imported from France.

In the center of the garden was a summer house, which was cov[e]red with morning glories and multiflora roses. The fence was covered with woodbine and yellow jessamine. The south garden had vegetables of every variety. The west garden was the orchard with a variety of fruit trees and a butter bean arbor running the entire width of the garden. My father often resorted to this butter-bean arbor to read and study.

(Today, the Adolphus Sterne Home in Nacogdoches is open to the public.)

Perhaps even more telling were the recollections that Louise Romberg Fuchs recorded in 1927 about her first home in Texas: "I had some work to do all my life, in the house, in the field, and in the garden. The garden always interested me and I always had flowers in the house, too. . . . My dear grandmother in Germany always sent me all kinds of flowers seeds: wonderful stocks, pinks, mignonette, hyacinth bulbs, all of which were my standing favorites." She goes on to remember: "On one side of our house, when we moved to the farm, was a thicket of trees, under-brush, and grapevines. Here we spent one Sunday afternoon with hoes and spades, and before the sun went down, after four hours of work, where there had been only brush and weeds there was now a nice roomy arbor, so thick covered with grapevines that no sunlight could come through. Before it a large round flower bed had been made and in the center of the bed stood a cactus plant . . . surrounded by prairie flowers. The arbor was soon improved by the addition of a table and bench."

In the *History of the Romberg Family*, Helene R. Mackensen, a Romberg granddaughter, recalled her grandparents' farm house where "[t]he path leads up past a rosebush with dark red, velvety roses, up to the old log house. Just in front of the walk is a trellis overgrown with madeira vine, fragrant with waxy, white blossoms, and with roses that grow in clusters in shades from the faintest pink into dark red, some even into blue." And in a letter she sent home to Germany in 1850, Elise Willrich asked for "[a]ll the bulbs you can get together (but no seeds) without causing you too much trouble, like Queenscrown, Lilies, Tulips, Hyacinths, Narcissus, etc., etc., packed in buckwheat chaff, also cuttings from Gardenias of good quality" (quoted in Ragsdale).

Typical early German-Texas home showing *fachwerk* construction technique, as seen at the San Antonio Botanical Center. **(Greg Grant)**

Left: Restored Ferdinand Lindheimer House at New Braunfels, Texas. (*William C. Welch***)**

Above: ***Gaura lindheimeri* (***Greg Grant***)**

Whatever their actual gardening skills, the Germans did give the impression of being harder workers than other Texan settlers. Often whole families worked together in the fields, and German farmers rarely used slave labor. The Germans also came to be famous locally for the speed with which they added to and improved their homes, and the German communities became showplaces for the immigrants' skills in working with wood, stone, and iron. This, along with a neat, regimented lifestyle, fostered the impression that the Germans were more cultured than their Anglo and Mexican neighbors. Frederick Law Olmsted described the small cottages in New Braunfels as "looking neat and comfortable." He also pointed out, in A *Journey through Texas*, that "[m]any were furnished with verandas and gardens, and the greater part were either stuccoed or painted." To this day, Texans of German ancestry tend to keep a manicured, orderly yard.

One of the most noted urban examples of skillful German craftsmanship and period architecture is the beautiful King William district of San Antonio. With the first house built in 1867 by Ernst Altgelt, founder of the Hill Country town of Comfort, it soon became the most prominent residential section in the area. The diverse architecture and stately atmosphere of this thirty-five-block neighborhood reflect the hard-earned wealth and refined taste of the city's first business elite. Designation as the state's first historic district has helped to spur extensive restoration, so that today the King William district ranks as one of the most beautiful neighborhoods in the United States and one of San Antonio's foremost tourist attractions.

As many of the German immigrants were college-educated (some were even university professors), they quickly made their mark in the educated professions. To several German naturalists, for example, gardeners owe much of primary research on Texas' native flora and fauna.

Among the most important of these pioneering naturalists was Ferdinand Jakob Lindheimer from Frankfort-on-the-Main. He spent fifteen years collecting and classifying previously undescribed plants around Houston, Galveston, San Felipe, Columbus, Cat Springs, New Braunfels, Fredericksburg, and San Antonio. Most of his collecting was done for Professor Asa Gray of Harvard and fellow German George Engelmann of the Missouri Botanical Garden. Considered "the father of Texas botany," Lindheimer's name has been honored in one genus of Texas wildflowers and twenty different native Texas plant species, including *Gaura lindheimeri* (commonly known as gaura or Lindheimer's gaura), now a popular garden perennial.

Carl Wilhelm August Groos House (circa 1880) in the King William District of San Antonio. (*Greg Grant*)

Lindheimer played an incidental but important role in the German colonization of the state. It is reported that he helped guide Prince Carl of Solms-Braunfels and his many immigrant followers to the site of present day New Braunfels on the Comal and Guadelupe rivers. But Lindheimer's greatest contributions were of a botanical and horticultural nature.

His dream (which he carried with him through all his moves around the frontier) was to establish Texas' first botanical garden. In a 1842 letter he stated: "I have kept back one specimen of every plant known to me. I must decide upon a more secure location somewhere here in Texas when I can establish an herbarium of indigenous plants. I must also have a botanical garden somewhere hereabouts where I can protect rare perennials" (quoted in Goyne).

Again in 1843 Lindheimer wrote: "During the winters I want to conduct classes mornings, study afternoons. Here it will be possible also for me to establish a nursery of botanical plants, namely perennials… also seeds of annuals about whose development I am curious; also shrubs whose blossoms or fruits I wish to acquaint myself with shall have asylum in it" (Goyne). In an 1845 letter he added: "Near the town here I have reserved a piece of land for my botanical garden of Texas plants, for an arboretum, especially for southern or tropical fruits and for an agricultural experiment garden" (Goyne).

After finally settling in New Braunfels, Lindheimer served from 1852 to 1872 as the editor for the *Neu-Braunfelser Zeitung*, the local German-language newspaper. Today Lindheimer's home in New Braunfels stands as a small museum with a garden such as he might have cultivated.

Also making a name for himself was Friedrich Ernst, who before coming to Texas had served as head gardener and bookkeeper for the Duke of Oldenburg. Ernst, who is considered "the father of German immigration" in Texas, founded and helped settle the town of Industry in 1838, the first German town in Texas. He is perhaps most famous for the overly enthusiastic letter he sent in 1832 to a friend back in Oldenburg, Germany, extolling the virtues of his newly beloved home, Texas:

The ground is hilly and alternates with forest and natural grass plains. Various kinds of trees. Climate like that of Sicily. The soil needs no fertilizer. Almost constant east wind. No winter, almost like March in Germany. Bees, birds and butterflies the whole winter through…Principal products: tobacco, rice, indigo grow wild; sweet potatoes, melons of an especial goodness, watermelons, wheat, rye, vegetables of all kinds; peaches in great quantity grow wild in the woods, mulberries, many kinds of walnuts, wild plums, persimmons sweet as honey, wine in great quantity . . . Meadows with the most charming flowers . . .

This letter was published in a number of newspapers throughout Germany. Ernst's enthusiasm proved contagious, spreading quickly and starting the first steady stream of German immigration to Texas. In 1836 the census showed 218 Germans in Texas. By the 1840s there were thousands.

Ernst's influence on Texas horticulture extended beyond his role as a cheerleader, however. He was known as a skilled gardener, and shared much useful information on fruit and garden culture.

In particular, Ernst is also considered "the father of the Texas cigar industry." He never did build his own "segar" factory, as he planned. But Ernst's enthusiasm for this project, and the advice he freely shared with others, is reflected in the fact that by 1892 there were cigar factories in twenty-eight towns in Texas, and by 1898 some 1,000 acres devoted to the production of suitable tobaccos. According to The Institute of Texan Cultures in San Antonio the largest tobacco experiment station in the world was established in 1902 at Nacogdoches by the United States Department of Agriculture. Today, Texas is the only state west of the Mississippi with a cigar factory, Finck Cigar Company in San Antonio, producing Travis Club cigars. In 1893, when H.W. Finck, son of a German immigrant, located

there, San Antonio supported eighteen other cigar manufacturers as well.

Another skilled gardener and an accomplished student of the natural sciences was the former Baron Otfried Hans Freiherr von Meusebach. Serving as second commissioner of The Society for the Protection of German Immigrants in Texas, the Baron dropped his title upon arriving in Texas and became simply John O. Meusebach. Meusebach is remembered for having founded the town of Fredericksburg, and while he lived there he was one of that community's leading citizens, forging a lasting peace treaty with the Comanche Indians of the Texas Hill Country, and serving as a state senator. He later moved to Loyal Valley, where his farm and garden became a showplace.

Visiting the Meusebach farm in 1877, N.A. Taylor wrote in *The Coming Empire*:

Loyal Valley is indeed a garden in a wilderness; a garden in which one can linger and be happy. Here is a nursery in which sixty varieties of roses grow, and hundreds of the finest flora of three continents; sixty varieties of pear, forty of peach, and an array of apples, plums, and grapes—all cultivated and arranged with taste and skill that cannot be excelled. It is curious to see such an industry in so isolated and remote a region; and nothing could possibly indicate so well the higher

Oxblood lily
(*Rhodophiala bifida*)
(*Greg Grant*)

civilization of the people of the valley, as the fact stated to me by the proprietor that he had liberal and profitable customers. I am sure, said John O. Meusebach, that our valley will soon have as fine vineyards, orchards and gardens as any country in the world, and I feel some little pride in the thought that it is I that am doing it. John O. Meusebach held that people could not be happy and really blessed until they had vineyards and orchards . . . in which view I heartily concurred.

In a letter dated March 14, 1884, Meusebach himself stated, "We have planted onions, [German] potatoes, beans, and sugar corn in the garden. We had plenty of turnips, and sold about $30.00 worth. As I bought no new trees this year, I trimmed all the old trees severely, and made 2000 cuttings of grape-vines, as well as 1000 of crepemyrtle and other shrubs" (*Wurzbach's Memoirs and Meusebach Papers*). His crape myrtles evidently presented quite a spectacle when in bloom. Describing the garden in her book, *John O. Meusebach*, Irene Marschall King, his granddaughter, states:

The avenue of crape-myrtle shrubs leading to the family residence had a graduation of color that would have pleased an artist. The path to the cow pen had rows of lilacs on either side, and Vitex [American lavender] surrounded the outhouses. Bamboo plants grew near the pond, and jujube plums or Texas dates, with their thick, thorny growth served as fences. Meusebach tended carefully a small-leafed boxwood, so that his wife could use the miniature leaves to decorate cakes for special celebrations. Trumpet vines flourished to attract hummingbirds. Bachelor buttons were made into dried bouquets for the winters; a pot of Parma violets usually stood in a sunny window to give fragrance to the winter air. The flowering willows provided thimbles for the children.

The naturalized offspring of Meusebach's flowering willows (*Chilopsis linearis*, and related to catalpas not willows) and jujubes (*Ziziphus jujuba*, also called Chinese date) remain on his old property today. These help the visitor form some idea of what the garden looked like in its heyday. But it is challenging to imagine the effect of another of the former baron's fancies—the open-air Roman bath constructed of whitewashed native stone and set beneath a bathhouse covered with purple and white wisteria.

Dr. Ferdinand von Roemer, a German paleontologist, was sent to study the limestone areas of west-central Texas and in 1849 published *Texas*, one of the most valuable early surveys of Texas flora, fauna, and geology. It is still considered a classic today. During his relatively short stay in the state he went on collecting trips and shared libraries with both Lindheimer and Meusebach.

Another influential German immigrant was the highly educated Louis Cachand Ervendberg, a Protestant minister who helped to establish the town of New Braunfels, building that immigrant community's first church and establishing an orphanage for the many children of those who died during the long hard trek in from the coast. Ervendberg led a movement to establish a German-English University near Industry, and as a prominent supporter of improved agricultural practices also sought to found a local agricultural school. In 1850 he succeeded in securing a charter for a Western Texas University that was to teach scientific agriculture near New Braunfels. Sadly, neither of Ervendberg's plans for institutions of higher learning was realized, and it wasn't until a full generation later, in 1876, that the founding of The Texas Agricultural and Mechanical College in College Station (Texas A&M University) gave the state its first agricultural school.

To supply the needs of their horticulturally minded neighbors, a number of German immigrants established nurseries, and several of these were to play important roles in the development of gardening within Texas. Particularly notable in this regard were Johann Joseph Locke's Nursery, founded in 1856 at New Braunfels; Johann Friederich Leyendecker's Pearfield Nursery, established in 1876 at Frelsburg; and Gustav A. Shattenberg's Waldheim Nursery established at Boerne before 1895. Locke's Nursery is still in operation today, run by Johann's ninety-plus-year-old grandson, Otto Locke, Jr. Numerous Leyendecker nursery catalogues, documents, and family papers are preserved in the Barker Texas History Library at the University of Texas in Austin. Shattenberg is credited for transplanting a number of bald cypress (*Taxodium distichum*) from the headwaters of the Blanco River to the site of today's San Antonio River Walk (Perry). He also had a large commercial pear orchard in Boerne. Surviving pear trees can still be seen along Interstate 10 west of San Antonio. Today, San Antonio sports a 30-million-dollar wholesale nursery industry and a host of farmers

Left: *Iris* x *germanica* (Greg Grant)

Above: Christmas tree at the Alamo. (Greg Grant)

descended from German immigrants. Despite marginal soils and an erratic climate, the Texas Hill Country claims the state's largest peach production area and the state's only apple industry.

At least one of these old time Texan-German plantsmen succeeded in establishing a truly international business. Peter Heinrich Oberwetter was an excellent botanist and a pioneer in the study and cultivation of bulbs, particularly amaryllids. His 1915 obituary termed him a "botanist of much renown" and noted that "the results of his field work were eagerly sought for by different educational institutions in America and elsewhere." But Oberwetter was more than a respected scholar; he also had a very real influence on gardens around the world. For he was by trade an importer of rare bulbs, an exporter of native bulbs, and a creator of new strains of bulbs by hybridization.

According to his granddaughter's recollections, Oberwetter journeyed to Mexico during the Civil War, and from there he exported bulbs to many parts of the world. He then returned to his home in Comfort and soon moved his family to Austin where he was reportedly the gardener for the Texas Deaf and Dumb Institute from 1866 to 1874. Beginning in 1889 the Austin City Directory listed him as a florist as well as a botanist. He is often credited with the introduction into the United States of the oxblood lily (*Rhododphiala*

bifida), a fall-blooming "miniature amaryllis" from Argentina that has appropriately naturalized throughout the German areas of Texas.

In addition to the oxblood lily, several other ornamental plants popular in modern Texan gardens can be linked to the influence of German pioneers. Such plants include the German, or bearded, iris (*Iris* x *germanica*), and a number of rose cultivars, including 'Crimson Glory', 'Eutin', 'Grüss an Aachen', 'George Arends', 'Skyrocket' (Willhelm), 'Leverkusen', 'Dortmund', 'Kordes Perfecta', 'Trier', 'Frau Karl Druschki', 'Tausendchon', and 'Veilchenblau'.

The Germans brought plants and they brought such customs tied to nature as the Christmas tree. In her *Memoirs of a Texas Pioneer Grandmother, 1805–1915*, Ottilie Goeth remembers:

Somehow our first Christmas seemed a little meager in comparison to our German Christmas celebration with its fragrant fir tree, always decorated with so much loving care by our good parents for us children. At Cat Springs, Texas, where we first settled, Father had nailed a large cedar limb to a stump. They were the only cedar trees in the vicinity. Homemade yellow wax candles and small molasses cookie figures, baked by my two older sisters—that was the entire decoration.

In 1839, Gustav Dresel, a German traveler, noted with dismay that Christmas and New Year's Day were not celebrated by Anglo-Americans in southeast Texas (Houghton). Of course, today, Christmas trees are a significant horticultural commodity in Texas and the rest of the United States.

The gardeners who introduced so many beloved plants are long gone. Yet while traveling the Germanic areas of Texas today, one cannot help notice the skillfully constructed limestone buildings, the traces of European *fachwerk* construction techniques, and the intricate patterns of the "gingerbread" that adorns the houses. Within the fine ironwork of the fences lie yards lush and neat—living legacies to the German immigrant's ingenuity, perseverance, and spirit of self-help.

In *A Journey through Texas*, Frederick Law Olmsted summed it up this way:

> In exile, but free, these men make the most of life. I have never before so highly appreciated the value of a well educated mind, as in observing how they were lifted above the mere accident of life. Laboring like slaves; (I have seen them working side by side, in adjoining fields,) their wealth gone; deprived of the enjoyment of art, and, in a great degree, of literature; removed from their friends, and their great hopeful designs so sadly prostrated, "their mind to them a kingdom is," in which they find exhaustless resources of enjoyment. I have been assured, I doubt not, with sincerity, by several of them, that never in Europe had they had so much satisfaction—so much intellectual enjoyment of life, as here. With the opportunity permitted them, and the ability to use it, of living independently by their own labor—with that social and political freedom for themselves which they wished to gain for all their countrymen, they have within them the means of happiness that wealth and princely power alone can never command.

The Germans loved life, gardening, and most of all their new home. In a final show of typical German-Texan pride and unity, John O. Meusebach had the strongest forces behind his existence inscribed on his tombstone near Loyal Valley in the Texas Hill Country: "TENAX PROPOSITI" (Perseverance in purpose) and "TEXAS FOREVER."

Bibliography

Bene, Louis. "Memorial of the Trustee of the German Emigration Company to the Legislature of the State of Texas." Verein Collection, University of Texas Archives.

Burkholder, Mary V. *The King William Area*. San Antonio: The King William Association, 1977.

Der Auswander nach Texas. Ein handbuch und Rathgeber fur Die, welche sich in Texas ansiedeln wollen, unter besonderer Berucksichtigung Derer, welche sich dem Mainzer oder Antweroener Verein anvertrauen. Bremen: 1846. Quoted in Otto W. Tetzlaff, "A Guide for German Immigrants." In Wilson (*Texas and Germany: Crosscurrents*) 14.

Geue, Ethel Hander. *New Homes in a New Land*. Baltimore: Genealogical Publishing, 1982.

Goeth, Ottilie Fuchs. *Memoirs of a Texas Pioneer Grandmother 1805–1915*. Burnet, Texas: Eakin Press, 1982.

Goyne, Manetta Altgelt. *A Life among the Texas Flora*. College Station, Texas: Texas A&M University Press, 1991.

Houghton, Dorothy Knox Howe, Barrie M. Scardino, Sadie Gwin Blackburn, and Katherine S. Howe. *Houston's Forgotten Heritage*. Houston: Rice University Press, 1991.

Jordan, Terry G. *German Seed in Texas Soil*. Austin, Texas: University of Texas Press, 1966.

King, Irene Marschall. *John O. Meusebach*. Austin: University of Texas Press, 1967.

Kunz, Virginia Brainard. *The Germans in America*. Minneapolis: Lerner Publications Company.

Lich, Glen E. *The German Texans*. San Antonio: The University of Texas Institute of Texan Cultures, 1981.

Loher, Franz. *Geschichte und Zustande der Deutschen in Amerika*. Cincinnati: Eggers and Wulkop; Leipzig: K.F. Kohler, 1847.

McDaniel, H.F., and Nathaniel Alston Taylor. *The Coming Empire; or Two Thousand Miles in Texas on Horseback*. New York, Chicago, and New Orleans: A.S. Barnes and Co., 1877.

Olmsted, Frederick Law. *A Journey through Texas*. New York: Dix, Edwards, 1857.

Perry, Garland A. *Historic Images of Boerne, Texas*. 1982.

Sterne, C.A. Statement quoted in "Diary of Adolphus Sterne, Rich in Texas History, Is Presented at Joint Session." *The Houston Chronicle*. February 15, 1925.

Ragsdale, Crystal Sasse. *The Golden Free Land*. Austin: Landmark Press, 1976.

Romberg, Annie. *History of the Romberg Family*, Belton, Texas.

Wurzbach's Memoirs and Meusebach Papers. San Antonio: Yanaguana Society Publications, 1937.

The Gardens of Old Salem:

The German Influence in Piedmont, North Carolina

FLORA ANN BYNUM

In the fall of 1753, a group of fifteen Moravian Brethren made the arduous trip from Pennsylvania to North Carolina. Their purpose was to begin settlement of a 100,000-acre tract of land that the Moravian church—one of the oldest German Protestant groups—had bought in the Carolina wilderness.

Above: Rosemary and sage (*William C. Welch*)

The garden behind the Miksch Tobacco Shop in Old Salem is an adaptation of the medical garden that existed at Bethabara, the original Moravian settlement (1753) in North Carolina. Both Bethabara and Old Salem are located today within the modern city of Winston-Salem, North Carolina. Note hops growing on poles behind the summerhouse. (*Darrell Spencer*)

Almost immediately after their arrival in November, the Brethren began to clear the land for crops, and fields soon surrounded the settlement, which had been named Bethabara. At the same time, the settlers began to lay out a garden. By July 1754, this garden was sufficiently developed that they could send a plan of it back to Moravian church headquarters in Germany. This plan followed the medieval geometric pattern of European gardening, and was laid out in neat rectangular beds with a central work path, small work paths between the beds, and a summerhouse at the end of the central path.

This first garden was expanded to serve the growing community, and in 1759 Christian Gottlieb Reuter, surveyor of the Moravian tract, drew a plan for it that exists today. This plan shows a large garden of a half acre, laid out in the medieval pattern, with large square beds, long rectangular border beds, and smaller rectangular beds for experimental crops and seed "brought personally from Germany."

The community's doctor laid out a medical garden and Reuter in 1761 drew a plan of that as well. This plan was also geometrical; and in this, it much resembles drawings of English Tudor gardens or European medicinal gardens. These two plans, both of which include complete plant lists, are preserved in Moravian church archives. As far as is known, they are the earliest drawn garden plans with plant lists to exist today in America.

By 1760, maps of Bethabara showed orchards, vineyards, a bottom garden (apparently more vegetables), summerhouses scattered at appropriate locations, cultivated fields, and roads lined with trees. Bethabara functioned as a communal economy, so the large gardens served the entire community, with Brothers and Sisters assigned to garden work.

In 1766, the central town of Salem was started and in 1772 the inhabitants of Bethabara moved there, leaving Bethabara as primarily an agricultural community. In Salem the communal economy was abandoned. The town was laid out like those of Europe, with a central square around which were the large community buildings. Homes for families were built close together on narrow lots, fronting directly on the street, with a swept yard behind the house that together with its outbuildings served as a service area, and behind that a garden. Again in European tradition, each household was assigned an out-lot outside of town where field crops could be grown. Three farms were developed near Salem, also to provide for the community.

The householders of Salem laid out their private gardens in a remarkably uniform manner, arranging the planting in "squares," or large rectangular beds, usually six to a garden. (The term garden "square" was not a

Moravian term, but was used throughout colonial America to refer to a garden plot.) As Salem lay on a ridge, the gardens generally stretched down a series of terraces, with two squares to a terrace. In these gardens, families grew the vegetables, herbs, and small fruits with which they fed themselves, but they also mixed flowers into the beds. This intermingling continued for a couple of generations at least, for contemporary records do not mention separate flower gardens as part of private lots until the late 1840s.

Much larger gardens, laid out in large squares, were behind the Single Brothers House, the Single Sisters House, the tavern, and the Community House, to serve the residents of these buildings.

Initially, Salem offered only one ornamental garden, and that was the Girls Boarding School Pleasure Garden, begun in 1804 for the use of the students of that institution. In 1849, the boys had their turn. In that year, a small flower garden was laid out, at the request of two students, in the front corner of the Boys School yard.

The Moravian Brethren were very conscious of the appearance of their community, lining the streets and lanes with trees, giving careful attention to the planting of the square. Visitors to Salem often commented on its neatness, its many flowers. Vacant lots in the town were often used for orchards, and usually each family planted fruit trees at the rear or along the fences of their yards. And every lot was fenced, for this was a strict requirement.

The Moravians were intensely interested in the plant material of the new land to which they had come. Many of the ministers and teachers, who often had been educated in Europe, filled their spare hours with "botanizing," that is, with collecting plant specimens and preparing herbarium sheets. These individuals compiled floras of the area, and maintained an active correspondence with others of similar interests throughout the country. Botany was taught in both the Boys School and the Girls School.

Today the old community of Salem is surrounded by the modern industrial city of Winston-Salem. In 1950, Old Salem Inc. was formed to preserve and restore the pioneer town, the area now known as Old Salem. In 1972, a program of landscape restoration was begun, to replant as much as possible the species of native and introduced trees mentioned in early Salem, to re-create, wherever possible, family gardens, to plant orchards, and to exhibit the early field crops.

Much of the land of the early town was long ago lost to modern development, but Old Salem Inc. hopes through its program of landscape re-creation to provide a proper setting for surviving buildings, and to create an impression of the early landscape. The modern planting is of authentic heirloom or antique varieties of flowers and vegetables. As much as possible, these are of types mentioned in the early Moravian records. Fencing has also been correctly restored. In all of this, the Moravian archives, letters and diaries, maps, drawings and paintings, and the early floras of native plant

"Salem from the North West," artist unknown, October 1832. When this watercolor was drawn, Salem was at its height as a trade and craft center. (*Courtesy of the Moravian Archives, Winston-Salem, North Carolina*)

A small garden in a corner of the Boys School yard. Pencil sketch by Maximilian Eugene Grunert, September 4, 1850. (*Collection of Old Salem Inc., Winston-Salem, North Carolina*)

material have been carefully researched and followed.

Only a few of the early buildings are still standing today in the first settlement at Bethabara, but the site is maintained by the city as Historic Bethabara Park, with stabilized ruins marking the early town. In 1985, a program was begun to re-create the Upland or Community Garden, following the plan drawn by Reuter in 1759 and supplementing this with archaeological research. Today, this garden follows the original form and serves the same purpose: it is used again as a community garden, with local citizens renting plots or garden squares in it. A program to re-create the Medical Garden, following Reuter's 1761 plan, was begun in 1993.

References

The historical data for this article are based on information in *Records of the Moravians in North Carolina*, Volumes I-III (Raleigh: North Carolina Historical Commission, 1922–43), Dr. Adelaide L. Frie, editor. The original Moravian records are located in the archives of the Moravian Church in America, Southern Province, Winston-Salem, North Carolina, and are principally in German.

Reuter's plan for The Upland Garden at Bethabara is in the archives of the Moravian Church, Northern Province, Pennsylvania. The plan for the Medical Garden is in the Moravian archives in Winston-Salem.

The Southern Cemetery as a Garden of Culture

GREG GRANT

The traditional Southern cemetery has not only served as a resting place for our deceased loved ones, but as a garden of heirloom plants as well. Unfortunately, these historic collections of local customs, artistry, and plants are rapidly becoming a phenomenon of the past. For today, the "perpetual care" cemetery, a depressing blanket of manicured turfgrass and rows of brightly colored plastic flowers has all but replaced our true Southern heritage graveyard.

Above: Johnson's amaryllis, or St. Joseph's lily (*Hippeastrum* x *johnsonii*) (*Greg Grant*)

Byzantine gladiolus
(*Gladiolus byzantinus*)
(*William C. Welch*)

Each Southern culture produced its own distinctive type of graveyard. Of particular interest are the Hispanic cemeteries with their multitude of brightly colored flowers, a profusion of crosses and religious icons, and many handmade markers of wood, cement, and tile. The German cemeteries typically offered a fine display of ironwork, and the graves were commonly bordered with hand-carved or hand-cut wooden curbing. The Anglo population was the least enterprising in this matter, and seems to have been the first to switch to the turfgrass-monotypic marker-plastic flower mode.

Instead of the mass-produced tombstones you find today, Southern cemeteries used to offer a wide variety of markers fashioned from a range of materials, including wrought iron, native stone, and wood, side by side with those professionally carved in granite and marble. And because curbing was popular (and not only with Germans) gravesites used to be perfect raised beds for planting shrubs and flowers. I like to think of this as "raised dead" gardening!

Gravesites were often (and still are in some areas) decorated with such things as sea shells, marbles, medicine bottles, and toys. The presence of such symbols in our cemeteries actually traces back to pagan influences. There's also evidence of our African heritage in the old-time Southern cemeteries, for that culture seems to have been the one responsible for scraping and sweeping to keep the soil surface there clean

and bare. Long before turfgrass, glyphosate herbicide, lawn mowers, and string trimmers, our cemeteries were kept meticulously barren of grass and weeds.

Plants of all kinds were planted in our cemeteries of the past. Many had religious connotations, such as evergreens, which symbolized everlasting life. Anything remotely resembling a lily was considered a flower of death, and crinums, amaryllis, lycoris, hymenocallis, and narcissus as well as true lilies all found their way into the cemeteries under this guise. Many of our cemetery plants were originally symbols of the Mediterranean "great mother," which later came to symbolize the Virgin Mary. Other common cemetery flowers included roses, crape myrtles, and irises. White flag (*Iris* x *albicans*), often planted on graves in the Middle East centuries ago, is still a frequent sight today in Southern cemeteries.

It was once a custom to plant a deceased one's favorite plant or plants on their grave. Long after their garden popularity waned, many of these plants cling to life in our older cemeteries today. Oftentimes these cemeteries may be the only source of certain cultivars and species. Many antique rose cultivars have been rescued and reintroduced into the nursery trade from cemeteries.

How sad it is today to see trees cut down, chain link fences erected, shrubs mutilated by string trimmers, roses sprayed with nonselective herbicides, and bulbs and wildflowers mowed before their season of bloom. Some senseless groups have even gone so far as to banish living plants from the cemetery! It's considered all right, however, to scatter hideous plastic reproductions all over the ground. Just because the people are dead, do the flowers have to be lifeless, too?

It's curious that in destroying the traditional cemeteries, we are violating exactly those causes to which modern Americans continually pay lip service. The old cemeteries are collections of regional culture—so why are we stamping them out? We used to maintain our cemeteries in annual get-togethers, when whole families would assemble to tend the graves of loved ones. That's at least a step toward the restoring of family ties, something we all worry about.

And who can argue against beautiful, low-maintenance, living plant material in a cemetery? Why not return our cemeteries to their old-fashioned role as family meeting places, cultural museums, and historic botanical gardens. Have the flowers really gone?

Heirloom Plants of the South

❋

And the Lord God took the man, and put him into the
garden of Eden to dress it and to keep it.

GENESIS 2:15

Gardening is one of those primordial forces in our lives that we can't hide from. Even the most brown thumbed is compelled to torture a house plant or wonder why the grass won't grow. Like love itself, horticulture speaks a universal language, recognizes no race or culture, and is free to all. Since the beginning of modern civilization, all peoples have gardened, first for food and then for flowers.

Above: Chinese trumpet creeper (*Campsis grandiflora*) (*Greg Grant*)

(William C. Welch)

This section of the book takes a look at a number of the most commonly cultivated plants in early Southern gardens. Although vegetables and fruits were certainly the first plants to be cultivated by our ancestors, we have chosen to focus primarily on the early landscape ornamentals. The growing of flowers is always a sign that culture has found its rightful place in horticulture. And of course they make better pictures as well!

In his *New Book of Flowers* (1866) Joseph Breck justifies the cultivation of flowers in saying:

Nonsense, sheer nonsense to tell us it is useless to cultivate flowers. They add to the charms of our homes, rendering them more attractive and beautiful, and they multiply and strengthen the domestic ties which bind us to them. We would not advocate the cultivation of flowers to the neglect of more necessary objects. Attending to the one, does not involve neglect of the other. Every man engaged in the culture of the earth, can find time to embellish his premises who has the will to do it, and we pity the family of the man who has not. Rob the earth of its flowers, the wondrous mechanism of the Almighty, and we should lose the choicest mementos left us that it was once a paradise.

Southern heirloom plants belong in Southern gardens. They've earned the right. These plants are still with us for two reasons. First of all they're tough and adapted. The testing has already been done. They want to grow here. Also, they're pretty. People don't save ugly plants. What more could we possible ask for? And we can't forget the nostalgia evoked by the sight or smell for plants that Grandmother grew or for those that we grew up with as children.

Another important aspect of these living antiques is that they are necessary components of accurate restoration projects. The days when we could surround a carefully restored Victorian house with a twentieth-century landscape are gone. If we believe that restoration involves the exact nails and original paint pigments, then we should have an appropriate landscape design and authentic plant materials as well.

Most of the plants included here, such as roses and honeysuckle, were grown for their beauty and fragrance. Others, such as figs and persimmons, were cherished for their culinary uses. Bill and I have included as many historically grown Southern heirloom plants in this section as we were able. Of course, our selection certainly isn't exhaustive. We relied on personal observation, historic garden documentation, early garden books, the advice of others (if we liked it), and old

Milton and Frances Parker garden, Beaufort, South Carolina. (*William C. Welch*)

nursery catalogues to come up with our entries. If your momma's favorite was left out, please forgive us and cherish it none the less.

Borrowing from the wonderful book *Passalong Plants*, by Steve Bender and Felder Rushing, our initials are included with each plant description to indicate its author.

If you take away nothing else from this book, we hope that you will at least gain a respect for those plants which have kept us gardening for over a hundred (sometimes a thousand) years.

May you stay young and your plants grow old. Enjoy.   —GG

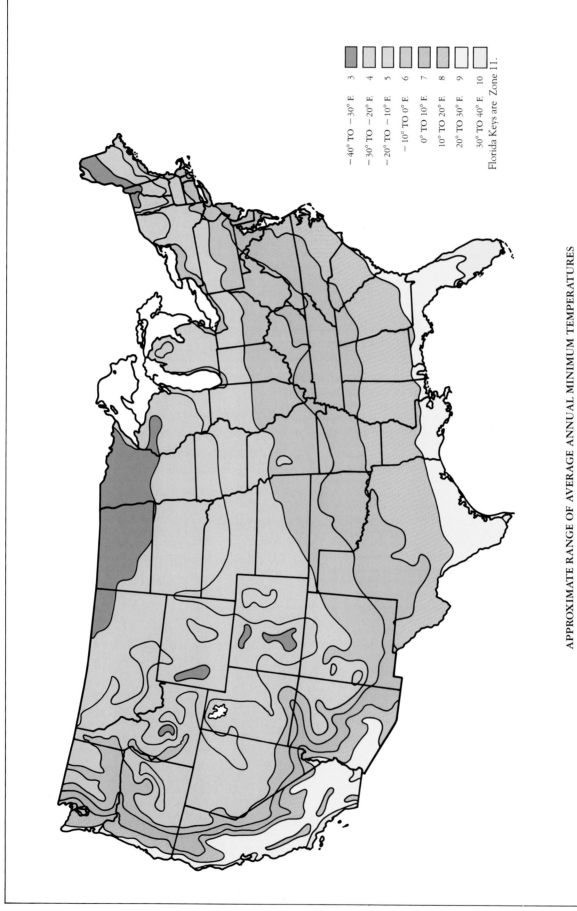

APPROXIMATE RANGE OF AVERAGE ANNUAL MINIMUM TEMPERATURES

−40° TO −30° F.   3
−30° TO −20° F.   4
−20° TO −10° F.   5
−10° TO 0° F.   6
0° TO 10° F.   7
10° TO 20° F.   8
20° TO 30° F.   9
30° TO 40° F.   10
Florida Keys are   Zone 11.

Mimosa (*Albizia julibrisson* 'Fan Silk') (*Greg Grant*)

Albizia jullibrison
Mimosa, Silk Tree
Family: Fabaceae (Pea)
Zones: 7–11
Bill and I debated whether to include the mimosa among our Southern heirloom plants—and I won. Having grown up running barefoot under my grandparents' "crying," fragrant mimosa and its flock of hummingbirds, I couldn't bear to omit this plant. It wasn't until college entomology that I learned those weren't tear drops falling on my head (as my Grandmother Emanis told me), but aphid poop instead! How sweet (and sticky!) childhood bliss truly is.

The mimosa is a native of China and India that reached England as "Acacia julibrisson" in 1745. Its introduction into South Carolina at the end of the eighteenth century is attributed to Andre Michaux, the French botanist who spent ten years collecting plants in the southeastern United States. Thomas Jefferson was among the earliest American gardeners to cultivate this tree; he noted in his garden diary planting seeds of "Mimosa Julibritzin" on April 13, 1809. Prince's Nursery of Flushing, New York listed the mimosa in 1823. The 1851–52 catalogue of Thomas Affleck's Southern Nurseries (Mississippi) also included an advertisement of the "beautiful Mimosa julibrisson," and in his letter to the editor of the *Natchez Daily Courier* on October 28, 1854, Affleck advised that "The *Acacia julibrissin*, or flowering Acacia, though by no means rare, is yet too showy, with its myriad of pink and yellow flowers, to be omitted in pleasure grounds, or even in small yards."

Other nurseries throughout the South picked up this tree—Langdon's Nurseries' (Alabama) 1881–82 catalogue described it as "Acacia Julibrissin …rapid growing shade tree, very beautiful." Over the years, the mimosa has naturalized in rural areas throughout the entire South, spreading its heady perfume and delicate blossoms from Texas to Georgia.

Mimosa is less popular with modern horticulturists, who criticize it as short-lived and susceptible to "mimosa wilt" disease. It is also prone to iron deficiency in alkaline soils. Otherwise, though, the mimosa's culture is simple. Stick it in the ground and wait for the blooms. Okay, it actually prefers acidic, well-drained, sandy loam soils. My "pappaw," the infamous Rebel Eloy Emanis and my original garden instructor, pollarded his mimosas regularly to give them a tight, umbrellalike crown. I did the same to my first mimosa as well.

Although considered a "trash tree" by most professional gardeners, I think the mimosa deserves a place at every Southern farm, cottage, and weekend home, even if it isn't long-lived. Unlike many garden trees, this one doesn't compete with the lawn below it—St. Augustine grass thrives in the mimosa's dappled shade. And when in bloom, mimosa is an eye-catcher. I now cultivate the 'Fansilk' (Flame) red mimosa from Fanicks Nursery in San Antonio. It's so pretty that the folks at the Arcadia Newbern Lodge #97 in East Texas had to ask my grandmother what it was. They've gotten used to wondering what I've planted.   —GG

Belamcanda chinensis
Blackberry Lily
Family: Iridaceae (Iris)
Zones: 6–9
The foliage of the blackberry lily so closely resembles that of its relatives the bearded irises as to fool the gardener—if the plant isn't in flower. For blackberry lily blossoms are quite distinctive: as much as two inches across, deep orange with red freckles. Individual blossoms last only a day, but dozens of buds gracefully adorn each of the airy flower stalks, and these continue to emerge from late spring into fall, ensuring a

Blackberry lily (*William C. Welch*)

Common box-wood (*Buxus sempervirens*) (Greg Grant)

long succession of flowers. The source of the blackberry lily's common name becomes apparent when the flowers fade in late summer and the fruit and seed form, producing a cluster that looks very much like a shiny, ripe blackberry. These seed structures are attractive as well as intriguing, and may be used fresh or dried in floral arrangements.

Originally from China and Japan, where the plant was used for medicinal purposes, the blackberry lily has made itself very much at home in most areas of the South and provides gardeners of that region with an attractive and easily-grown perennial. Blackberry lilies are effective when massed in borders or in containers. I was pleased to have the opportunity to collect a few specimens at Ingleside, former home of Thomas Affleck, the well-known writer and nurseryman of the 1840s and 50s, in Washington, Mississippi. Mr. Earl Rawlings, the current owner of the property and a distant relative of Affleck's wife, Anna Dunbar Affleck, showed me the plants, which were still growing near the ruins of the head gardener's cottage.

One reason for this plant's popularity is the ease with which it is propagated from divisions or seeds. To divide, lift and separate the rhizomes of mature plants in fall or early spring. Both divisions and seedlings usually bloom the first year after planting and continue to thrive for years.

Blackberry lilies prefer well-drained soils and a sunny location, but partial shade and less than ideal soils will do.
—WCW

Buxus sempervirens
Common Boxwood
Family: Buxaceae (Boxwood)
Zones: 6–10

And so with the Tree Boxes—the neatest and prettiest of evergreen trees; always fresh and pleasant to look on. They grow better here than even in their native climate; as does, also, the Dwarf Box, for edgings.
Thomas Affleck in a letter to the editor of the *Natchez Daily Courier*, October 28, 1854

This shrub has been in cultivation in America for over 200 years. It is the hedging and topiary box of many historic European and American gardens, including those of Colonial Williamsburg, and in the heyday of the *parterres* in the Southeast and the upper South, this was *the* plant. Supposedly, it is a native of both Europe and Asia, though some authorities speculate that

actually it may have been introduced to Europe in ancient times. I won't mention that the foliage of this species stinks; some like the smell of a wet dog.

Historically, two forms were cultivated: *B. sempervirens* 'Arborescens' (tree box, American box) and *B. sempervirens* 'Suffruticosa' (dwarf box, edging box, Dutch box, slow box). Tree box grows to be a good size shrub or even an attractive small tree, but the shorter, more compact dwarf box normally stops growing at a height of less than three feet. The dwarf is the one primarily used for edging and *parterres*.

According to Raymond Taylor's book, *Plants of Colonial Days*, Abigail Davidson advertised imported box "for edging of walks" in the Boston *Gazette and Country Journal* of March 12, 1770. Taylor also points out that Captain Ridgeley, of Hampton, Maryland, left a will in 1787 directing that his box gardens be maintained. I can't get anybody to look after my plants when I'm gone for a week, much less eternity!

Martha Turnbull made numerous references in her garden diary (1836–1895) to her boxwood and *parterres* at Rosedown Plantation in St. Francisville, Louisiana. On October 5, 1837, for example, she wrote "set out box in yard," while on November 15, 1841, she mentions trimming the box. She made a note of sticking box cuttings in January and November of 1849, while on October 20, 1855 she recorded a day spent "putting down box around my *parterre*."

Many early nurseries in the South,

Japanese box (*Buxus japonica*) *parterre* in a Dutch garden. (Greg Grant)

especially those of the Upper South and the East, carried boxwood. In an 1851–52 catalogue, Thomas Affleck's Southern Nurseries of Washington, Mississippi listed "Tree and Minorca" box (I don't know what minorca box is). Montgomery Nurseries (Wilson's Nursery) of Montgomery, Alabama listed dwarf box in an 1860 catalog while in an 1881–82 catalog, Langdon Nurseries, near Mobile, Alabama offered *B. communis*, *B. argentea*, *B. myrtifolia*, *B. latifolia*, *B. japonicum*, and *B. variegata*. As near as I can tell, though, common box was not very common in Texas.

Camellia japonica
'Pink Perfection'
(*Linda Askey*)

B. microphylla (formerly known as *B. japonica*), the Japanese or little-leaf boxwood was not introduced to Europe until 1860, but may have arrived in the American South somewhat earlier—an 1857 landscape plan of Henry Watson in Greensboro, North Carolina listed a Chinese box which could possibly be a very early use of Japanese boxwood. Today the little-leaf box is more common in modern Southern gardens than the common box, probably because the Japanese species is slightly better adapted to our region's constant heat and humidity.

All forms of boxwood require good drainage. They are susceptible to nematodes, and the newest leaves are prone to frost damage during severe winters or sudden cold snaps. Propagation is by cuttings.   —GG

Camellia spp.

Camellia
Family: Theaceae (Tea)
Zones: 7–10
Although camellias may be found in many modest gardens today, historically this group of shrubs has served as a status symbol in the South. The difficulty with which camellias are propagated has put this task beyond the skills of most amateur gardeners; in the past, even professional nurserymen found the propagation of camellias challenging, and for generations this was reflected in a relatively expensive price of nursery-grown stock. Cost and the difficulty of cultivation has prevented camellias from following the classic path of exotic plants introduced

into the South—camellias never filtered down from the gardens of wealthy collectors to the cottage gardeners' plots. Until recently, to have camellias blooming in your garden was a proud evidence not only of horticultural skill, but also prosperity.

Like so many of the South's cherished ornamental plants, camellias originated in China and came to North America via Europe, but in this case, the steps in that progression are not easy to trace. Two volumes have helped to guide me through the long and fascinating history of these beautiful and important plants. One of these is my copy of H. Harold Hume's *Camellias in America*, which came to me as a gift many years ago from Lynn Lowrey, a well-known horticulturist in Houston. My other resource has been *The Camellia: Its History, Culture, Genetics And A Look Into Its Future Development*, a handbook edited by David L. Feathers and published by the American Camellia Society in 1978, which is available from the society headquarters in Ft. Valley, Georgia.

The genus *Camellia* includes many species, but of these, three are of special importance and interest as heirloom Southern plants: *Camellia sinensis*, *Camellia japonica*, and *Camellia sasanqua*. Of these three, the one that evoked the most intense interest in the early days of the Southern colonies was *Camellia sinensis*, a shrub that, truth be told, is of no special ornamental value.

C. sinensis is a reasonably attractive evergreen shrub that bears single, cream-colored flowers. The blossoms were of no concern to colonial planters,

though; what they were interested in was the plant's foliage, which when dried and processed may be brewed into the popular beverage, tea. This was an ancient taste in China and Japan, and cultivation of the tea plant had been carried on in those lands since ancient times. Tea-drinking became the fashion in England in the late sixteenth century or early in the seventeenth century, but because the leaves had to be shipped in from China, for a long time tea remained an expensive luxury. In fact, tea was brewed only at the "best homes," and the leaves were stored in locked boxes. Still, the growing passion for tea led to a serious trade imbalance with China, whose merchants accepted payment only in silver and who showed little enthusiasm for British goods. The British, in turn, resolved to establish a domestic tea industry, and it was hoped that the new colonies in southern North America would prove a suitable site.

The famous Trust Garden in Savannah was the first to receive seeds of tea. This occurred in 1744, when a shipment came in from the East Indies; unfortunately, according to contemporary observer Francis Moore, these first seeds, "though great Care was taken, did not grow." Plants were sent to Georgia in 1772, and are recorded as growing on Skidaway Island, near Savannah before 1805. This attempt to grow tea near Savannah also failed, seemingly because of a combination of under capitalization and a climate which proved to be very unhealthy for the gardeners.

By 1813, a serious effort to grow tea was underway at Charleston, South Carolina, in the nursery of Philipe

Camellia sasanqua mix (Greg Grant)

Noisette. The planting did not flourish there either, nor did they prosper in Texas—there is a record by the Cat Springs Agricultural Society of unsuccessful attempts at tea culture by early German settlers there. Tea-growing never did become a viable industry in the Southern colonies, though curiously, an English company finally succeeded in establishing a successful plantation near Charleston long after independence. The Lipton Tea Company planted the tea bushes, whose foliage is harvested every year now and marketed under a private label. This success, however, has not been duplicated, for tea is not easily cultivated in North America, and has never been widely grown in the South.

The tea bush has a more beautiful relative, one which did take root in the American South, and that is *Camellia japonica*. This species is best known to Southern gardeners for its handsome foliage and elegant winter and early spring flowers. A native of Korea, China, and Japan, this camellia has flower colors that range from white to turkey red, with many variegated forms. Although well-adapted to much of the South, *C. japonica* has a reputation for being difficult to grow when exposed to less than its ideal growing conditions. It is, however, by far the most important species of the three in relation to our Southern gardening heritage, and specimens of *Camellia japonica* mark the site of many important plantations and old homesteads throughout the South. *Camellia japonica*'s less popular rival in the Southern garden is *Camellia sasanqua*, a shrub of Japanese origin.

Individual blossoms of the Sasanqua camellias, though beautiful, are much less spectacular than those of *C. japonica*. Nevertheless, *C. sasanqua* fills an important garden niche because it is fall blooming—*C. japonica* cultivars (known as "japonicas" in the South) bloom in late winter or early spring.

Of the two ornamental species of camellias, *C. japonica* was the first to arrive in North American gardens. Though frost sensitive, this plant actually made its first entry into the United States as a single red form imported by John Stevens of Hoboken, New Jersey, in 1797 or '98. Presumably Stevens succeeded in the cultivation of this plant, for in 1800 Michael Floy, a nurseryman across the river, in the Bowery of New York City, wrote to a friend that he had brought back from England that July another japonica camellia, "a plant of the Double White [later named 'Alba Plena'] for John Stevens, Esq. of Hoboken, New Jersey, who had two or three years previously imported the Single Red."

For a Northerner such as Stevens, camellias could only succeed as a greenhouse crop, and that was how they were viewed by nearly all the early importers, who were located in the coastal areas of the Northeastern United States. Boston, actually, was the first American center for camellia cultivation, for the wealthy gardeners of that city competed in obtaining new varieties as they moved from China into Europe. In addition, Boston's amateur growers succeeded in raising some new varieties of their own from seed, and

these too were introduced into the florist and nursery trade. The Massachusetts Horticultural Society took the lead in popularizing new camellias, but it was a New York nursery, William Prince's Linnaean Botanic Garden in Flushing, that in 1822 became the first American firm to list camellias in its catalogue. It advertised a stock of seventeen varieties, including one sasanqua camellia, "Lady Banks' tea leaved sasanqua."

Philadelphia soon overtook both Boston and New York as a center for camellia cultivation. That city's leading nurserymen, Robert Buist and David Landreth, both gave liberal space to camellias in their catalogues and were active in promoting these shrubs. In 1829 three camellia varieties were shown at the Philadelphia Horticultural Society Show, and by April 1830 the number of entries had grown to twelve.

It was from Philadelphia that ornamental camellias finally entered the South. David Landreth's nursery kept a representative in Charleston, South Carolina, and in 1819 opened a branch store in that city at 351-352 King Street. Clearly the Landreths took this venture seriously, for David Landreth, Jr., the son of the nursery's founder, took over the management of the King Street store, and continued to work there until April 22, 1862, when the real estate and stock were confiscated by an order of the Confederate States District Court.

Most importations of camellias into the South came from growers along the Atlantic seaboard from Washington D.C. north, though some were also imported from Europe. Plants from both sources were eagerly sought, and private camellia collections grew rapidly as planters realized how well adapted the plants were to the warmer and moister parts of the South. Plants often grew to a great size and age, and camellia blossoms became a part of plantation life in Charleston, Savannah, Wilmington, Mobile, New Orleans and ports of the Mississippi River. Of particular note among the early collections were those at Magnolia Gardens and Middleton Place near Charleston, South Carolina.

The birth of Magnolia Gardens came in 1848, when the Reverend J.G. Drayton, D.D., planted the first

camellias and azaleas of what were to
become remarkable collections. He
eventually assembled more than 300
camellia varieties, and many of these
were seedlings of his own raising. When
Hume wrote his 1955 book many of the
Magnolia Garden plants had reached a
height of twenty-five or more feet tall,
and had trunks measuring thirty inches
or more in circumference—such a
specimen might carry thousands of
flowers at its peak of bloom.

Magnolia Gardens' chief local rival
was Middleton Place, another Charles-
ton-area garden which boasts many fine
old camellias, although here they were
not among the garden's original
plantings. This was inevitable, for when
the landscape at Middleton Place was
first laid out in the years 1764–74,
camellias were not available anywhere
in America. But Middleton Place has
proven well adapted to camellia
cultivation, for these shrubs have
actually naturalized there, and in the
past thickets of "volunteers" formed
around seed-bearing specimens.

The most important name in the
history of Southern Camellias is that of
Prosper Julius Alphonse Berckmans,
who was born on October 13, 1830 at
Aschot, Belgium, and acquired a good
background in horticulture and botany
before immigrating to America. His first
stop on this side of the Atlantic was
Plainfield, New Jersey, but after a short
stay there he resettled in Augusta,
Georgia in 1857, purchasing a half
interest in a nursery that had been
started by D. Redmond. The following
year he bought up the other half of the
business, and he went on to build
Berckmans' Fruitlands Nursery into one
of the most important and influential
nurseries in the South.

Fruitlands introduced many fruit
and ornamental trees and shrubs such as
oriental persimmons, peaches, grapes,
roses, and azaleas into the South, and
was a pioneer in the popularization of
Southeastern natives. This nursery was
also a leading camellia-producer;
indeed, following the Civil War,
Fruitlands was for many years the sole
source for camellia plants in the South.
Berckmans and his sons, Louis, J.,
Robert, and P.J.A. Jr. (who followed him
into the business) kept in touch with

*Camellia
japonica* 'Alba
Plena' (*William
C. Welch*)

Hovey, Wilder, Landreth, and other
camellia experts in the North, and
regularly ordered their new introductions. But the bulk of Fruitlands'
camellias were imported from the
founder's native Belgium, which
throughout much of the nineteenth
century was the center for camellia
propagation and breeding in Europe.

Throughout its half century of
operation, Fruitlands served as a source
for prized camellia specimens all over
the South. After the nursery went out of
business, its site became part of the
Augusta Country Club, and as late as
1955, when Hume was publishing his
camellia guide, venerable plants of 'Prof.
C.S. Sargent', 'Lady Hume's Blush', and
'Alba plena' still flourished there.

Excellent growing conditions for
camellias are found all through the
coastal regions of North and South
Carolina, and Georgia, and along the
Gulf Coast through Mobile, Alabama.
They have been important garden
plants in the Mobile area since early
times. Actually, the southeastern Gulf
Coast as a whole is excellent territory
for camellias—the well-drained acid
soils, high humidity, and abundant
rainfall found there provide ideal
growing conditions.

As early as 1839, Gilbert R. Rotton
reported finding in Mobile "about fifty
varieties of camellias," many of which,
he said, had been imported from
England. In 1853, C.C. and D.W.
Langdon established Langdon Nurseries
about 28 miles north of Mobile, and
camellias were among the wide variety
of plant materials they grew. The

Langdon's catalogue for 1890–91 listed
thirty-nine varieties by name and
assured customers that it could get for
them many more. C. Ravier & Sons
established a florist business in Mobile
shortly after the Civil War and imported
and distributed large numbers of
camellias from France. Today, Mobile's
Bellingrath Gardens is known for a
collection of large old specimens.

Louisiana also has its share of
heirloom camellias. The finest of these
are found around St. Francisville in
West Feliciana Parish, a small Mississippi River village where in antebellum
days many fine plantation homes and
gardens prospered. Early plant introductions were brought upriver from New
Orleans by boat. Of all the gardens in
St. Francisville, the very finest, in its
heyday, was Rosedown, the beautiful
plantation home and garden that Daniel
Turnbull built for his bride, Martha in
1835.

In her garden diary Martha Turnbull
mentioned having 100 japonicas
(camellias) in November 1855. On
September 22, she had mentioned
having purchased commercially
propagated camellias, but also referred
to camellias she has budded and rooted
herself. In addition, Mrs. Turnbull grew
large numbers of camellias from seeds.
In her April 1858 diary entry she wrote:
"April we had 29 pretty japonicas, 59
from seed in ground, 45 seedlings in jars,
196 all together. Six of them are of
Augustus' propagation, 5 also cockade,
and besides thousands are coming up
from seed, two layers of the pretty white
by the summerhouse." The original

Camellia japonica 'Rose Dawn'
(*Greg Grant*)

garden covered twenty acres, and the remnants of those plantings, which are open to the public now, contain many heirloom plants, in particular many fine old camellia specimens. Aged plants of 'Alba plena' and 'Fimbriata' are also reported to exist in the cemetery of the Grace Episcopal Church in St. Francisville.

South of St. Francisville along the Louisiana coast is Avery Island, and the former estate of E.L. McIlhenny of pepper sauce fame. This enterprising businessman was a noted authority on camellias, and a collector who was also active in the propagation and dissemination of the plants. There are many old specimens surviving at his Jungle Gardens today.

The camellia's historical progress across the South eventually culminated in Houston, Texas, the point that marks the far western edge of suitable climate and soils. In tracing the history of camellia cultivation in that city I have had the help of Sadie Gwin Blackburn, whose research in the River Oaks Garden Club archives has yielded intriguing insights. What she has found is that although there are mentions of camellia plantings in Houston before the turn of this century, the real japonica craze did not start until the birth of the River Oaks Garden Club

Azalea Trail in 1936. One of the favorite stops in the early days of the tour was the four acre estate garden of Mr. and Mrs. John E. Green, Jr. The interesting feature of the Green garden was the collection of 150-plus camellias there, plants that had been transplanted from old gardens across the South or else imported from Belgium and France. In addition to such historic favorites as 'Lady Hume's Blush', 'Purple Dawn', 'Alba Plena', 'Chandleri Elegans', and 'Magnoliaflora', the Greens also cultivated a specimen of 'Leucantha', which had been planted in 1898 according to a 1936 *Houston Chronicle* article.

Another Houston garden of note was that of Mr. and Mrs. H.R. Cullen. According to a March 1937 article from the River Oaks Garden Club archives, the six-acre Cullen garden contained over 8,000 plants of azaleas and camellias, which made it the largest known collection of these plants outside of Bellingrath Gardens.

CAMELLIA CULTURE
Camellias require a soil that is both well-drained and yet sufficiently moisture-retentive to maintain the plants through dry spells. If an existing soil is too heavy or sandy, it should be modified by the addition of organic materials. For healthy camellias, the soil must also be acidic, and any water used for irrigation should also be acidic or at least neutral in pH. Mulches are beneficial, since they help insulate the soil from temperature and moisture extremes. Camellias are happiest in a spot that is protected from the hot

afternoon sun, especially during the summer months. Large pine trees are excellent for providing such protection, as long as they are not planted too closely together.

Propagation is by seed, cutting, or grafting. When propagating superior clones by grafting, seedling plants of *C. japonica* or *C. sasanqua* are commonly used as understocks. Grafts are usually made just before growth begins in spring or when plants go dormant in August.

Although they are quite specific in their cultural requirements, camellias are not otherwise demanding. Southern gardeners who can meet camellias' basic needs should certainly try these handsome and historic shrubs. Camellias were featured in the cottage gardens of the past and for generations remained the preserve of the wealthy. But advances in nursery techniques and in our understanding of the camellias' needs have brought these shrubs within the reach of the average gardener. Why not let them add some elegance to your period plantings?   —WCW

Campsis radicans
Trumpet Creeper, Trumpet Vine, Trumpet Flower, Cow–itch
Family: Bignoniaceae (Bignonia)
Zones: 5–11
The native trumpet creeper is a common sight on fence rows over the entire South. This tenacious, deciduous vine will not be denied—it grows where it wants. Fortunately, it is showier and not as rampant as kudzu, and the hummingbirds like it. If trumpet creeper grew like kudzu, we'd have to fog the hummingbirds like mosquitos.

Madame Galen trumpet creeper
(***Campsis* x *tagliabuana* 'Madame Galen'**)
(*Greg Grant*)

Trumpet creeper (*Campsis radicans*)
in an eighteenth-century illustration.
(**Atlanta History Center**)

Chinese trumpet
creeper (*Campsis grandiflora*) in a
San Antonio,
Texas, garden.
(*Greg Grant*)

According to Raymond Taylor's *Plants of Colonial Days*, this species was sent to England as early as 1640 as *Tecoma radicans*. A century later, early American plant collectors Mark Catesby, William Bartram, and Thomas Walter were collecting it as *Bignonia radicans*. It has always been cultivated in the South and was offered by a number of early southern nurseries. Today there are several forms of *Campsis radicans* available including the yellow variety, flava.

The Chinese species, C. *grandiflora*, was found by Engelbert Kaempfer, chief surgeon to the Dutch East India Company, in Japan as early as 1691 but not introduced to England until 1800. It has very large, showy flowers and is only hardy to zone 7. Hybrids between the Chinese and American species were developed in France and are known as C. x *tagliabuana*. The most common and popular of these, a cultivar that was introduced in 1889, is 'Madame Galen'. This plant bears huge showy red-orange flowers.

In its 1881–82 catalogue, Langdon Nurseries near Mobile, Alabama listed "Bignonia radicans-orange scarlet trumpet flower" and "Bignonia grandiflora-Japan trumpet flower." The 1906–07 catalogue of Fruitland Nurseries in Augusta, Georgia listed "Bignonia grandiflora" and "Bignonia hybrida."

Our native crossvine, *Bignonia capreolata*, was also cultivated in old-time Southern gardens. A member of the same family, it was often offered by Southern nurseries along with the trumpet creeper. A spectacular bright-orange-flowered cultivar named 'Tangerine Beauty' is now becoming available in the Southern nursery trade as well.

My first experience with C. *grandiflora* was in San Antonio at Fanick's Nursery. They had a beautiful unidentified specimen which had been propagated with some difficulty from a large plant in town. I was told by several horticulturists that it was the true 'Madame Galen'. After several years of researching it, however, I finally

concluded that it was the Chinese trumpet creeper. It clearly was not of our native species, for like the handful of other Chinese trumpet creepers scattered around San Antonio, the nursery specimen was dwarf in stature.

Several years ago, Dr. J.C. Raulston of North Carolina State University brought the same plant back from the Orient. He has since introduced it into the North Carolina nursery trade. This spectacularly flowered, shrubby vine holds tremendous potential for Southern gardens. Bill was familiar with the plant from his childhood and provided me with the following recollection:

"As a teenager I often visited relatives in the south-central Texas town of Yoakum. Among the plants

Chinese trumpet
creeper (*Campsis grandiflora*) in a
San Antonio,
Texas, garden.
(*Greg Grant*)

Catalpa (*Catalpa bignonioides*) in Old Salem, Winston-Salem, North Carolina. (*Flora Ann Bynum*)

observed were some spectacular specimens of trumpet creepers, most of which were trained as shrubs or small trees, something like wisterias. The huge flowers were a lovely tint of melon-orange and were borne in large terminal clusters. I was told that Mr. Rice, a well known local horticulturist, had been propagating them by grafting onto native trumpet creepers since the 1930s. For a number of years Stevens Nursery sold the plants and in a recent telephone visit with Phil Stevens, son of the original owner and now in the nursery business himself in Yoakum, he remembered being paid by the plant to graft them when he worked for his father back in the 1960s. Much later, in the 1970s I asked my two gardening aunts, Aunt Bern and Aunt Edna, to bring cuttings the next time they came to College Station. They approached an elderly friend who had a handsome specimen of the plant trained into bush form and obtained permission to take cuttings.

"The cuttings were neatly packed and arrived in perfect condition. They rooted easily and I couldn't wait to finally have this plant I had enjoyed seeing but never grown. To my surprise, the cuttings began growing wildly, like the native form. I checked with my aunts to make sure that we had not miscommunicated about just what plant

I had wanted and they assured me they had taken cuttings from the correct plant. Some of the cuttings finally bloomed and were lovely, although more like 'Madame Galen', the form grown by the wholesale nurseries. I was confused and disappointed by the plants which later sprouted vigorously in our flower beds and became a weedy pest, much like the native form.

"Several years ago Greg brought me a plant rooted from a similar beautiful specimen in San Antonio. It has performed like its parent and is beautiful as a large, container-grown specimen near the front entrance of our College Station home. Dr. Dan Lineburger, Professor and Head of our Horticultural Sciences Department here at Texas A&M and Dr. Wayne McKay, Texas A&M Research Horticulturist at El Paso are experimenting with production of the Chinese trumpet creeper in tissue culture. Apparently the plant has both juvenile (running) and adult (bushy) forms. Hopefully the technicalities of its propagation will soon be worked out.

"In recent years the several specimens I enjoyed observing in Yoakum have disappeared, but thanks to Greg and his work in propagating this plant at Lone Star Growers in San Antonio, I have three healthy specimens. They never fail to attract plenty of attention when in bloom. So far they have not

reverted to wilder growing forms, but I will never really trust them."   —GG

Catalpa bignonioides
Southern Catalpa, Common or Easter Indian Bean; Cigar, Fishbait or Worm Tree
Family: Bignoniaceae (Bignonia)
Zones: 6–9

As I began researching catalpas to add to my personal experiences with this tree, I was reminded by a friend that Flora Ann Bynum has a special interest in this species. Flora Ann is chairman of the landscape restoration committee of Old Salem Inc., the organization that has restored the Moravian congregation town of Old Salem in Winston-Salem, North Carolina. She became interested in catalpas when the committee had to locate specimens of this Southern species to replant Salem Square after a major storm in 1989. She proved to have compiled a considerable file of information on catalpa history and culture, and generously shared the following essay:

The Southern catalpa was once highly regarded as an ornamental tree in the Southern landscape; a long and handsome double row on the Palace Green at Colonial Williamsburg attests to the tree's former glory. Today, the Southern catalpa is seldom planted and is sometimes considered a weed tree. In fact, it can be found growing wild throughout the southern United States.

"Catalpa" is a Latinized version of a Cherokee Indian name, and it was in Cherokee country that the naturalist Mark Catsby discovered this species in 1726. He introduced the plant to gardens in America and England, and included an illustration of it in Volume 1 of the work he published in 1731, *The Natural History of Carolina, Florida, and the Bahama Islands*. In this book he wrote:

This tree was unknown to the inhabited parts of Carolina until I brought the seeds from the remote parts of the country. And though the inhabitants are little curious in gardening, yet the uncommon beauty of this tree had induced them to propagate it and 'tis become an ornament to many of their gardens and probably will be the same to ours in England.

There is some evidence that catalpas were planted at the Governor's Palace in Williamsburg as early as 1737, and there is a reference in a journal from 1782 to the catalpas at the palace. Those growing there today were planted after 1930 as part of the restoration.

Eliza Lucas (later Eliza Pinckney) mentions in a 1743 account of William Middleton's gardens at Crowfield near Charleston, South Carolina "…a large square boleing [sic] green…with a walk quite round composed of a double row of fine large flowering Laurel and Catulpas which form both shade and beauty.…"

We have a copy of a page from a 1789 Baltimore, Maryland, newspaper with a nursery advertisement listing "Catalpa Flower-tree" for sale. And George Washington is known to have planted two catalpas at Mount Vernon in 1785.

The Moravians in Salem, North Carolina (the area of Winston-Salem known today as "Old Salem") obviously prized the catalpas, as their records mention this tree a number of times. So, the records mention the planting of catalpas on the square in 1782, the planting of a double row running from

the Girls School to the Parish Grave-yard in 1809 and 1815, and in the graveyard itself in 1820; a catalpa struck by lightning in front of the Pottery in 1809; and so on. In the front yard of the Stauber farm in Bethania, another Moravian settlement near Winston-Salem, are two tremendous old catalpa trees that, judging from their size and alignment with the house, must have been planted when the house was built in 1852. The larger tree stands 64 feet tall, with a trunk 180 inches around at a height of 4 ½ feet from the ground. The spread of the crown is 52 feet.

The southern catalpa has a limited natural range, and is thought to be native only to western Georgia, western Florida, Alabama, and eastern Mississippi. It has large, broad, heart-shaped of triangular, light green leaves that end in a tapering point. In late May and the first week of June here (Atlanta) the showy flowers appear in large pyramidal clusters. Orchidlike and ruffled on the edges, the blossoms seem to be all white at first glance, but closer scrutiny reveals yellow striping and purple-brown spotting inside the flowers. A few weeks after the flowers are gone, long, thin, green, beanlike pods hand in clusters all over the trees.

The other American species of catalpa is the northern or western catalpa (*C. speciosa*) which is native to the Mississippi Valley from Indiana to the Gulf. When settlers began moving into that area and found catalpas, they thought these belonged to the same species as the Southern catalpa. However, Dr. John Ashton Warder of Cincinnati, Ohio, the publisher of *The Western Horticultural Review*, recognized the new trees as a distinct species, and published the first description of the northern catalpa in his magazine in 1853.

Distinguishing the two species is difficult, especially when the trees are young and not in flower. Even foresters sometimes confuse the two. When, following a major storm, we had to replant Salem Square in Old Salem, we were determined to use the species known to the early Moravians. We could not locate any commercial source of the Southern catalpa, however; one of the big nurseries in the Tennessee Valley told us that this species froze out

in their are and so they would only grow northern catalpas. Finally, at a car wash in a neighboring county, we found a large catalpa surrounded by many nice, smaller trees, which the owner said we could dig. So in late fall we obtained several specimens for the square and other locations in Salem.

Yet a doubt still lurked in my mind: had we collected the Southern catalpa or its northern relation? Tree manuals pointed out minor differences in seed pods and leaf size—but added "sometimes and not always." The definitive differences are in the flower structures. Our trees were too small to bloom, but the next year, in early June, I gathered a bucket of fragile blossoms from the tree at the car wash and took them to Dr. R.L. Wyatt, a botany professor at Wake Forest University here. He had his botanical manual all laid out, waiting, and they confirmed that we had the true Southern catalpa. I breathed a sigh of relief!

I have since discovered easier ways for an amateur like me to distinguish the two species. The northern catalpa is a much taller tree, growing straight up like a hickory, and may reach a height of one hundred feet. The Southern species has a much broader crown, and at maturity may measure sixty feet tall. In addition, the Southern catalpa starts branching very low on its central trunk, so that its heavy, stout, trunklike branches form a loosely rounded crown. Its bark is dark-grayish, thin and scaly, while that of the northern catalpa is thick and ridged. But for the amateur the easiest distinguishing mark of the northern catalpa is that it blooms two weeks earlier than the Southern catalpa.

We never see the northern catalpa here except as a garden tree. The Southern catalpa, by contrast, is much naturalized and can be easily spotted from the roadside, as its large leaves are of a much lighter green than the rest of the woodland foliage. The only tree that the Southern catalpa resembles is the also-much-naturalized paulownia, or princess tree.

Catalpas are easy to move, even from the wild, and can be transplanted almost bare-root. They grow rapidly, and a large Southern catalpa in full bloom is a magnificent sight.

Salem Square catalpa in Old Salem. (*Darrell Spencer*)

Far left: Splendid cockscomb planting in Old Salem. (*Flora Ann Bynum*) Left: Cockscomb (*Celosia cristata*) in a Texas garden. (*William C. Welch*)

If catalpas have today lost their fame as an ornamental tree for Southern gardens, they are still beloved by fishermen as a source of catalpa worms, which are prized as freshwater fishbait. The worm is a three-inch-long, greenish yellow caterpillar similar to the tobacco worm, and when mature it exhibits distinctive, horizontal green and black stripes. Their appetite matches their size, and an infestation of catalpa worms may defoliate a tree entirely—fortunately, the tree soon recovers, rapidly producing a new crop of leaves.

Apparently, not all catalpa trees attract worms. The ones we have planted in Salem Square, for example, have so far been wormless, and we hope they remain that way, for defoliated trees are not attractive and the tourists would surely not enjoy the worms. I am told that you can "prime" a tree to produce fishing worms by introducing a few half-grown caterpillars onto it.

So, a tree once valued as an ornamental still brings pleasure to Southerners as a fishbait tree!

—WCW

Celosia cristata
Cockscomb
Family: Amaranthaceae (Amaranth)
Zones: Warm season annual
The name *Celosia* comes from the Greek word kelos, meaning burned; this, apparently, refers to the look of the flowers in some species. Come to think of it, my entire garden in San Antonio looks pretty "kelos" this summer.

In China this flower is called chi kuan ("cockscomb") where it is extensively cultivated. Most believe

Celosia cristata developed from *Celosia argentea* which is listed as native to India but is common in the wild in China. Cited by the English herbalist Gerard in 1633 as "Velvet Floures Gentle (*Amaranthus pannicula incura holifera*)," it was also known in early times by the names of purple amaranth, floramor, and flower gentle. Under any and all of these names, cockscomb has been grown in American gardens since the eighteenth century.

Three forms were introduced into England from Asia in 1570. In 1709, John Lawson, author of *A New Voyage to Carolina*, noted "Prince's Feather very large and beautiful" in the gardens of Carolina. According to Raymond Taylor, it was in Virginia in 1739. In 1760, "Indian Branching cockscombs" were listed for sale in Boston while Thomas Jefferson sowed seeds of cockscomb on April 2, 1767 at Monticello.

There are two types of cockscomb,

the crested and the plumed. My favorite has always been the crested or fasciated type; maybe because of the long line of cockfighters in my family. Flowers of both types may be red, pink, orange, yellow, or variegated, and there are attractive red-leafed varieties as well. Although there are many dwarf cultivars available today, the original types were fairly tall plants. My dear friend Flora Ann Bynum found one over seven feet tall this summer in North Carolina. And I thought everything in Texas was bigger.

The particular cockscomb I grow has been seen in numerous gardens throughout the South and was collected in the older section of San Antonio. Fanick's Nursery, a third generation family-operated nursery in San Antonio, was once known as a producer of cockscomb seed for seed companies, as well as for its introduction of new varieties.

The old form I grow has dark rose-

Cockscomb (*Celosia cristata*) and perilla (*Perilla frutescens*) (*William C. Welch*)

red combs and reaches around three feet tall while producing multiple side stalks. The leaves and stems also have a reddish tinge, especially in bright light. Due to the long stiff stems it makes an excellent cut flower, fresh or dried.

Apparently the branching type has been in and out of favor. Joseph Breck, in his book *The Flower Garden* (1851), writes, "There are the tall and the dwarf varieties, and some that are somewhat branching; but these last should be rejected." But this opinion is directly contradicted by a Thomas More, Esq. in an article in *Floral Magazine* which I found quoted in a book of 1906—the *Hortus Veitchii* by English nurseryman James Veitch. More wrote that "It is not improbable the more branched…forms, if carefully selected might in time yield a plumy crimson variety analogous to the golden one we already possess; and this is the result at which growers should aim, rather than to obtain large expanded combs which take away from the elegant aspect of the plant."

Whether your cockscombs are branched or unbranched, old or new, they require full sun and adequate moisture. Cockscomb is easily propagated from seed collected in the fall and sown in late spring. This plant self-sows and may become something of a weed, though it is very easy to pull. It's like purslane and perilla—if you're going to have weeds, they might as well be pretty ones.   —GG

Chaenomeles speciosa, Cydonia oblonga, and *Pseudocydonia sinensis*
Quinces
Family: Rosaceae (Rose)
Zones: 5–9
The chief attraction of the flowering quinces is their early bloom—the flowers appear on bare twigs, before the leaves emerge in spring. These blossoms may be red, white, pink, or salmon. The flowers are followed in late summer by oblong to rounded, yellowish green fruits that somewhat resemble pears. These fruits have a pleasant aroma and though very hard have been used for making conserves and marmalades. Fruiting on the flowering quinces is erratic, however, in quality and quantity.

Flowering quince (*Chaenomeles speciosa*) (William C. Welch)

Flowering quinces form a thorny, multistemmed clump and vary from three to six feet or more tall and wide, depending upon the cultivar and the growing conditions. There is an orangish-red cultivar sometimes sold as "Texas Scarlet" that is compact in form and grows well even under poor conditions. My experience with other cultivars is that they prefer well-drained, acid soils and sunny or partially shaded exposures. Propagation is from cuttings or division of mature clumps.

These plants are of Chinese and Japanese origin and were introduced to western gardening in 1796 by Sir Joseph Banks of the Royal Botanic Garden at Kew under the name of *Pyrus japonica*. This was only the first of several names, however; for a time the ornamental flowering quinces were classified as *Cydonia* but now seems to have settled under *Chaenomeles*. Many gardeners still refer to the flowering quinces as "japonicas," and the situation is confusing for anyone trying to trace these plants back through historical documents and descriptions.

Complicating this problem still more is the existence of a second group of garden plants, the tree quinces, which grow much taller than the flowering quinces, forming (as the name suggests) a small tree. These, which have played a bigger role in the history of Southern gardens, are currently listed under two separate genera. I have invested considerable effort in determining "the correct" name for the heirloom tree quinces, and believe that common quince of European origins is properly identified as *Cydonia oblonga*, while the

Chinese quince, which is similar in appearance and habit, is named *Pseudocydonia sinensis*.

Taxonomists point to several differences between the two species. Most apparent are that *C. oblonga* has no serrations on the leaf margins and keeps its sepals in the fruit. *P. sinensis* has deeply serrated leaf margins and deciduous sepals. Both of these tree species differ in several ways from the flowering shrub, *Chaenomeles speciosa*. One difference is that the tree types have no thorns.

Chinese quince, *Pseudocydonia sinensis*, is an attractive small tree. Pink flowers, peeling reddish bark, and outstanding fall leaf color add to the landscape value of the tree, which usually reaches fifteen to twenty feet. Fireblight has been reported as an occasional problem with quinces. Lynn Lowrey, well-known horticulturist and nurseryman from Houston, has extolled the virtues of Chinese quince for many years and successfully planted them as far south and west as New Braunfels, Texas.

The pedigree of this species as a Southern garden plant reaches back well into the last century. This I learned from a reference I found in the Cherokee Garden Library in Atlanta, W.W. Meech's book of 1888, *Quince Culture*. In the section titled "Varieties of the Quince," Meech stated that "CHINESE QUINCE (*Cydonia sinensis*) is a variety cultivated for ornament. In the Southern States it is in favor for its fruit, which sometimes attains a weight of two and a half pounds. I have found the quality good for a preserve, though the

Flowering quince
(*Chaenomeles
speciosa*) (*William C.
Welch*)

grain is a little course. The tree grows to the height of thirty feet or more. The foliage assumes a beautiful red tint in autumn. The flowers are rosy red, with a violet odor. It blooms in May. The fruit is a very large, smooth, oblong-oval, and of a greenish yellow. The flesh is firm; and when preserved turns a beautiful pink. It ripens late, and keeps a long time in sound condition.

"This quince was taken to Holland at the close of the last century, and to France in the beginning of this, and fruited in the Jardin du Roi in 1811. It proved hardy in Paris, but the season was short for its fruit to ripen well. It succeeds in the West Indies, and in the United States south of Maryland. To swell some catalogues the Chinese quince trees have been called Hong Kong and Lutea." (The name for Chinese quince was changed to *Pseudocydonia sinensis* around 1990.)

An even earlier reference to the Chinese quince comes from a book of 1851 titled *The Fruit Garden*, by P. Barry. In a section titled "Quinces for Ornament," Barry remarks: "Chinese…quite different in appearance from other quinces. The leaves are glossy, sharply

and beautifully toothed; the fruit is large, oblong, bright yellow, and keeps until spring; little used. The flowers are large and showy, with the fragrance of the violet; worked on the other sorts, rather tender, requiring a sheltered situation. Usually cultivated for ornament. A very tardy bearer."

Bill and Florence Griffin of Atlanta procured a handsome specimen of quince for the Tullie Smith garden at the Atlanta History Center. Serrations on the leaf margins indicate that this specimen is *Pseudocydonia sinensis*. The fruit of this tree is ovoid in shape and when ripe is golden yellow in color and from four to six inches long. I also remember nice specimens of this species planted by Emory Smith at his garden on Highland Road in Baton Rouge (now Hilltop Arboretum). The fruit is highly aromatic and was traditionally displayed in bowls in the home. Its pink flowers and handsome fruit make it an attractive small tree. *Cydonia oblonga*, the second species of tree quince prominent in Southern gardens is the common fruiting quince naturalized in the hills and woodlands of Italy, the south of France, Spain, Sicily, Sardinia,

and North Africa. According to the ancient Roman encyclopaedist Pliny, "There are many kinds of this fruit in Italy; some growing wild in the hedgerows, others so large that they weigh the boughs down to the ground."

The Romans boiled the fruit of this plant with honey, much as modern cooks make marmalade. Today, *Cydonia oblonga* is important as an understock for pears as well as for its own fruit.

Flora Ann Bynum, Secretary Treasurer of the Southern Garden History Society, lives in Old Salem, North Carolina. After visiting the quince at the Tullie Smith garden in Atlanta, Flora Ann wrote in a letter to me dated October 17, 1990, about a quince that appears to be *Cydonia oblonga*:

There is an old quince tree here in a yard in Salem, which I trotted up to see as soon as I got home Tuesday; it is in leaf much like the Tullie quince, but the edges of the Tullie quince leaves are very serrated, while the leaves of the Salem quince have a smooth edge. Also, the Salem quince has one glorious fruit on it, a beautiful golden yellow, shaped just like a very, very large Golden Delicious apple, but

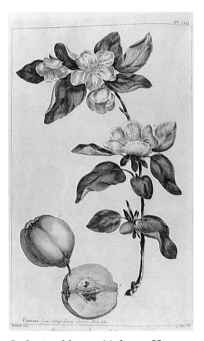

Cydonia oblonga (*Atlanta History
Center*)

Pseudocydonia sinensis **in the Tullie Smith garden at the Atlanta History Center. (William C. Welch)**

little care, and the fruit is often knotty and inferior. This practice is a very erroneous one. No tree is more benefitted by manuring than the quince. In a rich, mellow, deep soil, even if quite dry, it grows with thrice its usual vigour and bears abundant crops of large and fair fruit. It should, therefore, be planted in deep and good soil, kept in constant cultivation, and it should have top-dressing of manure every season, when fair and abundant crops are desired. As to pruning, or other care, it requires very little indeed—an occasional thinning out of crowding or decayed branches, being quite sufficient. Thinning the fruit, when there is an overcrop, improves the size of the remainder. Ten feet apart is a suitable distance at which to plant this tree.

Gilbert Onderdonk was a well-educated and successful nurseryman who resided in Victoria County, Texas. He was influential in all areas of the nursery business but specialized in fruit. In his Mission Valley Nurseries descriptive catalogue for 1888 he wrote concerning quinces, "When properly treated the quince does well here. Nothing turns up its nose quicker at a poor soil than the quince. Plant in rich soil, apply a little salt on the surface of the ground each year. The Apple or Orange quince is well tested here. Priced 50 cents." Judging from his description, the quinces Onderdonk was describing were probably *Cydonia oblonga*.

For a tree that once was listed in almost every nursery catalogue in the South, quinces are surprisingly rare today. This is especially true in the case of *Cydonia oblonga*; the Chinese quince (*Pseudocydonia sinensis*) is certainly not common, but is found more often than *Cydonia oblonga*. Fireblight, quince rust, and other diseases seem to be responsible for this near disappearance of a once-classic plant.

Yet there are faint promises of a return. Lynn Lowrey in Houston reports little or no fireblight on the Chinese quinces he has planted, and Flora Ann

flatter. The fruit was obviously mature because of the color, but nowhere near the size or shape Florence Griffin tells me the Tullie quince gets.

The selection of quinces available to gardeners of the last century seems to have been rich, at least in Georgia. In the collection of antique nursery catalogues at the Cherokee Garden Library in the Atlanta History Center, I found references to the following: Fruitland Nursery (1858) had 'Portugal' and 'Angers' varieties; Pomona Hall Nursery (Clarksville, Georgia, 1856) listed pear-shaped quince, apple-shaped quince, and 'Angers'; and Downing-Hill Nursery in 1855–56 noted Apple, Orange, Portugal, and Cocksackie, while in 1870–71 they listed Apple, Orange, 'Angers'.

In my own files, I also turned up some indications of the availability of quinces in other areas of the South. For example, Affleck's Southern Nurseries, near Natchez, Mississippi, in their 1851–52 catalogue lists both Chinese quince and *C. oblonga*: "Quince-Apple-shaped, Lemon, Portugals, Pear shaped and Chinese; a handsome and hardy

plant; fruit very large and excellent .75 cents." Another listing came from nearer my home, in the catalogue of Fairview Fruit Farm in Brenham, Texas, which in its 1875 catalogue advertised "Quinces—Angers, Apple or Orange, and Chinese—of immense size, rather coarse, but desirable for its magnificent appearance."

Martha Turnbull provided forty-eight years (1837–1895) of illuminating details of her gardening activities at Rosedown Plantation near St. Francisville, Louisiana. She refers several times to "eating quinces" and described growing plants from seed. Mrs. Turnbull also refers to specific quinces as "Aunt Sarah Quince" and "Aunt Isabelle's" quince (1864).

A.J. Downing, in his classic *Fruits and Fruit Trees of America* published in 1857, provides considerable insight into the culture of quinces:

The Quince grows naturally in rather moist soil, by the side of rivulets and streams of water. Hence it is a common idea that it should always be planted in some damp neglected part of the garden, where it usually receives

Desert willow (*Chilopsis linearis* 'Bubba') in a San Antonio garden. (*Greg Grant*)

Bynum reported of the specimen in Old Salem that as of the summer of 1994 it was thriving and loaded with fruit. The quinces were once an important part of the Southern landscape and cuisine—perhaps they will be again.   —WCW

Chilopsis linearis
Desert Willow, Flowering Willow
Family: Bignoniaceae (Bignonia)
Zones: 8–11 (particularly the southwest)
I had first encountered this native tree as a xeriscape plant for the Southwest, and had assumed it was a modern discovery—so imagine how surprised I was to learn that almost every early Texas nursery carried desert willow.

As is so often the case, the common name for this plant is deceptive. The desert willow is not a willow at all, though it looks somewhat like one, with its narrow foliage and somewhat weeping habit. Native to dryland habitats in west Texas, the southwestern United States, and Mexico, desert willow is a drought-tolerant, deciduous small tree that blooms from summer till frost, bearing lavender and white, snapdragon-like blossoms.

A purple form and a white one were listed in Gilbert Onderdonk's 1888 Mission Valley Nurseries catalogue from Nursery, Texas. About the white the catalogue says: "A new variety, now for the first time introduced to the public. It was found by Dr. Atlee of Laredo, Texas in the sand of the Rio Grande near the seminary at Laredo. We obtained it from him, and now have a few plants for sale. It will be considered very beautiful by all who see it. The

foliage is of a paler green than the purple which we began to disseminate when we first started our nursery in 1870."

By 1898 this same nursery was also offering the cultivar Major, "the largest flowering variety." Other early Texan nurseries that carried the desert willow were D.G. Gregory and Son's Val Verde Nurseries at Alleytown, J.F. Leyendecker's Pearfield Nursery at Frelsburg, G.A. Shattenberg's Waldheim Nursery at Boerne, W.A. Yates' Nursery at Brenham, F.T. Ramsey's Austin Nursery at Austin, and Anna B. Nickels' Arcadia Garden at Laredo. I also found it listed by P.J. Berckmans' Fruitland Nurseries of Augusta, Georgia.

Desert Willow was grown and admired by early German-Texan John Meusebach, who was a naturalist, nurseryman, politician, and founder of Fredericksburg, Texas. This tree has naturalized around his old homesite and nursery in Loyal Valley.

Several years ago Texas A&M University released a number of new cultivars of desert willow, but none seems to have caught on in the trade. Two dark-flowered selections named 'Burgundy' and 'Burgundy Lace' are available in the wholesale nursery trade, however. In addition, Lone Star Growers of San Antonio, Texas has also introduced a Paul Cox (San Antonio Botanical Center) selection named 'Bubba', which has dark early blooming flowers, darker green foliage, and an uncharacteristic compact, upright habit.

Desert willow is very easy to grow on any site with well-drained soil and full sunlight. Nor is the desert part of its

name coincidental—this is an extremely drought-tolerant species. Use it in the landscape as you would a crape myrtle. Propagation is by seed or cuttings of improved selections.   —GG

Citrus spp., *Fortunella* spp., and *Poncirus* spp.
Citrus
Family: Rutaceae (Rue)
Zones: 9–10
There are at least sixteen species and several genera that compose plants that we call citrus. All are native to south and southeast Asia and the Malay Peninsula.

Most citrus species are tropical in origin and are killed outright or severely damaged when temperatures drop below freezing. They are highly prized for their fruit, but, with their large, shiny, evergreen foliage, and highly fragrant white to purplish flowers, are also valuable as ornamentals. Some are best cultivated as shrubs while others are useful as small trees. Most are grown as grafted plants with the common understocks being sour and trifoliate orange.

The Spanish are usually credited with bringing citrus to North America. The sweet orange (*Citrus sinensis*) had been introduced into the lands of the western Mediterranean region by the Romans around the first century A.D., following their conquest of the Near East. Columbus is known to have taken orange, lemon, and citron seeds from the Canary Islands with him to Hispaniola on his second voyage in 1493. Thirty years later Oviedo's testimony stated that sweet oranges were already abundant in Hispaniola. Spanish colonists subsequently introduced the trees into coastal areas near Charleston; Savannah; Mobile, Alabama; New Orleans; St. Augustine, Florida; as well as into South Texas, California, and Mexico. Commercial production of oranges, grapefruit, lemons, limes, satsumas, mandarin oranges, and kumquats have all been successful in the South at various times.

The appeal of their fruit and their ornamental qualities had also led to citrus trees' cultivation well to the north of their natural, warm-weather range. Once again, the Romans were pioneers in this, building houses glazed with sheets of mica to cultivate citrons as early as the first century A.D. Special glasshouses, later known as "orangeries," designed for growing sweet oranges were common features of northern Italian estates by the fourteenth century, and by the seventeenth century, orangeries were appearing throughout northern Europe. The various kinds of citrus continue to be grown as container and greenhouse subjects over much of the world.

A greenhouse is not necessary for growing citrus in much of the South, if the gardener is willing to experiment with the less familiar sorts. Some citrus species are considerably more cold hardy than others. Satsumas and tangerines (*C. reticulata*), kumquats (*Fortunella* sp.) and calamondins (*C. Citrofortunella mitis*) are probably the most cold hardy edible citrus.

The trifoliate orange (*Poncirus trifoliata*) has inedible fruit but the plant is prized for its hardiness as an ornamental into zone 7. Its green stems, large and fragrant white flowers and ease of culture make it useful for very thorny hedges and specimen plantings all over the South. It is an aromatic small tree that can reach 30 feet tall. The fruit is like a small, pubescent, thick-skinned orange.

A native of China, the trifoliate orange was introduced into England in 1850, and by 1894 was listed in the catalogue of J.F. Leyendecker's Pearfield Nursery, Frelsburg, Texas. Leyendecker recommended this species as an ornamental shrub or hedge plant. The ease with which trifoliate oranges are cultivated may be deduced from the fact that they have escaped cultivation in some areas of the South to flourish in the wild. Flying Dragon (*P. trifoliata* var. *monstruosa*) is a well-known variety of trifoliate orange that has a most interesting zigzag branching pattern. It is popular as an understock for other citrus or as a specimen landscape plant.

Pamela Puryear, a garden historian from Navasota, Texas, remembers a handsome four-foot clipped hedge of *P. trifoliata* that used to grow at the Presbyterian manse (c. 1869) in Navasota. It was destroyed in the 1970s when the home was demolished to make

Clockwise from upper left: Meyer lemon (*Citrus Limon* 'Meyer Lemon') (*William C. Welch*) Nagami kumquat (*Fortunella margarita*) (*Greg Grant*) Trifoliate orange (*Poncirus trifoliata*) (*Greg Grant*)

way for a new building. Trifoliate oranges are also used for breeding with other citrus for their ability to withstand freezing temperatures.

The Kumquat (*Fortunella* sp.) is named for Robert Fortune, the great Scottish plant explorer of the mid-1800s, who introduced it to Europe. It has never been found in the native state but is said to be indigenous to China, where it has been cultivated for many years, as it has been in Japan, Indochina, and Java. There are two common forms of kumquats; Nagami (*F. margarita*), which are oblong, and Meiwa (*F. margarita* x *japonica*), which are round. They form dense shrubs that can reach ten to twelve feet in height and spread to about eight feet, but may also be kept smaller for many years by confining the roots in containers.

Kumquat trees flower and fruit much of the year and are prized as container plants, shrubs, hedges, or specimens. The fruit of the kumquat is about 1½ inches in diameter, and is sweet and edible when fresh—the entire fruit is eaten, skin and all. Kumquat fruits are also commonly preserved,

either as whole fruits or in a high-quality marmalade.

Kumquats are usually budded onto trifoliate orange rootstocks. Although hardier than most citrus, they occasionally freeze or are damaged by cold in zone 9. Kumquats are extensively used in the restored *parterre* garden of the Hermann-Grima House in the French Quarter of New Orleans.

Grapefruit is now considered to be a hybrid between the pomelo and the sweet orange. The production of grapefruit is a major enterprise in Florida, South Texas, and California. It is a fruit primarily of American origin with major varieties being developed in the last fifty years or so in the states where they are produced. Grapefruit are among the least cold hardy of citrus.

Sweet oranges were especially important to the early gardens of Charleston, South Carolina, where they were grown commercially as well as in many of the famous courtyards of the city. The devastating freezes of 1898–99 killed most of the trees in the area. New Orleans also has a tradition of orange trees that go back to the Spanish period,

Mayhaw orchard
(*Cratageous opaca*)
(*Marty Baker*)

and are esteemed in various localities."

The mayhaw is native to wetland areas across much of the South. As a teenager in the 1930s, Marvin Baker (Marty Baker's father) rode twelve miles on horseback from Burke, Texas to Taggert's Flat, located two miles east of the Neches River in Angelina County to gather mayhaw fruit in late April. The fruit was gathered from flooded, flat river bottoms filled with one to three feet of water for nine months of the year. After being swept from the water's surface, the mayhaws were put into cotton sacks. At home, Marvin's mother would boil the whole fruit in water to

and remnants of a thriving area of commercial orange production still remain below New Orleans in Plaquemines Parish.

Lemons (*C. Limon*) and limes (*C. aurantifolia*) are even less cold hardy than oranges and can be grown outdoors only in tropical areas. 'Meyer Lemon' is slightly more cold hardy than other lemons and are productive when grown in containers as well as in the ground. Most limes are propagated as seedlings and are named for their point of origin, such as Key, West Indian, or Mexican limes. Limes are also useful as container plants since they are compact in growth and have fruit or fragrant flowers many months of the year. Citrus trees grow best in well-drained soils and require vigilant pest and weed control to thrive and produce well. Scale insects, white flies, and numerous diseases attack the fruit and plant. —WCW

Crataegus opaca
Mayhaw
Family: Rosaceae (Rose)
Zones: 4–9

This is an attractive and unusual small tree, an asset to almost any garden. Yet its interest for our ancestors lay in its fruits. In the mid 1800s and early 1900s, Southerners relied mainly on the native fruits that were growing close by, and ate whatever was in season. Therein is the mayhaw's special value: it is the first native tree to flower in the late winter, and so the first to ripen fruit, yielding its harvest in early spring (April and early May).

The mayhaw fruits are unfamiliar to most Southerners today, and for

information on them we turned to Marty Baker, Extension Horticulturist at the Texas A&M Research and Extension Center in Overton. He has a special interest and expertise in mayhaws and has provided the following information on them:

Ripe mayhaws signal the end of winter in the South. This event comes in April or May, when the small (⅝–1 inch in diameter), applelike, fragrant fruits are gathered and processed into syrups, jellies, pies, wine, and vinegar. The fruit has ornamental value while still on the tree, and the showy white blossoms that precede them (opening in January and February) are especially welcome. L.H. Bailey in his *Sketch of the Evolution of Our Native Fruits* (1898) refers to mayhaws as thorn-apples and states: "Several of these thorn-apples produce fruit of great beauty, and some of the fruits are pulpy and edible,

Mayhaw (*Cratageous opaca*) (*John Lipe*)

The following recipes are from J.S. Akin, Sibley, Louisiana and Billie Jean Capps, Diboll, Texas:

MAYHAW SYRUP
1 cup mayhaw juice (as for jelly)
½ cup sugar
½ cup white Karo (to prevent jelling)

Rapid boil 18-20 minutes.

MAYHAW JELLY
To cook mayhaws
1 gallon of mayhaws and 1 gallon water

Cook until tender; strain through a cloth; squeeze out all juice. This should make 10 cups of juice. If not, add enough water to make 10 cups.

To make jelly
5 cups mayhaw juice
7 cups sugar
1 box Sure-Jell

Cook as directed on Sure-Jell instructions.

Far left: Greg's grandmother's milk and wine lily (*Crinum x herbertii*) (*Greg Grant*) Left: Milk and wine lily (*Crinum x herbertii*) in a Jefferson, Texas garden. (*William C. Welch*)

make syrup, which was the first fresh fruit product to appear on the table after the cold winter months.

Selections have been collected from various regions—from the Neches River bottom, in flooded flats north of Buna and in groves close to Deweyville, Texas; in the Pearl River swamps of Mississippi; in lowlands around Logansport, Louisiana; and in groves near Thomasville, Georgia—and planted in upland orchards to produce numerous clones, some of which are available today. Although native to wetlands, mayhaws also thrive on drier sites and are sufficiently attractive to plant in shrub or herbaceous borders, where they will form fifteen- to thirty-foot trees. They grow best in acid soils.

Mayhaw seed viability varies greatly from tree to tree. Pulped fruit from trees with viable seeds can be fermented from three to six days at warm room temperatures above 75 degrees F. The seeds are then removed from the pulp and washed with water through a screened collander. These seeds generally have excellent germination percentages. A more tested method is to clean the seed and store in damp sand at about 35 degrees F. for eight months before planting. Also, many gardeners have had success by removing the pulp from fresh fruit and planting seed under intermittent mist systems.

Mayhaw cuttings can be rooted under intermittent mist or in a humidity chamber during the summer. Dipping in a root-promoting hormone may facilitate rooting. Plants grafted onto understocks or rooted from cuttings will produce fruit like the plant from which

the cutting or graft was taken.

After World War II, a few hobbyists and farmers tinkered with mayhaws and marketed small amounts of jellies and syrups at roadside stands. The mayhaw's full potential has not been recognized yet, but they are receiving a degree of attention now. In at least four states, including Texas, agricultural scientists are learning how to manage the mayhaw as a crop, like apples, pears and other fruit. Unfortunately, the plants are proving susceptible to fireblight, cedar apple rust, and other problems that challenge fruit crops.

Cultivation may be important to the mayhaw's survival, for many native stands have been destroyed or threatened by development and changes in natural drainage patterns. This tree is a distinctive part of our Southern heritage, it is worth cultivating in our landscapes as an ornamental or edible fruiting plant. —WCW

Crinum spp.
Crinum, Crinum Lily, Milk and Wine Lily
Family: Amaryllidaceae (Amaryllis)
Zones: 7–11

The various species of Crinum belong to the most important, the most beautiful and the most popular of Florida garden plants. No plants grow so easily, with so little attention, and no plants are so floriferous and so deliciously fragrant.
Henry Nehrling, *Bailey's Standard Encyclopedia of Horticulture*, Volume 2, 1917

Although they do not rank among the oldest horticultural heirlooms of our region, in the past hundred years, crinums became synonymous with Southern gardens. In many ways, they remind me of Texas and the South. They're huge, the biggest of all bulbs. They're so showy and fragrant that they border on being obnoxious. They're so tough that Bill claims none have ever died—and he may be right.

As members of the amaryllis family (not the lily family, as the common names might lead you to expect), crinums are often found listed as *Amaryllis* in old references. According to *Hortus Third*, there are about 130 species of crinums, native mainly to the tropics and South Africa. Originally grown as greenhouse specimens, these bulbs became common Southern dooryard plants around the turn of the century.

Most early crinums made their trip to the United States by way of the Caribbean, some as early as the mid 1800s. Many were introduced through Florida nurseries, and the first U.S. nursery to list crinums was Reasoner's Royal Palms Nursery at Manatee, Florida, which began selling the bulbs as early as 1886. Some crinums also arrived by way of Dutch nurseries such as Krelage and Van Tubergen. Around 1837 Krelage listed seven crinums, including *Crinum americanum* and two forms of *C. bulbispermum*.

C. americanum, known as the southern swamp lily, is our only native crinum. As the name says, it's native to local wetlands. It is often confused with our native white spider lily (*Hymenocallis*).

Crinum powellii album in Mr. Kesel's garden in Paige, Texas. (**William C. Welch**)

C. *bulbispermum* (formerly C. *capense*, C. *longifolium*, and *Amaryllis longifolia*) is our most commonly cultivated species, and the most cold hardy as well. A native of South Africa, it is often found naturalized in ditches, cemeteries, and around old homesites in the South. Its rather small, drooping, trumpet-shaped flowers may be white, pink, or striped. Normally the first crinum to bloom in spring, it may continue flowering until frost. Its wide, straplike, blue-gray foliage, which cascades and twists upon the ground, reminds me of a giant allium. This species is one of the parents of most of our common hybrid garden crinums, which inherit C. *bulbispermum*'s mounding foliage, along with its cold hardiness. It seems that this may be a very old garden plant, for in 1629, John Parkinson made reference to a *Narcissus Marinus Exoticus*, "the strange sea daffodil," which may have been C. *bulbispermum*. In 1859, this crinum also won a mention in Charles Darwin's *Origin of Species*, as part of the great naturalist's discussion of William Herbert's work with the pollinization of C. *bulbispermum*.

This work deserved a mention, for Dean William Herbert (1778–1847), an English minister, botanist, naturalist, artist, and reform politician, has been called the "father of the Amaryllis family." His 1837 *Amaryllidaceae* is considered the greatest taxonomic treatment of this family ever undertaken, and until recently the record for breeding the greatest variety of crinum hybrids indisputably belonged to Herbert.* Certainly, the most commonly cultivated hybrid crinums in the South are C. x *herbertii*, a hybrid he first produced around 1837 by crossing C. *scabrum* and C. *bulbispermum*. A number of others later produced different variations of this same hybrid. Plants of this group typically have cascading, slightly glaucous-green foliage, large flowers stalks, and drooping, candy-striped flowers—the source of the common name, "milk and wine lilies." These bloom heavily from summer to fall, shortly after any rain or irrigation.

Like many crinums, C. x *herbertii* clones are very fragrant. As a child, I always thought they smelled like my mom's hand lotion. To this day when I smell them, they take me back to my grandmother's porch where the two large clumps on both sides of the steps bathed us with their perfume as we rocked in the swing. In addition to many unnamed forms, I cultivate one called 'Carroll Abbott', which is big, early and very free blooming. My granny's form will always be my favorite though.

* Today, the record is probably held by two Texans, Dr. Thad Howard of San Antonio and David Lehmiller of Kountz, Texas.

It is possible that some of Herbert's material filtered into Florida by way of Bermuda or other British possessions. Crosses between C. *zeylanicum* and C. *bulbispermum* are also considered milk and wine lilies, along with just about any that have striped flowers.

The most common hybrid crinum in the upper South is the relatively cold hardy C. x *powellii*. This cross between C. *moorei* and C. *bulbispermum* was described in 1887 and introduced in 1888. A number of variations of this hybrid exists including the varieties album (white), roseum (pink), and rubrum ("red"). Van Tubergen listed three clones in 1895. C. x *powellii* has neater foliage than C. x *herbertii* and tall slender flowers stalks with more erect flowers, not quite as gaudy. C. x *powellii* is a summer bloomer. It is available from a number of commercial bulb sources.

Another hybrid commonly encountered in the South is 'J.C. Harvey'. This plant is a cross between C. *kirkii* and C. *moorei* or C. *kirkii* and C. *yemense* that was developed late in the last century by J.C. Harvey in southern California and afterwards grown by him on the Isthmus of Tehuantepec in Mexico. It was first marketed by the Reasoner Brothers of the Royal Palms Nursery in 1902. 'J.C. Harvey' has neat, cornlike foliage and blooms in summertime, bearing light pink flowers similar to those of C. x *powellii* on slender stems. Though it multiplies rapidly, it is a rather shy bloomer, which probably explains why most crinums given away turn out to be 'J.C. Harvey'. I once rescued a whole clump sitting cheerfully by the roadside

Crinum x 'Ellen Bosanquet' (**Greg Grant**)

amongst discarded trash, because I knew better than to be daunted by the former owner's rejection. Another frequently found, fairly hardy hybrid is 'Ellen Bosanquet', a Louis Bosanquet introduction. It is apparently a cross between *C. scabrum* and *C. moorei*, and has semi-erect and wavy green foliage that may burn a little on hot, sunny sites. From summer to fall 'Ellen Bosanquet' bears, attractive dark pink flowers that are as close to red as a crinum gets. It makes a very striking cut flower and has a nice scent—my grandmother loves this one.

There are a number of rather common hybrids of *C. americanum*, including 'Elsie', which Elizabeth Lawrence originally found in an Atlanta garden. This cultivar is reportedly common in old gardens of coastal North Carolina. Like most of our enduring hybrids, its other parent appears to be *C. bulbispermum*. Another crinum, one that is common in South Texas, is a milk and wine type which goes by the name of 'Royal White'. 'Royal White' was apparently a Luther Burbank introduction. These *C. americanum* hybrids have loose, somewhat spidery blossoms and of course a pleasing fragrance. Their flowers stalks have a bad habit of falling over under the weight of the blossoms, however.

There are many other cultivars of crinums. Unfortunately, most are hard to come by or are quite expensive—some cost as much as $100 per bulb. One of Bill's favorites is 'Mrs. James Hendry', a Henry Nehrling introduction, whose delicate pink blossoms are known for their delicious fragrance. I consider Henry Nehrling to be the father of amaryllid culture in the South.

Crinums are very easy to grow throughout the South. They multiply best however in loose, sandy loam soils. Although quite drought-tolerant, they bloom best with regular irrigation. Many of the everblooming types tend to bloom after each rainfall or heavy irrigation. A light application of high-nitrogen fertilizer can also stimulate repeat blooms, as well as promoting healthy, lush foliage. When my crinum foliage grows ragged or becomes infested with insects, as it periodically does, I cut it off at the base. The plants quickly replace the loss with healthy, new

leaves. Propagation is by division with a good strong back and a sturdy sharp shooter!

In addition to Herbert, other breeders of classic crinums were Henry Nehrling of Florida, Luther Burbank of California, Cecil Houdyshel of California, and Theodore Mead of Florida, who reportedly received a collection of nearly one hundred different crinums from India around 1900.

I don't know of any plant which has been so ignored by the modern gardeners of the South as have been the crinums. There is probably no other flowering perennial that adapts well to either extreme drought or aquatic conditions, all the while providing stunning displays of fragrant, cut flower quality blossoms. Crinums belong in the South, so I say plant them whether you like them or not. When I was actually reading one of the books in my collection recently, I ran across an author who, describing crinums, saw their potential early on:

> They are, however, in many respects especially interesting, and when the time comes that plants are grown for what there is in them, rather than for what can be made from them, in way of profit, we shall expect to see many of the Crinums pretty generally cultivated.
> C.L. Allen, *Bulbs and Tuberous-Rooted Plants*, 1893

I'm waiting.   —GG

Deutzia scabra
Fuzzy Deutzia, Deutzia
Family: Saxifragaceae (Saxifrage)
Zones: Zones 6–9
Deutzia was named for J. Deutz, a sheriff of the Dutch city of Amsterdam, and was introduced to western gardens from Japan and China in 1822. The species name, *scabra*, refers to the roughness of the leaves, which in this plant's native country, Japan, are used by cabinet makers in polishing the finer kinds of woods. The plant is a graceful, deciduous shrub with a height and spread of eight to ten feet that bears showy, upward pointing, cylindrical panicles of beautiful white flowers in midspring. The arching branches have attractive,

Deutzia (*Deutzia scabra*) (Greg Grant)

peeling brown bark. They seem better acclimated to the middle South than zone 9 and the coastal areas. Deutzias are easily propagated by cuttings, divisions, or layers. A related species, *D. gracilis*, grows only three to four feet tall and blooms earlier in spring, often with tulips and daffodils. In describing both these species of deutzias, nurseryman Peter Henderson wrote in *Practical Floriculture* in 1890 that they are "exceedingly showy when in blossom, and are two of the most desirable shrubs in cultivation." He further extolled the value of *D. gracilis* as a plant to force in winter and spring for the cut flower trade.

As a landscape plant deutzia lends itself well to massing in shrub borders or, occasionally, to planting as a specimen or hedge. They provide a lovely background for bearded irises, which bloom about the same time as the deutzias. Deutzia flowers last about two weeks in spring and after that, aside from their rather interesting flaking brown bark, these shrubs provide little visual benefit to the garden for the rest of the year. They prefer good, well-drained loamy soils but are tolerant of a fairly wide range of soil pH. Once established, deutzias are quite drought tolerant.   —WCW

Eureka persimmon (*Diospyros kaki*) (*William C. Welch*)

Diospyros kaki, and *D. texana*

Persimmon
Family: Ebenaceae (Ebony)
Zones: 7–9

With their bright orange fruits borne on naked stems, persimmons have few rivals for fall display. They are practical, too: persimmons are among the longest-lived and least troublesome of the fruit trees that may be grown in the South. And the fruit, once thoroughly ripe, is delicious—the botanical name for this tree, *Diospyros*, which means "fruit of the gods," is no exaggeration.

The type of persimmon commonly seen in the produce section is the fruit of a Chinese species, *Diospyros kaki*, which has a long history of cultivation in Japan. This species was brought to Europe in 1796, and travelled to North America in the nineteenth century, so it is an authentic planting for historic gardens. But the species that should be of special interest to the Southern gardener is our native *D. virginiana*, the species name of which refers to the colony of Virginia. Don't be misled by this, however; this persimmon is indigenous and common all over the South.

The persimmon is dioecious, that is, the male and female flowers are borne on different trees and only female trees bear fruit. This fruit is oblong in shape and ranges in size from ¾ to 1 ½ inches in diameter. Fruit size and quality varies markedly from tree to tree, as does the season of maturity. Some trees start ripening their fruit as early as August, while others aren't ready for harvest until February. In any case, the fruit should not be picked until soft and dead ripe, for under-ripe fruits are highly astringent and pucker the mouth like alum. When fully ripe, though, the native persimmons can be sweet, tasty and nutritious, as good as the fruit of the grocery store Japanese types, even though much smaller.

Early settlers and explorers knew and appreciated native persimmons. They were mentioned in writings of De Soto in 1539, Jan de Laet in 1558 and John Smith in the seventeenth century. These pioneers probably learned of the persimmon from Indians, who mixed persimmon pulp with crushed corn to make a kind of bread. Nor is the fruit the persimmon's only valuable product—woodworkers prize the hard, tough wood which has been used to make tool handles and golf clubs. In addition, many species of birds and animals find the fruit attractive as a food source.

Texas or Mexican persimmon (*D. texana*) is an interesting plant that is native to south Texas and Mexico. The fruit is somewhat smaller than that of the eastern persimmon and is black when ripe, at which time it is sweet and may be used in the same ways as that of *D. virginiana*. The foliage of the Texas persimmon is smaller, too, and unlike the rough, alligator-skin-like trunks of the eastern persimmon, that of the Texas persimmon is smooth and gray, with thin layers of bark flaking off the surface. Reaching a height of forty feet, the Texas persimmon is a handsome tree that is sometimes used for landscape purposes, especially in areas of alkaline soil, where this species thrives. It is also important as a source of food for wildlife.

Persimmons have a taproot system that makes them difficult to transplant. Early Southern gardeners sometimes grafted wood from superior fruiting types onto small seedlings or more mature trees. *Diospyros virginiana* varies in size but can reach forty to fifty feet under ideal conditions.

Excerpts from nursery catalogs give insight into the adaptability and interest in persimmons: Pearfield Nursery (Frelsburg, Texas, 1888): "Japanese Persimmon—lists six types including 'Masugata.'...This variety we received from the Agricultural Department, Washington, D.C. in 1878. Produced its first fruit in 1881, and has not failed since." Mission Valley Nurseries (Victoria County, Texas, 1888): "Japan Persimmon—We planted trees of this fruit in 1878. They are thrifty and productive. We believe this fruit will prove an acquisition to Southern Texas." The Austin Nursery, F.T. Ramsey (Austin, Texas, 1907): "Japan Persimmon grafted on native persimmons, Hachiya, Hyakume, Okaume, Tane Nashi, Yemon."

Waldheim Nursery, Boerne, Texas, 1895–96: "Japan Persimmons. A new and valuable fruit. It is perfect adaptability throughout the South coupled with the extreme oddity and delicious flavor of its fruit, the later somewhat resembling that of a date or fig when

Japanese persimmon (*Diospyros kaki*) (*William C. Welch*)

dried, makes it a very desirable fruit for this section. The tree is rather dwarfish in growth with large, glossy foliage and bears very young often at the age of 2–3 years and is enormously productive; the fruit will ship safely to the most distant market and will stay on the tree until frost. There are a number of varieties varying in shape and color. Price .50 cents."

And in a letter from the Department of Agriculture, Washington, D.C., February 10, 1879 to J.F. Lyendecker, Pearfield Nursery, Frelsburg, Texas: "Dear Sir: I take pleasure in forwarding you a package of tea plants and two persimmons…" The Pearfield Nursery 1888 catalogue further states: "We have some other varieties which we are now testing. At the Dallas Fair and Exposition in 1886 we received a premium and diploma for the best display of Japan Persimmons. The secretary of the Exposition writes: They attracted marked attention being such a novelty. Hundreds and thousands of people stopped in wonder and admiration and asked me questions. Many could hardly believe their eyes, and a few even asked if they were 'wax'." —WCW

Pearlbush (*Exochorda racemosa*) (William C. Welch)

Exochorda racemosa
Pearlbush
Family: Rosaceae (Rose)
Zones: 7–9
When my friend Cleo Barnwell from Shreveport provides me with a plant and suggests in her gracious way that it is an "overlooked gem" for our Southern gardens, I take notice. Such is the case with pearlbush. Although I am sure that my two plants of pearlbush would be happier in the moister, acid soils of the Southeast, they have adapted well to both our country and city

Celeste fig (*Ficus*) (John Lipe)

gardens in Central Texas.

This plant's common name evokes the five-petalled blossoms that this ten- to fifteen-foot tall shrub bears on terminal branches in early spring. The expanding flower buds, which appear soon after this deciduous shrub's first flush of spring growth, do indeed look like pearls, and in this stage of their development they make fine cut material for floral arrangements. Pearlbush prefers a sunny or partially shaded location and loamy, well-drained soil. Adapting well to both acid and alkaline soils, this shrub is also quite drought-tolerant once established.

Pearlbush comes to us from eastern China and was introduced to England in 1849. Propagation is by seed (a cold treatment for thirty or sixty days improves germination), or by semi-hardwood cuttings taken and rooted under mist in summer. The genus name, *Exochorda*, describes the structure of the fruits, which are suspended by cords and consist of five small compressed bony carpels adhering around a central axis in a starlike manner.

In 1890, Peter Henderson described pearlbush as "a beautiful hardy shrub, from China, introduced a few years since, and as yet comparatively little known…. It is still a rare plant in the United States, chiefly because it is difficult to propagate, and in consequence is not easy to get. It is propagated by seeds, layers, or suckers."

In older references you will find pearlbush classified as *Spiraea grandiflora*, and this is the alias under which it appears in historic garden plans. Best landscape use is probably in the shrub

border or as a specimen; be sure to allow it ample space, for it can become a substantial plant. The largest plant I have seen is in Madison, Georgia, and that specimen had a multibranched, rounded form, and stood about fifteen feet tall and nearly as wide. After the relatively short bloom period in spring, pearlbush offers little other landscape interest. Still, though short-lived, the blossoms are beautiful enough to earn this plant a place in the garden. Pearlbush has never been common, but once experienced, it is never forgotten. —WCW

Ficus carica
Fig
Family: Moreaceae (Mulberry)
Zones: 7–11
Figs are believed to have originated in Syria, but wild forms now occupy a much larger area than they did in the past. Today, they are commonly found growing wild from eastern Iran to the Canary Isles and through the Mediterranean. In cultivation, the figs' range is much wider—truly cosmopolitan, in fact. The ancient Phoenicians seem to have begun the process of exporting the plant, taking it to the east and the west, and figs soon passed along the early trade routes to China and India. Their arrival in the Americas was more recent, dating to the arrival of the Spanish colonists who introduced figs into Florida and Mexico. From there they quickly spread to other areas of the South.

When the cultivation of figs began is unknown, but drawings of the fruit found in the Giza pyramids date back to

Old Salem figs (*Flora Ann Bynum*)

several centuries before the birth of Christ. Figs were known in Babylon and the fruit is mentioned three times in the Odyssey. The Greek geographer Strabo, who attended school near the present town of Aidin, the center of the Smyrna fig district, reported that the figs of that region were already highly esteemed in his day and brought the highest price in the market. According to W.T. Swingle (1908), "this record goes to show that fig culture has been the principal industry in this region for two millennia, the oldest fruit industry of which we have any record, for the date orchards that were the admiration of Herodotus at Palmyra and Babylon perished ages ago" (quoted in Ira Condit's *The Fig*).

Today figs are cultivated extensively in Spain, Turkey, and Italy. They are also grown commercially in California and, until recently, in Louisiana and Texas. The fig's fruit is popular for eating fresh, and dried figs stuffed with walnuts, almonds, small pieces of orange or citron are a delicacy in many parts of the world. Figs were also put up as preserves in the American South, and wine was sometimes made from this fruit by early gardeners of this region.

Figs have been grown in the south of France at least since the time of Thomas Jefferson, who visited Marseilles and Toulon in 1787. In his memoranda he wrote that the most

delicate figs known in Europe were those growing about this district, where they were known as "figues Marcellaises" to distinguish them from others of inferior quality. Jefferson was also familiar with a homegrown product, too. In a letter he sent to William Drayton from Paris, Jefferson stated: "The fig and mulberry are so well known in America that nothing need be said of them. Their culture too, is by women and children, therefore, earnestly to be desired in countries where there are slaves" (quoted in Condit).

In the South, figs were once found in nearly every home garden. Both John Bartram (1765–66) and William Bartram (1791) ran across fig trees in their travels. Some forty miles north of Mobile, Alabama, William Bartram observed "the fig trees were large as well as their fruit, which was then ripe (August), of the shape of pears and as large, and of dark purplish colour." In 1821, James G. Forbes observed that a Dr. Andrew Turnbull had established a colony of 1500 Greeks and Minorcans at New Smyrna, Florida in 1763, and that the colonists had grown grapes, figs, and pomegranates, all familiar fruits in their native land.

Figs were, evidently, familiar to George Washington from earliest childhood. Charles A. Hoppin (1926), in his writings about the birthplace of George Washington at Wakefield, Virginia, stated that in 1851, in the midst of a 200-acre cornfield, stood a mammoth fig tree and a stone slab inscribed: "Here the 22nd of February, 1732, Washington was born." Close by was a thicket of shrubby fig trees covering a circular space nearly fifty feet in diameter, thickly matted together, the largest being three inches in diameter at the base and eight to ten feet high.

As an adult, General Washington planted fig trees at Mt. Vernon, probably cuttings from the bushes at his boyhood home. In 1830 Edith Sale visited Mt. Vernon and found some "upshoots" of the original fig tree. She stated that a "row of fig bushes stands beside the box hedge and doubtless the children after lessons would delight in their abundance" (Condit).

Figs also make their appearance in the writings of early nurserymen. Thomas Affleck, when he visited

Washington, Mississippi in 1842 reported that he found "figs now in perfection, the last certainly the greatest luxury in the fruit line I ever partook of." A year or two later, when he settled at Washington, six miles from Natchez, Affleck planted an orchard of fifty fig trees. Still later, he published a series of *Rural Almanacs and Garden Calendars*, and the one for 1852 lists fifteen varieties of figs.

The fig industry in Texas was based primarily upon one cultivar known locally as "Magnolia." This came into the state with a tree peddler who travelled through the coast country selling trees that were labeled "Magnolia" and that he sold as specimens of that favorite Southern ornamental. Purchasers soon learned that what they had bought were in fact figs, but the name remained attached to the cultivar. Its fruit was admired by J.C. Carpenter, when he arrived in Houston in 1900. Upon settling at Aldine, Carpenter set out ten acres of "Magnolias," eventually increasing the planting to twenty-three acres. In 1902 he started a preserving business that was the real beginning of the commercial fig industry in Texas.

Although occasionally damaged by cold, these trees are sufficiently hardy to be successfully grown several hundred miles inland from coastal areas. There are more than 700 varieties of figs in cultivation, but only a handful were common in gardens of the old South. Prominent among these are 'Brown Turkey', 'Magnolia', 'Celeste' and 'Texas Everbearing'.

Figs grow fairly quickly to a maximum of fifteen to twenty feet, and they prefer fertile, well-drained soil, though they adapt to most soils and moisture conditions. Pruning is not necessary for good fruit production, but shaping and removal of crossing limbs makes the trees neater and more acceptable as landscape plants. I remember visiting the Jamison commercial fig orchard about thirty years ago below Houston at Pearland where the trees were pruned to a height of about seven feet with single trunks and scaffold branches much like peaches. The result was very attractive.

Occasional hard freezes can kill the branches, but the trees recover quickly and are soon back in production since they bear fruit on new growth. As the trees mature, their cold tolerance increases. But in areas where their hardiness is questionable, figs are most safely grown against south-facing walls. Espaliering a fig tree against a sunny wall not only protects the plant against frost, it also allows the gardener to cultivate the plant in much less space than it would occupy if allowed to grow free.

I remember figs trained as small trees when I was growing up in Houston. They were fun to climb but the leaves were irritating to the skin. 'Magnolia', with its very large reddish brown, pink-fleshed fruit was the preserving fig of choice in my family. Recent years have seen less interest in 'Magnolia' because it is an open-eye fig, which has a small hole at the tip of the fruit. This makes it susceptible to attack by the dried fruit beetle, which causes the fruit to sour. Closed eye types like 'Celeste', 'Texas Everbearing', and 'Alma' form a drop of clear, sticky material in the eye that prevents entry of the damaging insect.

Figs are among the easiest fruiting plants to grow. They benefit from a mulch placed over the roots in summertime to help keep the soil moist, and to watering during prolonged dry spells. Figs often produce for long periods, bearing a first crop in June on the last year's growth and then afterwards a second more prolific crop in August and September on the current season's growth.

Nematodes are sometimes a problem in sandy soils and over-fertilization can cause fig trees to produce an abundance of foliage and little fruit. Stress from lack of moisture can cause fruit drop. In addition, cultivating the soil around the base of the tree may damage the figs' shallow roots. Figs are easily rooted from cuttings taken during the trees' dormant period and stuck deeply into good garden soil. Newly rooted plants often bear the third year.

Many Southern nurseries listed fig trees for sale in the late 1800s and early 1900s. Among them was Waldheim Nursery, Boerne, Texas, who, in their 1895–96 catalogue listed Celestial, Brown Turkey, Adriatic, and San Pedro. The Alvin Fruit & Nursery Co., Algoa, Texas, offered the following: "50,000 fig trees in Nursery, We have the largest

commercial orchard of figs in the South and make a specialty of growing the trees. Varieties listed…Brunswick, Celeste, Lemon, Green Ischia, & Magnolia (Magnolia is the most profitable fig known…Don't fail to plant a few Magnolia figs."

—WCW

Gardenia jasminoides
Gardenia, Cape Jasmine, Cape Jessamine
Family: Rubiaceae (Madder)
Zones: 7–11

In May, 1879, I had the first opportunity to enjoy its beauty in almost every garden at Houston, Texas. The effect was not only very delightful, but I was charmed with its dignified and noble appearance, its wealth of powerfully fragrant flowers and its dense masses of large thick glossy leaves. I saw that the gardens were replete with it, as single specimens, in groups, and as borders around the cemeteries. Everywhere, wherever planted, it added a peculiar charm to its surroundings.
Dr. Henry Nehrling, *My Garden in Florida*, 1944

There are certain floral fragrances that slap you in the face and say, "I'm from the South, dammit!" Gardenia, along with magnolia, sweet olive, banana shrub, butterfly ginger, and Japanese honeysuckle all do that for me.

Though this shrub has been called cape jasmine, it is not from the Cape of Good Hope (or Cape Cod or Cape Fear,

for that matter), nor is it a jasmine. This plant actually originated in China and belongs to the same family as coffee, pentas, firebush, and ixora. Its more popular name, gardenia, commemorates Dr. Alexander Garden of Charleston, South Carolina, who studied medicine and botany in Scotland. More importantly, he was also an enthusiastic pupil and friend of Linnaeus, who was the plant's namer.

Gardenias were originally adopted by western gardeners as greenhouse specimens that were cherished for their creamy white blossoms and heavenly fragrance. Originally known as *Gardenia florida*, the gardenia's exact date of introduction into North American is unknown. The Brooklyn Botanic Garden's 1968 handbook, *America's Garden Heritage* (Volume 23, Number 3) lists no date but says it was introduced during colonial days. Certainly there are plenty of references in our early garden literature. In 1806 the Philadelphia nurseryman Bernard M'Mahon mentioned planting seeds of gardenias in his book, *The American Gardener's Calendar*. Martha Turnbull of Rosedown Plantation referred to trimming her cape jessamine hedge on February 2, 1841 in her detailed garden dairy. In 1860 Robert Buist made note of *G. florida flore pleno* as the cape jasmine in his *American Flower-Garden Directory*. He also listed *G. radicans*, the dwarf cape jasmine, *G. longifolia*, *G. multiflora*, *G. latifolia*, *G. fortunii*, and *G. camelliaflora*, all as greenhouse plants and probable varieties of *G. florida*.

Almost all early nurseries of the South listed the cape jasmine. Thomas

Cape jessamine (*Gardenia jasminoides*) (Greg Grant)

The following caption is original to this illustration and provides interesting insight into the early discovery of the cape jasmine (*Gardenia jasminoides*). It is from Philip Miller's book *Figures of the Most Beautiful, Useful and Uncommon Plants described in The Gardeners Dictionary exhibited on Three Hundred Copper Plates, Accurately Engraven after Drawings taken from Nature* (London, 1760).

Property of and courtesy of the Atlanta History Center, Cherokee Garden Library.

"This plant was brought from the Cape of Good Hope by Captain Hutcheson, who discovered it growing naturally a few Miles up the Land from the Sea, being drawn to it by the great Fragrance of the Flowers, which he smelt at some distance from the Plant, which was then in full Flower; so he caused it to be taken up and planted in a Tub of Earth, and carried on board his Ship, and brought it to England, where it has flowered Three Years in the curious Garden of Richard Warner, Esq., at Woodford in Essex, who was so oliging as to favour us with Branches of this curious Plant with Flowers to make the Drawing. It is a Plant unknown to the Botanists, having never been described in any of their Books; nor was the Plant known to the Person who has the Care of the Dutch garden at the Cape of Good Hope, though it was found growing but a few miles from it."

Hip gardenia (*Gardenia thunbergia*) (*William C. Welch*)

Hip gardenia (*Gardenia thunbergia*) at Rosedown. (*William C. Welch*)

Affleck's 1851–52 Southern Nurseries catalogue listed "cape jessamine, the old double" and a "fine new variety, a Southern seedling." An 1860 catalog from Montgomery Nurseries (Wilson's Nursery) of Montgomery, Alabama also offered cape jessamine along with dwarf cape jessamine. Gilbert Onderdonk's Mission Valley Nurseries catalogue of 1898–99 called gardenia "the most charming flower of the South."

Rosedown and Oakley Plantations of St. Francisville, Louisiana both have what they call the "hip gardenia" naturalized on site. My good friend Dr. Neil Odenwald of Louisiana State University has identified this as *G. thunbergia* from South Africa. It bears single white blossoms, narrow foliage, and in the fall produces an attractive red-orange fruit that somewhat resembles rose hips. I would like to compare this to the plants used as understocks in the alkaline soils of Florida, to see if they are the same species.

Today there are a number of cultivars on the market, including the dwarf *G. jasminoides radicans*, 'August Beauty', 'Mystery', and 'Veitchii', a less hardy, earlier blooming type historically used for cut-flower production. My favorite is still the original big leafed, large growing, big flowered *G. jasminoides*, the perfume of the South.

Gardenias are a little troublesome to grow but their fragrance makes them well worth the effort. An acidic, well drained, sandy loam soil amended with organic matter is essential. Some filtered shade during the hottest part of the day is also beneficial. In alkaline soils iron chlorosis is a severe problem. The most common pest encountered is the white fly. Propagation is from cuttings or by seed in the case of fruiting types.

—GG

Gelsemium sempervirens
Carolina Jessamine, Yellow Jasmine
Family: Loganiaceae (Logania)
Zones: 7–11
This state flower of South Carolina is native to the southeastern United States from the Carolinas all the way to Texas. Though often called yellow "jasmine," this vine is not a true jasmine, nor is it even closely related to that genus. The

Carolina jessamine (*Gelsemium sempervirens*) (*William C. Welch*)

average gardener doesn't care about such distinctions, though. All that he or she knew was that this vine bore beautiful, yellow, and powerfully fragrant flowers—and that's why it has been cultivated in the South from the beginning of our ornamental gardening heritage.

On August 12, 1786 Thomas Jefferson wrote to Richard Cary, his kinsman and friend in Virginia, requesting a number of plants, including *Bignonia sempervirens* (this was the original botanical name for this species; it also passed under the name *Gelsemium nitida* for a while). Bourne's 1833 *Florist's Manual* states "The *Bignonia sempervirens*, or Yellow Jasmine, is a very beautiful shrub or tree…That of the Southern States gives out a delicious fragrance in the night. In New-England it is reared with some difficulty. It is, however, generally found growing in our gardens, and is much admired."

There is a listing for yellow jessamine in an 1860 catalogue of Montgomery Nurseries (Wilson's Nursery) of Montgomery, Alabama. Langdon Nurseries, also of Alabama, lists *Gelsemium nitidum* and *Gelsemium nitidum, Fl. Pl.* in an 1881–82 catalogue in which he states about the latter: "This is the well known Carolina Yellow Jasmine, differing from the proceeding

[sic] in that the golden yellow flowers are as double as a tube rose. Hardy, grows rapidly, flowers freely early in the spring, and though not new, has not received that degree of attention to which its merits entitle it. We are not aware that it is offered by another Nursery in the country, but think it worthy of cultivation wherever a rapid evergreen vine is wanted." I assume that this is the same as the cultivar sold today as 'Pride of Augusta' that Wayside Gardens of South Carolina carries.

I often associate plants with the people from whom I obtained them. In the case of yellow "jasmine," I remember how excited I was when my first grade teacher Mozelle Johnston, an avid gardener, shared two plants of yellow jasmine with me. I planted one on the gas lamp in the front yard and one at the base of a double-trunked post oak.

The double-flowered jessamine I've got growing in my garden now came from J.C. Raulston of the North Carolina State Arboretum. Dr. Raulston also shared a pale yellow-flowered form with me which I think he obtained from Dodd's Nursery in Alabama. I also cultivate G. *rankinii*, a southeastern native that Lone Star Growers of San Antonio propagates and sells. It blooms two weeks later than the yellow jessamine in my garden, but has no fragrance. I plan to plant all four forms together on a dog pen. Dogs could

always stand a little culture.

Carolina jessamine is very easy to cultivate. Although native to acidic woodland soils, it grows quite well in alkaline types as well. It is quite shade-tolerant, although it blooms best in full sun. Due to its vining habit, it shows to best advantage when trained up a supporting structure. Propagation by cuttings under high humidity is possible, but fairly difficult. Look for a sucker springing from the soil at the base of a plant—that can be detached and transplanted with ease. —GG

Gladiolus spp.
Gladiolus
Family: Iridaceae (Iris)
Zones: 4–11

The heirloom gladiolus which is most common in Southern gardens is *Gladiolus byzantinus*. This species thrives in old cemeteries, abandoned homesites, and along ditch banks, for unlike the fussy modern hybrids, G. *byzantinus* is a survivor, and a true perennial. The color of its blossoms is, typically, a beautiful magenta-purple, though there is also a white form which is found here and there. I have not been able to establish exactly when this plant—a native of Turkey—first appeared in our gardens, but it does seem to have arrived in the American South sometime in the early 1800s.

If G. *byzantinus* is to thrive, it must be given a sunny location, and it prefers a well-drained soil. The corms are much smaller than those of the hybrids commonly advertised in nursery catalogues today. It multiplies readily and may be divided as the foliage dies in

Byzantine gladioli (*Gladiolus byzantinus*) (*William C. Welch*)

Parrot gladiolus (*Gladiolus natalensis*) (*William C. Welch*)

early summer. The disappearance of the foliage at that season makes it risky to delay digging G. *byzantinus*' corms until fall or winter, the season generally recommended by growers of modern gladioli. For unless you are well enough organized to have marked the place where the plants were growing, you probably will not be able to find the corms.

Another species gladiolus occasionally found in old Southern gardens is G. *natalensis* (sometimes listed as G. *psittacinus*) an African native that is sometimes called parrot gladiolus. The source of this common name is the hooded, orange and yellow flowers. Borne on three-foot-tall stems in April, these blossoms make striking cut flowers. This species thrives in loamy or clay soils.

Evidence of the parrot gladiolus' use in mid-nineteenth century American gardens may be found in Joseph Breck's book, *The Flower-Garden or, Breck's Book of Flowers*, which was published in Boston in 1851. Breck remarked that "*Gladiolus natalensis*, called by some *psittacinus*, has not been known many years among us, and was considered, when first introduced, as being very superb: but it has such a propensity to increase, that it has become very

common, and is now looked upon with indifference. The flowers are scarlet, on a greenish-yellow ground, produced in long, one-sided spikes: the stems sometimes four feet high, with fifteen or twenty buds and blooms." Elsewhere Breck also refers to G. *byzantinus*, noting that even in coastal New England it was winter hardy, so that its corms might be left in the ground year round.

The name gladiolus derives from the Latin word *gladius*, which means "sword"—this refers to the bladelike foliage. Various names commonly used for this plant are hardy glad, corn flag, sword-lily and Jacob's ladder. The old-time species types are more compact in growth than the hybrids and usually require no staking. Bloom time is usually April along with the bearded irises.

Traditionally, gladiolus were often planted in rows in the vegetable garden as well as flower borders. Both species described here were common in Southern cottage gardens of the nineteenth century. They deserve widespread use as perennials in period and modern gardens, though at present they are difficult to obtain from commercial sources.   —WCW

Gomphrena globosa
Bachelor's Button, Globe Amaranth, Gomphrena
Family: Amaranthaceae (Amaranth)
Zones: Warm season annual
Once again common names are likely to lead us astray. Go shopping in the catalogues for bachelor's button and you are liable to end up with a northern European weed (also called corn

flower), *Centaurea cyanus*, which has become popular in the wildflower meadows so fashionable in recent years. What you want to get is the real Southern bachelor's button *Gomphrena*, which has also been known as globe amaranth, and immortelle. Gomphrena isn't native either, but since it comes from tropical Asia, it likes our climate, and it's got roots here, too.

Actually, some authorities insist that gomphrena is really native to South America or Australia. Who knows? But what is sure is that gomphrena has been in Southern gardens a long time.

This flower is a warm season annual which is easily grown from seed planted in a sunny location after all danger of frost has passed. It is useful as a bedding plant and/or for cut flowers, and is famous for its cloverlike clusters of brightly colored bracts that can be pink, white, or purple. There are early references to a violet and a striped variety—I would very much like to locate seed of that. In all gomphrena flowers what appear to be the blossoms are really colored bracts that hide the true flowers, which are small and inconspicuous.

The normal height for this plant is approximately two and one half feet, although several dwarf cultivars are now available, including 'Buddy', a purple-flowered sort, and 'Cissy', a white. Both of these grow approximately one foot tall.

Gomphrena, or bachelor's button as many gardeners will persist in calling it, is very popular as an "everlasting flower," as its "flowers" hold their color after drying. The plants are very easily

Bachelor's buttons (*Gomphrena globosa*) (*Greg Grant*)

Bachelor's buttons (*Gomphrena globosa*) with Mexican bush sage (*Salvia leucantha*). (*Greg Grant*)

dried by harvesting them at their peak of bloom and hanging them upside down in a warm, dry, dark area. Early Southern gardeners took advantage of the gomphrena's year-round beauty by growing the plants in their garden until fall and then using them for indoor dried bouquets throughout the winter. The following spring, the dried flower heads were crushed, releasing the seeds which were then resown into the garden.

The gomphrena is reportedly used as a heart remedy in Central America. It always does my heart good to look at them! There are also references to the leaves being boiled and eaten as food.

I've also found a number of references to the cultivation of gomphrena in eighteenth- and nineteenth-century American garden handbooks. In 1847 Thomas Bridgeman listed it in *The Young Gardener's Assistant*, while Joseph Breck mentions it in *The Flower Garden* (*Breck's Book of Flowers*, 1859), stating that "Globe Amaranth—white, purple, and striped are desirable. A popular immortelle."

Thomas Jefferson grew this Southern bachelor's button in his garden at Monticello. On April 2, 1767 he recorded in his garden book: "Sowed

Carnations, Indian Pink, Marigold, Globe Amaranth, Auricula, Double Balsam, Tricolor, Dutch Violet, Sensitive Plant, Cockscomb, a flower like the Prince's Feather, Lathyrus."   —GG

Hemerocallis spp.
Daylily
Family: Liliaceae (Lily)
Zones: 2–11

Athough many people may think of the daylily as a modern flower, in fact this perennial's roots run way back into the history of our gardens. As early as the year 70 A.D., the Greek herbalist Dioscorides made reference in his writings to a form of the plant we now know as lemon or custard daylily. The plant he was describing had to have originated from cultivation, for this species is of Asian origin.

According to Chinese literature, various forms of daylilies have been cultivated by that nation's gardeners for thousands of years. The earliest references date back as far as 2697 B.C. and the Materia Medica commissioned by Emperor Hyang Ti, when the daylily was already in use as a food crop as well as a source of medicines. The consumption of daylily plants and flowers was thought to benefit the mind and strengthen willpower as well as to "quiet the five viscera." The flower buds, which may still be found on the shelves of oriental markets, are palatable, digestible, and nutritious. The root and crown were widely employed as a medicine to relieve pain and, later, juice extracted from the fresh roots by pounding was administered to patients suffering from cirrhosis and jaundice.

Carolus Linnaeus, the "Father of Botany," in his *Species Plantarum* of 1753 chose *Hemerocallis* as the scientific name for the daylily. This choice reflects a peculiarity of the flower; the name combines two Greek words meaning "beauty" and "day," and as this suggests, an individual daylily flower opens for only a day. However, since each scape (flower stalk) bears many buds, and these open in series, a single plant maintains a display over a number of days.

Daylilies resisted hybridization until this century, and old time gardeners were limited in their choices to just a

few kinds. There was the lemon daylily, *H. asphodelus*; the tawny or common orange daylily, *H. fulva*, and the double orange daylily, *H. fulva* 'Kwanso'. These were probably the only daylilies available to most Western gardeners until the 1920s.

Despite this lack of variety, daylilies have been popular garden plants in Europe for many centuries. The late sixteenth century botanist, Mathias de l'Obel (who also styled himself as de Lobel or Lobelius) of France, noted that by 1575 both the lemon daylily and the tawny daylily had been introduced into European gardens. Writing from London in 1733, Philip Miller in *The Gardener's Dictionary*, says of the lemon and tawny lily:

> The species are:
> 1. LILIO-ASPHODELUS, luteus
>   The Yellow Day Lily.
> 2. LILIO-ASPHODELUS, puniceus
>   The Red Day Lily.
> These plants are very common in most of the old English gardens. The first is called the Yellow Tuberose, from its being a very agreeable scent; but the other is called the Day Lily, or the Tuberose Orange lily in most places.

According to some sources, daylilies were extensively used in early American

Redouté's portrait of a lemon daylily.

Daylilies (*Hemerocallis fulva*) (William C. Welch)

1601, according to Clusius, 'Europa' was commonly found in the gardens of Austria and Germany. The Swedish botanist, Linnaeus, first considered 'Europa' a hybrid (1753), but later (1762) classified it a species with the name *H. fulva*.

The double form 'Kwanso' is almost as durable and well adapted as the single-flowered type, and its blossoms marks many deserted homesites and cemeteries throughout the South. By 1860 this double form had been introduced from Japan, where it had been noticed by European travelers since 1712. A variegated green and white foliage form was introduced in 1865.

I remember my excitement as an early teen when I learned that there was a double daylily. Mrs. Brewer drove the school bus I rode each day, and she knew of my gardening interests. One day she left me a grocery sack full of 'Kwanso'. Those plants bloomed that same year and thrived for as long as we lived in our Houston home.

For meadow gardens and naturalistic plantings, these species-type daylilies still make valuable additions to the designer's palette. In the eighteenth and nineteenth centuries, many gardeners relegated daylilies to out-of-the-way areas of the garden—they were sometimes known as "privy lilies" because they were commonly used to line the path to that outbuilding. Since the early 1930s, however, the activities of British and American hybridizers have revolutionized this ancient flower.

According to research conducted by

settlements. Alice Lockwood, in a caption for a picture of *H. asphodelus* in *Gardens of Colony and State* (Vol. 2), says, "Used in all gardens from the seventeenth to the twentieth century." Yet from the mid- to late nineteenth century, daylilies were conspicuously absent from American gardening literature. Perhaps this was because American gardeners were distracted by the huge influx of new plants coming into our country at that time.

I have found two references to daylilies from that period. The first is in Jane Louden's *Gardening for Ladies: and Companion to the Flower Garden*, New York, 1845, where the author praises daylilies as "handsome perennial plants with yellow or copper-coloured flowers. They are quite hardy and only require a moist soil and a shady situation. They are propagated by dividing the roots."

In the same year, Robert Buist wrote glowingly of daylilies in his *American Flower Garden Directory*, published in Philadelphia (in 1845). According to him, daylilies "flower well and are remarkable among the border flowers for their large yellow or copper-coloured corollas, some of them almost six inches in diameter; bloom from May to July and will grow in almost any soil." The lemon daylily has narrow, grasslike foliage and grows to three feet or less. Its lemon-yellow, four-inch trumpets are known for their sweet scent. Joseph Breck in his *Breck's Book of Flowers*, published in 1851, (Boston) described the species this way: "Yellow Day Lily,—has brilliant yellow lily-shaped flower in June: two feet high; leaves long keeled,

linear." Although known as a very reliable and low maintenance perennial, the lemon lily is difficult to find and what is sold under this name in today's nursery trade often proves not true to type.

Hemerocallis fulva, the tawny daylily, has naturalized so successfully throughout much of this country that it now functions as a wildflower in many areas. It is almost beyond belief that this plant could spread so successfully and so far only by root spread, yet the fact is that this particular species is a triploid "mule" and cannot produce viable seed. Actually, there are several cultivated clones and various wild forms included under the specific name *H. fulva*.

The oldest, most common and best known of these is the clone 'Europa', which was described by Lobel in 1576 as having cinnabar-red coloring in the flowers and as being distinctly different from *H. flava*, the lemon daylily. By

Daylilies (*Hemerocallis fulva*), Raleigh, North Carolina. (*William C. Welch*)

Hemerocallis fulva 'Kwanso' (*Greg Grant*)

Nell Crandall of Houston, the first hybridization of the daylily was done in 1877 by George Yeld, an English school teacher and hobby gardener. His cultivar 'Apricot' (*H. flava* x *H. middenforffi*) was first exhibited in 1892. A. Herrington of New Jersey registered the first known American clone, 'Florham', in 1899 (*H. aurantiaca Major* x *H. thunbergi* hybrid). Luther Burbank of California is credited with introducing four cultivars, which were introduced between 1914 and 1924.

Dr. A.B. Stout was the acknowledged pioneer of this new era of research on the genus *Hemerocallis*. His work began in 1921 as a result of his friendship with Dr. Albert Steward, who while teaching botany at the University of Nanking met and taught many of China's young botanists. Steward's home became the center of activity for people of many interests, and through them Stout was able to procure plants and information about daylilies that had been previously unavailable outside of their native land. Dr. Stout received twenty-seven living plants and seeds from central China in 1924 and between 1920 and 1942 received a total of fifty more parcels of living plants and seeds from China. With this unprecedented wealth of material he was able to produce viable seed from a number of species, often for the first time. *Hemerocallis fulva*, for example, he propagated by introducing its pollen into the flowers of fertile relatives.

Dr. Stout's work literally opened the door and laid the foundation for the modern breeding work with daylilies.

Since his initial efforts, many scientists and amateurs have become involved in hybridizing daylilies, and tens of thousands of new cultivars have resulted. Whereas daylilies formerly offered the gardener only a yellow and an orange, this flower is now available in countless shades of near-whites, yellows, oranges, pinks, vivid reds, crimson, purples, pastels, and handsome blends. As of the end of 1993, there were 36,486 cultivar names registered in the Daylily Check List.

Most of the new introductions soon fall by the wayside and are soon displaced by the continuing supply of new cultivars. One of the early hybrids, however, has remained popular since its introduction in about 1925. 'Hyperion' was developed by Franklin B. Mead and is considered by many to be unexcelled in its class. 'Hyperion' stands about four feet tall, blooming midseason with fragrant, large, widely open, canary yellow flowers with a green-flushed throat and prominent stamens. It is often confused and sold as the old lemon daylily, but that has daintier flowers, is smaller, and has more grasslike foliage. Another difference is time of bloom; Elizabeth Lawrence, in Charlotte, North Carolina gives the earliest date of first bloom for 'Hyperion' as June 3, and the latest date of first bloom June 26, whereas first bloom for the lemon lily she sets as early as April 19 and as late as May 10. In addition, the lemon daylily sometimes repeats in fall.

Recent daylily breeding is focusing on tetraploids. From 1960–65 there

were only seventeen tetraploids registered with the Daylily Society, but now the registered count exceeds 5,000. This explosion of popularity has to do with the tetraploids' greater potential. Since they have twice as many chromosomes as the normal plant, the tetraploids offer a correspondingly greater array of genetic material with which breeders can produce brighter flowers colors, stronger and sturdier scapes, more flower substance, etc. Not all gardeners are agreed, however, that tetraploids are universally desirable. Plant historians and traditionalists point to the simple beauty and natural adaptability of the species forms of daylilies and wonder why it is necessary to "mess with a good thing." In reality, both interests are valid and worthy of support. The beauty of some of the new hybrids is truly impressive, but so is the long history and elegant simplicity of the species forms.

Daylilies are fibrous-rooted, hardy, herbaceous perennials. Their roots are fingerlike to large, round, and fleshy. There is a crown at the spot where the roots and leaves join. The foliage is narrow and long, and assumes the shape of a fan. Basically, all daylilies fall into one of three types, according to their foliage. There are daylilies of dormant type, which lose their foliage completely during the winter; daylilies of the evergreen type, which retain their green foliage all year unless there is an unusually severe winter; and semi-evergreen daylilies, which lose part or most of their leaves during the winter. As a rule, the evergreen daylilies perform best in hot climates, while the deciduous types prefer cooler locations, although there are exceptions.

Species and older daylily cultivars are known for their ease of culture. Propagation is by division, with fall being the ideal time to divide and reset existing clumps. Division is necessary to maintain the growth and vigor of newer cultivars, but the species and early types described here can go many years without being disturbed. Like most plants, they respond favorably to good, well-drained soils and garden culture, but the luxuriant stands of daylilies flourishing along countless roadsides, and in cemeteries and abandoned

Far left: Confederate rose (*Hibiscus mutabilis*) (William C. Welch)
Left: Confederate rose (*Hibiscus mutabilis*) (Greg Grant)

homesites attest to this perennial's ability to cope with less than ideal conditions.

Daylily foliage is attractive all season long and their flowers appear with onset of our late spring and summer heat—in other words, just as the flowers of most other perennials and spring annuals are fading. Surely these privy lilies deserve a better spot in Southern gardens.*   —WCW

* Special thanks to Florence P. Griffin and the Cherokee Garden Library of Atlanta for their assistance in researching the heirloom daylilies. I also appreciate the assistance and support of Nell Crandall of Houston and the American Hemerocallis Society

Hibiscus mutabilis
Confederate Rose
Family: Malvaceae (Mallow)
Zones: 7–11
A native of South China, the Confederate rose was once a highly popular plant throughout the South. Sometimes known as "cotton rose" because its flowers, foliage, and growth habit recall those of the cotton plant, the Confederate rose will form a large shrub or even a small tree in areas where winters are not severe. It is root hardy in colder areas of the South and performs in the garden as a large perennial. Although still common in Southern gardens, the Confederate rose is rarely seen in nurseries.

There are several forms of Confederate rose, including 'Rubrus', which has deep pink flowers; 'Plena', which has double white flowers that turn pink or red the second day; and the species type,

which bears double flowers that open white in the morning and gradually blush pink in the afternoon before closing at night. All the forms are showy landscape plants with flowers that frequently measure six inches in diameter. They bloom most heavily in late summer and early fall.

Propagation is by cuttings, which root easily in soil or water during spring and summer. Confederate roses are not particular about soil and tolerate a wide range of moisture conditions. Cotton root rot can be a problem in alkaline soils where cotton has been cultivated.

Hibiscus moscheutos, the common rose mallow, is native to wetland areas of the South and has also been used as a perennial. It is root hardy as far north as zone 5 and provides a long season of garden color. Breeders have developed giant flowering forms of the rose mallows which are available today from seed or plants.

Another popular native species is

H. coccineus, the Texas star hibiscus. This bears single, red flowers about three inches in diameter atop branches of palmately lobed leaves with three to seven segments. Propagation is from seed or by cutting, and Texas star hibiscus thrives in most any garden soil. Like *H. moscheutos*, the Texas star hibiscus freezes back in winter and should be cut to ground level after the first hard freeze.

All four of the hibiscuses mentioned here were formerly common in Southern landscapes, especially in cottage-type gardens where they were often mixed with other perennials and annuals.   —WCW

Hibiscus syriacus
Althaea, Althea, Rose of Sharon
Family: Malvaceae (Mallow)
Zones: 5–11
These beautiful shrubs have been neglected and their advantages for lawn decorations, as single

Althaeas (*Hibiscus syriacus*) at the San Antonio Botanical Center. (William C. Welch)

Althaea
(*Hibiscus
syriacus*
'Helene')
(*Greg Grant*)

plants or in clumps or hedges, overlooked. They bloom from May till fall, during our hottest, driest weather, when flowers are scarce. They do not require watering, and demand little attention. They are decided acquisitions to any flower garden. Rosedale Nurseries Catalog, Brenham, Texas, 1899

A native of India and China, *Hibiscus syriacus* has been cultivated in the latter nation for as long as records exist. In China, both its flowers and leaves were used as food. In 1597, the English herbalist John Gerard recorded that he had planted seeds of the "Tree Mallow," and in 1629, John Parkinson, one of the first English garden-writers, mentioned that he had cultivated this plant. In the 1759 edition of his monumental *Gardener's and Florist's Dictionary*, Philip Miller described seven kinds:

the most common hath purple Flowers with dark Bottoms, another hath bright purple Flowers with black Bottoms, a third hath white Flowers with purple Bottoms, a fourth variegated Flowers with dark Bottoms, and a fifth pale yellow flowers with dark Bottoms but the last is very rare at present in the English Gardens; there are also two with variegated leaves which are by some much esteemed.

In 1778 John Abercrombie, author of *The Universal Gardener and Botanist*, called the plant "the greatest ornament of the autumn season, of almost any of the shrubby tribe." Double-flowered forms aren't mentioned until 1838, when J.C. Loudon said they were common in his *Arboretum et Fruticetum Brittanicum*.

This "greatest ornament" has been equally as popular in the American South—althaeas have been in Southern gardens from the beginning of our gardening heritage. Thomas Jefferson planted althaea seeds at all his homes—at Shadwell in April of 1767, at Monticello in March of 1794, and at Poplar Forest in December of 1812.

Althaeas were carried by almost all the early Southern nurseries dealing in ornamentals. In a survey of catalogues from nineteen nurseries covering the years 1851–1906, I found that sixteen of them offered althaea. That makes it the most popular Southern nursery plant; it ranked just ahead of arborvitae, honeysuckles, and roses. Typical of the listings was that of Thomas Affleck's Southern Nurseries in Washington, Mississippi, which advertised "fine new double Althaeas, a dozen sorts" in the 1851–52 catalogue. Montgomery Nurseries (Alabama) also listed althaea in their 1860 catalogue, as did Rosedale Nurseries of Brenham, Texas. Founded in 1860, Rosedale was one of the first commercial nurseries in Texas, and by 1901 its catalogue was advertising that "we can supply about twenty named varieties in Single and Double; White, Pink, Red, Purple, and all their modifications and combinations; also the

Variegated-leaved, with purple flowers."

Althaeas, in all their forms, are still supremely adapted to today's gardens. What's more, the future holds promise of even better things. In the 1960s, the late Dr. Donald Egolf, formerly of the National Arboretum in Washington, D.C., and well known for his work with crape myrtle hybrids, developed a series of sterile triploid althaeas that have larger, earlier flowers, and yet develop little or no seed. Sterility ensures that the plant's energy is spent on flower production instead of seed. The Egolf althaeas are: 'Diana' (white), 'Helene' (white with maroon throat), 'Minerva' (lavender), and 'Aphrodite' (pink). These new types have grown just as well for me as the old standards. They seem to bloom a bit earlier, have slightly larger flowers, and are more compact in height. I have observed some seed development, however.

There is also an almost true (if pale) blue althaea named 'Bluebird', which I am using as the background of the blue section of my newly evolving rainbow border. Unfortunately, I'm having trouble finding enough glass Milk of Magnesia bottles for my blue bottle tree, the "focal point" of the border. What would Gertrude Jekyll think?

Althaeas are very easy to cultivate

Althaea (*Hibiscus syriacus*)
(*Greg Grant*)

in just about any soil that is well drained and located in part to full sun, preferring the latter. They are, however, susceptible to cotton root rot in areas with alkaline soils. They can be grown as either shrubs or limbed up to make small trees. Propagation is by seeds (if you aren't particular about the quality of the offspring) or by cuttings rooted under high humidity.

Most people have quit using althaeas today in favor of the more popular crape myrtle. In this new era of plant diversification and with the renewed popularity of old-fashioned plants, the time is right for the rose of sharon to obtain her rightful place as the queen of the Southern garden—or at least as a princess.   —GG

Hippeastrum spp.
Amaryllis
Family: Amaryllidaceae (Amaryllis)
Zones: 7–11
In her book *Through the Garden Gate*, Elizabeth Lawrence tells of Henry Nehrling's unforgettable experience:

> I love Dr. Henry Nehrling's description of seeing Johnson's amaryllis for the first time, on a April day in 1879. He had just come from the still-wintry streets of Chicago, and was wandering about in the flowery fragrance of Houston, Texas, "half dreaming, half in joyful rapture," when he saw two long, glowing strips of red in a distant garden. "In the background, surrounded by magnolias, there was a low house with roses and jasmine climbing

Oxblood lily (*Rhodophiala bifida*) (*Greg Grant*)

> over the veranda. On both sides of the broad path, leading to the house, there appeared broad beds with great, beautiful, trumpet-shaped flowers, which glistened and shone in the light of the southern sun as if strewn with gold dust. There was not a hundred, no, a thousand of the flowers, which rose about two feet high over the somewhat short strap-shaped leaves that came forth in thick masses. The flowers showed a broad white stripe on every flower-petal, and gave off a very lovely aromatic fragrance.

The amaryllis is most likely my favorite flower. Each year when I was a child my mother would give me a Christmas present fit for a budding horticulturist—and one year this gift was a boxed Dutch amaryllis. I'll never forget the magic as the stalk emerged

from the seemingly lifeless bulb. I was so impressed that each year thereafter I requested and got a new amaryllis. Eventually, the collection grew so large that I had to have a greenhouse in which to keep it, for the amaryllis bulbs weren't cold hardy at my home in northeast Texas.

With my eyes opened to the attractions of these flowers, though, I came to realize that there was some kind of amaryllis growing in many of the yards out in the country, an amaryllis that *was* cold hardy. It was a spring blooming plant that bore narrower trumpets than those of the Dutch amaryllises, and in color these Texan flowers were bright red, and striped white on the inside. I began asking nurserymen what this flower was, and where I could buy it. Nobody knew. Finally my grandmother secured some bulbs from a friend and shared them with me. I'm still multiplying that stock today.

It wasn't until I went to work for Texas A&M that I found out what the plant truly is. Incredibly, it is the first hybrid amaryllis that was ever produced, a plant developed by an English watchmaker named Johnson sometime around 1790. A cross between *A. vittata* and *A. reginae*, it is known scientifically as *Hippeastrum* x *johnsonii* (formerly *Amaryllis johnsonii*), and is commonly referred to as Johnson's amaryllis or the St. Joseph's lily. As is typical of a first generation hybrid, this plant is a very strong grower and sets little or no seed.

Without a doubt, Johnson's hybrid is the finest amaryllis for garden culture in

St. Joseph's lily (*Hippeastrum* x *johnsonii*) in a Texas garden. (*William C. Welch*)

Roman hyacinth (*Hyacinthus orientalis albulus*) (Greg Grant)

the South. The combination of the brilliant red flowers, the spicy fragrance, and its unbelievable toughness makes it a bulb without equal. Although many early nurseries and catalogues offered this plant, it is unfortunately no longer in the trade. It still thrives, however, in many gardens and cemeteries in the South, and the persuasive gardener should be able to secure a stock (as my grandmother did) from those sources.

Sprekelia formosissima (*A. formosissima*), another member of the amaryllis family, is an even older garden flower than the St. Joseph's lily. This odd looking native of Mexico was described in John Parkinson's *A Garden of Pleasant Flowers* as *Narcissis Jacobeus flore rubro* ("The red Indian Daffodil") in 1629 and in Gerard's 1633 herbal as *Narcissis jacobeus indicus* ("the Indian or Jacobean Narcisse"). Bernard M'Mahon, an early American nurseryman, sent Thomas Jefferson "6 roots of the *Amaryllis formosissima*" in 1807 and for cultural information referred Jefferson to his *American Gardener's Calendar*, where the Sprekelia is referred to as the "Scarlet Amaryllis." On December 24, 1834, William Prince and Son of Flushing, New York, sent "six splendid scarlet Amaryllis or Jacobean Lily" to Rosedown Plantation in St. Francisville,

Louisiana. Today it is commonly called the Aztec or Jacobean lily.

Another amaryllis relative which can be found in older gardens is *Rhodophiala bifida* (formerly *Amaryllis advena*), the oxblood lily. Supposedly introduced into the United States by the German-Texan botanist Peter Heinrich Oberwetter around the turn of this century, this miniature red "amaryllis" from Argentina has naturalized throughout the German settled areas of Texas. It blooms in the fall much like *Lycoris* and tolerates all types of soils. It is an excellent naturalizing perennial for beds, lawns, and even roadsides. Texas bulb expert Scott Ogden, of New Braunfels, says, "No other bulb can match the fierce vigor, tenacity, and adaptability of the oxblood lily."

Amaryllis and its relatives are of easy culture. Although not particular about conditions, they grow and multiply best in a well-drained, loose soil with at least part to full sun. Propagation is by division.   —GG

Hyacinthus orientalis albulus
Roman Hyacinth, French Roman Hyacinth
Family: Liliaceae (Lily)
Zones: 7–11
Roman hyacinths were one of the first flowers I ever grew. I dug them from the old Wheeler place in Arcadia (ironically, that's where I sit writing this) where my dad kept his cows. There were both blue and white hyacinths there—I also got my first Byzantine gladiolus from the same site. All were growing

beneath a mimosa tree along with 'Grand Primo' narcissus. Those hyacinths have been a favorite of mine since the first time I smelled them.

They are not, I hasten to add, the flowers you see in the Dutch bulb catalogues. Those Dutch hyacinths do not perform as true perennials in the majority of the South and in the lower South often have to be replanted yearly. In the upper South Dutch hyacinths may return for a number of years but each time they will be smaller.

The fragrant, smaller-flowered hyacinth I was digging at the Wheeler place, the Roman kind, is native to southern France. It is a dependable perennial for the South, the only kind of hyacinth that is. In our region it naturalizes freely both in flower beds and in the grass, and though they're not as showy as those outsized Dutch hyacinths, you'll only have to plant Roman hyacinths once in your lifetime.

Hortus Third says the flowers of Roman hyacinths are white to bright blue. I've also seen a pink form, which is scarce today but still persisting here and there; people often recall it was in their mother's or grandmother's garden. The blue-flowered form is much more common in old Southern gardens and seems to be the most vigorous. Several shades of blue can be found, ranging from the most common soft medium blue, to light blue, bright blue, deep blue, and rarely, a dark almost purple shade.

Bailey's *Standard Cyclopedia of Horticulture* (1917) offered three

Aztec lily (*Sprekelia formosissima*) (William C. Welch)

Roman hyacinth (*Hyacinthus orientalis albulus*) (Greg Grant)

Yet by the 1970s, Roman hyacinths had all but disappeared from the nursery trade. Recently, a number of bulb companies have begun carrying them again. However, various friends (yes, I have more friends than just Flora Ann) have grown these commercial bulbs for three or four years now, and report that they do not resemble the Roman hyacinths of old garden origin. The blue ones come nearest, the white looks like a "petered out" Dutch hyacinth, and the pink misses the boat altogether. Time will tell if these commercial forms are truly adapted to the South. I don't allow wimps in my garden.   —GG

illustrations of Roman hyacinths, including one portrait that covers a full page. In the accompanying text, the book observes that "instead of one large truss from each bulb, the Roman Hyacinth produces three or four smaller but more graceful flower-spikes. By reason of its beauty and exquisite fragrance, its earliness and easy culture, the white Roman hyacinth is the most popular of winter-blooming plants. Several millions of these bulbs are grown annually by the florists of the large cities for winter cut-flowers." Elsewhere, the *Standard Cyclopedia* mentions *Dutch* Roman hyacinths, which it describes as "smaller sized bulbs of the ordinary Dutch hyacinths."

My good friend, Flora Ann Bynum of Winston-Salem, North Carolina, is the queen of Roman hyacinths. She has devoted a considerable amount of her time to researching them and to the hunt for a double-pink form. Any project she takes up she pursues with

religious dedication, and if there's not a double-pink one, she'll know why.

Roman hyacinths bloom outdoors in late winter in the South and are very easy to grow in a well-drained soil. The blue-flowering form requires no care at all. Older gardeners say that the white and especially the pink need to be fertilized annually and divided from time to time, and perhaps that is why they have tended to disappear. I started with mostly whites and a few blues. Now I have mostly blues and a few whites. The white blooms first, followed by the blue. Propagation is by division.

These bulbs were widely advertised in Victorian bulb catalogues, not only for outdoor use but also (and especially in the case of the white form) as a forcing bulb for use at Christmas. During the early part of the twentieth-century, the name "French Roman hyacinth" began to be used in catalogues, perhaps because the bulbs came from France.

Hydrangea macrophylla
Hydrangea, French Hydrangea, Hortensia
Family: Saxifragaceae (Saxifrage)
Zones: 7–10

My grandfather Emanis's favorite plant was the big blue hydrangea near the end of the porch, by the swing. Now that he is gone, I've grown to cherish hydrangeas as well. My oldest brother wants to cut his down. He says it looks messy. I told him he couldn't cut down Momma's hydrangea, people in San Antonio (where I live now) would kill (literally!) to grow hydrangeas. So take it to San Antonio, my brother says. I better get a cutting for my blue border while I can.

The showy shrub we call the "French" hydrangea is not from France, or at least not originally. In fact, *Hydrangea macrophylla* is a native of Japan. The French were responsible, however, for much of its breeding around the turn of this century. The

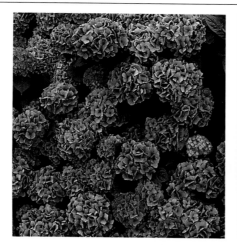

Far left: French hydrangea (*Hydrangea macrophylla macrophylla*) (William C. Welch)

Left: Lacecap hydrangea (*Hydrangea macrophylla normalis*) (William C. Welch)

Pee gee hydrangea (*Hydrangea paniculata grandiflora*)
(*Greg Grant*)

Oakleaf hydrangea (*Hydrangea quercifolia*)
(*William C. Welch*)

results have been divided into two distinct groups, the hortensias and the lacecaps (not to be confused with the hortensias and the McCoys).
The two types of macrophylla hydrangea are easy enough to distinguish. Hortensias bear clusters mostly of showy sterile flowers, which give them their large "mophead" look. Lacecaps have a center of non-showy fertile flowers surrounded by a ring of showy sterile flowers. There are many cultivars of both types, but hortensias are by far the most common type of hydrangea in Southern gardens, and are also popular as a source of dried flowers.

I could not find a date for the introduction of the *Hydrangea macrophylla* into American gardens, although I did learn that the species was in Europe before 1800. However, my nursery catalogues gave some indication of what was available locally by the late nineteenth century. An 1881–82 Langdon Nurseries catalogue (near Mobile, Alabama) listed *H. hortensis* ("an elegant well-known plant"), *H. imperatrice eugenia* ("a new variety"), *H. paniculata grandiflora* ("new, from Japan"), and *H. japonica*. Frank Vestal of Little Rock, Arkansas listed *H. paniculata* in 1896. A 1906–07 Fruitland Nurseries catalogue (Augusta, Georgia) listed the hortensia cultivars 'Japonica', 'Otaksa', 'Otaksa monstrosa', 'Ramis Pictis' or 'Red Branched', 'Rosea', and 'Thomas Hogg'. This nursery also advertised *H. paniculata grandiflora*. Known as the pee gee hydrangea, this

species with large, white flowers is frequently cultivated in gardens of the upper South today.
The first hydrangea in the South, if not in Southern gardens, was *H. quercifolia*, the oakleaf hydrangea, which is a native of southeastern North America. This plant was named by William Bartram and introduced into English gardens in 1803. In addition to the showy white flowers it bears in summer, this shrub's foliage colors well in the fall. There are nice specimens at Rosedown and Oakley Plantations in St. Francisville, Louisiana. 'Snow Queen' is a very popular cultivar today.

Hydrangeas require a loose, well-drained organic soil and plenty of moisture to thrive. These shrubs should be pruned back annually to keep them from looking "messy," but make your cuts right after the bushes bloom, for pruning later in the season or especially in wintertime removes the buds that make the following season's flowers. And hydrangeas are not near as pretty without the flowers, although I always thought the foliage smelled good. The hortensia is unique in that it serves as a sort of living litmus paper: acid soils cause it to bear blue flowers, while alkaline soils turn the flowers pink. Shades between the two are often seen as well. Aluminum sulfate, a soil acidifier, may be added to the soil to obtain blue flowers, and lime may be added to create pink ones. Make them any color you want, just don't cut them down. —GG

Iris x germanica, I. pseudocorus, I. albicans
Bearded Iris, Yellow Flags, Cemetery Whites, Louisiana Iris
Family: Iridaceae (Iris)
Zones: 5–9

Among the most beautiful and cosmopolitan perennials in the world, bearded iris thrive in all of the South except those areas that lie within a hundred miles or so of the coasts. Even there, some varieties are worth growing—some of the older types may succeed there, too. For, as with daylilies and roses, the older forms of iris, those favored by our

Iris x germanica 'Southern Comfort'
(*William C. Welch*)

Iris x *albicans* (William C. Welch)

Bearded iris (*Iris* x *germanica*) (William C. Welch)

ancestors, are easier to grow and longer-lived than the hundreds of new hybrids that fill catalogues today.

All of the irises discussed here are rhizomatous and have swordlike foliage. The flower-bearing stalks appear mostly in springtime and the blooms are very showy, six-petaled and often fragrant. The three upright petals are known as standards and the lower three as falls. Their form is the pattern of the fleur-de-lis, known as the symbol of French royalty. In bearded irises, brightly colored hairs (the whiskers of the "beard") emerge from the falls and serve as attractants to pollinating insects. The name Iris is for the Greek goddess of the rainbow and suggests the iridescent colors found in the flowers of this genus.

Probably the most common bearded iris grown in the South is *Iris* x *albicans*, better known as "Cemetery Whites." They are a naturally sterile hybrid and are extremely hardy, often marking abandoned homesites and old cemeteries, where for several weeks each spring they command the attention of all passersby. Originally from Yemen, these irises have naturalized so extensively in the South and become such a fixture of our rural landscape that many people consider them native.

Another iris that is commonly found on old homesites and cemeteries in Texas and the Gulf South are the "Early Purples." These are thought to be a form of *Iris* x *germanica*. Both this and the "Cemetery White" thrive over a broad area, even in areas close to the

coasts where excessive humidity and moisture limit success with other bearded irises.

Bearded irises are drought tolerant but resent poorly drained soils. They perform best when their rhizomes are only partially covered by well-drained soil and prefer a spot where the sun bakes their roots for at least half of each day in summertime. Dividing plants every three to five years helps keep them vigorous and flowering while providing a source for more plants. Each division should have a growing point and fan of foliage.

Probably the first iris imported from the Old World to America was *I. pseudocorus*, better known as the yellow flag. This was commonly grown during the seventeenth century and early American gardeners are known to have secured stock from Europe. Part of their appeal was their supposed medicinal value, for this plant was used in the treatment of "weak eyes" and ulcers. Undoubtedly, though, colonial gardeners prized this plant for its beauty as well, for the bright yellow flowers appear in April, displaying the classic fleur-de-lis form.

The yellow flag's foliage is much taller than that of the bearded irises and may reach four to five feet under ideal conditions. Unlike the bearded irises, yellow flags thrive on wet sites and naturalize along the edges of ponds and streams, in much the same fashion as the native Louisiana irises. Yellow flags prefer the moisture and humidity of the

coast, but will thrive anywhere in the South.

Louisiana irises can be grown successfully in every area of the South. The source of this adaptability no doubt lies in their parentage, for the Louisiana irises were bred from species found native in Arkansas, Louisiana, and Texas. Their historic use as garden plants outside their native range was minimal until recent years. But in the last generation, modern breeding methods and a strong national support group has produced hundreds of new cultivars.

Yellow flag (*Iris pseudocorus*) (William C. Welch)

The flower stalks of the Louisiana irises may vary considerably, from one to six feet, and the flowers may measure from three to seven inches across. Because all the primary colors are inherent in the various species that contributed to this group, there is no limit to the color range. The Louisianas, for example, include the purest form of red of any iris.

Louisiana irises prefer an acid soil in the range of 6.5 or lower. They like large quantities of both fertilizer and water but their greatest need for both of these comes during the naturally cool and moist fall and winter seasons. They are among the few irises that will thrive in poorly drained soils. Louisiana irises can be effectively used along streams and lakes in areas that are inundated periodically by changing water levels. Their foliage is lush and requires heavy fertilization to remain healthy and productive. Some cultivars go dormant during the heat of summer, leaving dead foliage that should be cut back or removed. New foliage will appear again in the fall.

Fall is the best season for transplanting. Beds should be well tilled and amended with large amounts of compost, peat, or pine bark. Rhizomes should be planted just below ground level and kept moist until well established. Clumps spread quickly, and individual rhizomes should be spaced several feet apart to avoid need for annual division.

The Historic Iris Preservation

Louisiana iris (*William C. Welch*)

Society (HIPS) was founded in 1988 to provide dates of introduction and other pertinent information relating to heirloom irises. For membership information refer to the index section on plant sources and organizations.

—WCW

Jasminum spp.
Jasmine, Jessamine
Family: Oleaceae (Olive)
Zones: 8–11 (mainly tropical)

The overpowering scent of jasmine has proven so alluring throughout the ages that anything that smelled or looked like jasmine was generally called such. Sometimes the plant in question *was* a jasmine: the vine that George Washington called "Persian Jessamine" in his diary was *Jasminum officinale*, more popularly known as the poet's, white, or common jasmine. Lady Skipwith,

another colonial Virginian, also grew "white jasmine" while Thomas Jefferson grew both "jasmine white" and "jasmine yellow." This last was not a true jasmine, as it happens. What is popularly called Carolina yellow jasmine is actually a native species of *Gelsemium*—lovely, but not a jasmine.

Jasmines weave their way through the history of Southern gardens, appearing in our earliest handbooks and catalogues. Bernard M'Mahon made numerous references to jasmines in his *American Gardener's Calendar*. An invoice dated February 27, 1837, from nurserymen William Prince and Son showed that Martha Turnbull received the following at Rosedown Plantation: "Spanish or Catalonian Jessamine, Jasminum Revolutum, Jasminum gracile, and Jasminum undulatum" Thomas Affleck's Southern Nurseries catalogue

Confederate jasmine (*Trachelospermum jasminoides*) (*Greg Grant*)

Sambac jasmine (*Jasminum sambac*) (*Greg Grant*)

Far left: *Jasminum polyanthum* (Greg Grant) Left: Yellow jasmine (*Jasminum nudiflorum*) (*William C. Welch*)

(Mississippi) listed "Hardy Jessamines, several varieties" in 1851–52 and Arnold Puetz's "Lily Nursery" (Florida) offered "Cape, Arabian, Grand Duke, and others" in 1881—the cape jasmine being a gardenia, of course. Langdon Nurseries (Alabama) offered *J. officinale* and *J. nudiflorum* in 1881–82.

Jaminum nudiflorum was a gift of the famous plant explorer Robert Fortune, who brought this sprawling shrub back from China between 1843 and 1861. Arnold Petz's Arabian jasmine was undoubtedly *J. sambac*, which seems to be the species most commonly cultivated in the coastal South today. Its cultivars, 'Maid of Orleans' and the double, buttonlike 'Grand Duke of Tuscany', are especially popular.

Other jasmines cultivated in the South include *J. mesnyi*, the primrose jasmine, and *J. floridanum*, the Florida jasmine. And there is the host of jasmine imposters which have traditionally been part of the Southern garden: *Trachelospermum jasminoides*, the Confederate or star jasmine; the heavenly scented *Cestrum nocturnum*, the night-blooming jasmine; *Tabernaemontana divaricata*, the crape jasmine; and *Murraya paniculata*, the orange jasmine.

Jasmines, and most of the imposters as well, are generally very easy to grow under most conditions. Some are cold-tender pot plants, some are vines, and some are fairly hardy shrubs. Propagation is easily accomplished by rooting cuttings.

The heavy scent of jasmine is like that of paperwhites: tawdry and overpowering. Some lust after it while others gasp for air. Personally, I fall in the lust category, especially when the jasmine scent is drifting through a garden. Not surprisingly, the extraction of perfume from jasmine flowers is an ancient industry—though today it is an artificial jasmine scent that we splash on everything from potpourri to your car's upholstery. Unfortunately, it smells like melted plastic to me. There's just no substitute for the real thing. —GG

Juniperus virginiana
Cedar, Red Cedar, Eastern Red Cedar
Family: Cupressaceae (Cypress)
Zones: 3–10

First of all, what we all call cedar is not a true cedar but a juniper instead. True cedars belong to the genus *Cedrus*, while our native red "cedar" belongs to the cypress family, which of course does not include the bald cypress—bald cypress is not a true cypress and has its own family. An honest, true cypress would belong to the genus *Cupressus*. See why you're a gardener and not a botanist?

How many cedars are there marking abandoned homesites, lining avenues, and standing guard at cemeteries in the South today? They're everywhere. The fence post guys haven't even made a dent in them. The cedar ranks right up there with the magnolia and the live oak as a popular evergreen tree in the South. Although it may be less popular in urban gardens, it is probably the king of evergreens in rural areas.

It was king especially at holiday time, when traditionally it supplied the Christmas tree for rural families. Back when my dad was in charge of cutting a "Charlie Brown" tree for the Grant family, it was what we always had. Thanks to the affection of its needles for my mom's carpet, we switched to loblolly pine. Today I cultivate leyland cypress for our trees, so that holiday visitors will think we have store-bought stuff for a change. One year when I wasn't around to cut us a tree, my mother went into town to the Christmas tree farm to get us our first bought tree. She looked for hours but couldn't find one as ugly as we were used to and came home empty-handed. It was just like old times because my dad was sent out to the pasture again to make an "acceptable" emergency selection.

In a letter to the editor of the *Natchez Daily Courier* on October 28, 1854, Thomas Affleck tried my same futile bit of botanical education, writing that "the cedars are very beautiful. And, by the way, what we know as the Red Cedar, is a Juniper." He went on to add, "The Junipers, headed by our own beautiful native, the so-called Red Cedar (*J. virginiana*), are indispensable. In the 'Red Cedar' there is a great diversity of foliage and habit of growth; some being open and loose in habit, others upright and compact. The latter I have always selected from the seed-bed. They should have room to grow, and be allowed to sweep the ground with their branches; not pruned up into the likeness of a gigantic broom!" That advice is just as good today.

Far left: Eastern red cedar (*Juniperus virginiana*) (*Greg Grant*)
Left: Eastern red cedar (*Juniperus virginiana*) (*William C. Welch*)

Most of the early nurseries in the South carried the red cedar. The ones that didn't probably knew that their customers would just dig them from the wild. Early Southern nursery catalogues in which I have found mention of this tree include Affleck's Southern Nurseries, of Washington, Mississippi, 1851–52; Langdon Nurseries, near Mobile, Alabama, 1881–82; Denison Nurseries, of Denison, Texas, 1885–86; Mission Valley Nurseries, of Nursery, Texas in 1888; Waldheim Nursery, of Boerne, Texas in 1895–96; and Frank Vestal-Florist and Nurseryman, of Little Rock Arkansas, 1896.

I'm sure everybody realizes that our native "cedar" is very easy to grow, since they flourish along fence rows throughout the South. Propagation is from seed, or you may dig the young trees from the woods or the fence rows, with permission of course. Don't dig mine in Arcadia though. I use them to make posts for fences, bird houses, bottle trees, and such. —GG

Kerria japonica 'Pleniflora'
Kerria, Japanese Rose
Family: Rosaceae (Rose)
Zones: 4–9
William Kerr first brought the double-flowered form of this plant from China to Kew in 1805, so perhaps it is only fair that it was named for him. Although in point of fact, the kerria was already known in Europe from descriptions written by Kaempfer in 1712 and Thunberg in his *Flora Japonica* in 1784. If the kerria was a novelty to westerners,

however, it was thoroughly familiar to the gardeners of temperate Asia. A native of China, it had, by the eighteenth century, been long cultivated in Japan.

Towards the end of the nineteenth century, kerrias with gold and silver variegated foliage were discovered and soon became a common sight in American gardens. Peter Henderson remarked in 1890 that kerria was "an old favorite in the garden, with both single and double flowers, to which has lately been added a very pretty variety with variegated leaves."

The plant form is that of a spreading shrub, six to eight feet tall. The stems are green year-round and are an asset to the winter garden, but the kerria's flowers are the feature that popularized this plant. The individual blossoms are about 1½ inches in diameter, and are borne singly at the ends of short stems produced during the previous year's growth. The kerria's heaviest period of bloom lasts for two or three weeks in April or early May, though flowers also appear sporadically throughout the growing season. In Bob McDonald's garden in Mangham, Louisiana, kerria is mixed with mock orange and white Lady Banks' roses, creating a spectacular spring display for several weeks each year.

Kerria flowers are sometimes

confused with those of the yellow Lady Banks' rose. Both plants thrive in our region, and since both are members of the rose family, the flowers have a superficial similarity. But the kerria bears flowers of much more of a golden color than the pale straw-yellow blossoms of the Lady Banks' rose. Propagation is from cuttings in summer or fall. Pruning should be carried out immediately after the spring flower season. Kerrias prefer well-drained

Kerria (*Kerria japonica* 'Pleniflora') (*William C. Welch*)

Winter and summer views of crape myrtles (*Lagerstroemia indica*) in Baton Rouge, Louisiana. (*Greg Grant*)

loamy soils that are neutral or slightly acid. High fertility can result in excessive growth and little flowering. They much prefer a location with protection from the afternoon sun—the flowers burn otherwise—and kerrias will actually bloom well in the shade.

—*WCW*

Lagerstroemia indica
Crape Myrtle, Lilac of the South
Family: Lythraceae (Loosestrife)
Zones: 7–11

> Deservedly one of the most popular shrubs in America. In the South it takes the place of the lilac of the North, but is far more beautiful....
> Gilbert Onderdonk's 1898–99 Mission Valley Nurseries catalogue, Nursery, Texas

It was suggested by a knowledgeable expert and garden writer that lilacs be included in this book. Lilacs as in "the North," I asked? He quickly quoted historic examples of lilacs in the South. I responded by pointing out that most plants have been grown in the South somewhere by somebody at sometime. That doesn't make them Southern though. Anyway, we have our own "lilac of the South," the crape myrtle.

Every self-respecting gardener knows that you grow lilacs in the North and crape myrtles in the South. Even that Yankee from Michigan, Liberty Hyde Bailey, knew this. In his 1917 *Standard Cyclopedia of Horticulture* he stated that "The crape myrtle, *Lagerstroemia indica*, is to the South

what the lilac and the snowball are to the North—an inhabitant of nearly every home yard." Saying the lilac is a Southern heirloom plant is like saying "Yankee Doodle" is the state song of Georgia. Amen.

The crape myrtle received its common name for its superficial resemblance (although no relation) to the true myrtle (*Myrtus*) and for its crapelike flowers. The Latin name of the genus, *Lagerstroemia*, was given to the tree in 1759 by the Swedish botanist Linnaeus, in honor of his friend Magnus von Lagerstroem (1696–1759), Director of the Swedish East Indies Company and an avid naturalist. The species name *indica* is a misnomer, for the crape myrtle is not native to India, but to China.

According to *Hortus Third*, there are about fifty-five species of *Lagerstroemia*, all native to Asia and the Pacific Islands. Of all of these, only three are cold hardy through most of the South, and these three are *L. indica*, *L. fauriei*, and *L. subcostata*. Traditionally, *L. indica* has monopolized the attention of Southern gardeners, but this is changing. *Lagerstroemia fauriei*, a species native to Japan, is the parent of a breeding program carried out at the National Arboretum in Washington, D.C. This tree boasts small but fragrant white flowers and an incredible, cinnamon-colored exfoliating bark, but its resistance to disease was of greatest interest to the National Arboretum's breeder, the late Dr. Donald Egolf. From *L fauriei* he bred a strain of mildew-

resistant hybrid crape myrtles, which he named after American Indian tribes ('Natchez', 'Tuscarora', etc.). The North Carolina State University Arboretum has also introduced a cultivar of *L. fauriei* named 'Fantasy', which has proven cold hardy in that northerly part of the crape myrtle's range. There is a huge, spectacular specimen there at that arboretum whose trunk alone is worth the trouble of a visit.

L. subcostata is a native of Taiwan and China. It apparently was used in breeding the National Arboretum hybrids as well. It has very small white flowers and an extremely attractive smooth tan colored bark. Its bark color looks like a mixture of cinnamon and sugar. There is a very nice specimen just inside the entrance of Louisiana State University's Burden Research Plantation in Baton Rouge. The cold-tender queen's crape myrtle, *L. speciosa*, is widely cultivated in tropical regions for its large clusters of huge flowers in shades of purple, pink, and white.

Of course *L. indica* is the queen of Southern gardens. It is very likely the most popular small flowering tree in the entire South. It has been cultivated in its native Southeast Asia for thousands of years. Our crape myrtle was supposedly introduced to the Royal Botanic Gardens at Kew, England in 1759. Its exact date of introduction into the United States is unknown. Credit is often given to Andre Michaux, who established a nursery around Charleston, South Carolina, around 1786. Apparently George Washington was one of

Far left: Crape myrtle (*Lagerstroemia indica*) at Middleton Place gardens in South Carolina. (*William C. Welch*) Left: 'Tonto' crape myrtle, a National Arboretum semi-dwarf hybrid.

the first to attempt to grow the crape myrtle here. Records at Mount Vernon show that a ship arrived in Philadelphia in April 1799 carrying two plants and seed of *L. reginae*, as well as seeds of *L. indica*. Bernard M'Mahon mentioned *L. indica* in *The American Gardener's Calendar* in 1806. Crape myrtle was listed among the plants cultivated in 1811 at the famous Elgin Botanic Garden in New York. It wasn't long before it began to spread across the South. Records at Prince Nursery in New York show that they were offering the crape myrtle for sale in 1827. Martha Turnbull's records from Rosedown Plantation in St. Francisville, Louisiana show that she ordered a number of different plants from the Prince Nursery. Thomas Affleck mentioned the crape myrtle in a letter to the editor of the *Natchez Daily Courier* in 1854 but didn't have it listed in his 1851–52 Southern Nurseries catalogue in Washington, Mississippi. Montgomery Nurseries of Montgomery, Alabama offered the crape myrtle in its 1860 catalogue. Langdon's Nurseries, near Mobile, offered four varieties (pink, purple, crimson, and white) in its 1881–82 catalogue. In Texas, T.V. Munson's Denison Nurseries listed pink, crimson, and purple crape myrtle in 1885, while in Frelsburg J.F. Leyendecker's Pearfield Nursery catalog of 1888 said it was "too well known to require description."

Almost every abandoned early homesite in the South is marked by at least one surviving crape myrtle. It always fascinated me as a child to see

the crape myrtles, jonquils, and garlic growing by themselves in the middle of the pastures. This toughness and survivability has lead to their use as a frequent cemetery ornamental and a common street tree.

Crape myrtles are very easy to cultivate in any type of soil as long as they have direct sunlight. If the highway department, the cemetery dead, and Bill can grow them remarkably well, the rest of us have an overwhelming chance of success. Unfortunately, they are often overpruned and in this way horribly disfigured. Actually, the only pruning they require is to remove unwanted suckers to show off their beautiful bark and branching structure. Seedpods may also be trimmed off on smaller trees to promote reblooming.

When looking for crape myrtles at nurseries you will find various plants described as "pixie," "dwarf," "semi-dwarf," standard," and "tall." In fact,

crape myrtles are available in all sorts of sizes, with different cultivars stopping at heights of anywhere from three to thirty feet. Propagation is by seed, dormant cuttings, or leafy cuttings under mist.

—GG

Laurus nobilis
Greek Laurel, Cooking Bay, Bay Tree
Family: Lauraceae (Laurel)
Zones: 9–11

Many plants pass under the name of laurel, but this is the only one properly so called. Though many other common names have attached themselves to *Laurus nobilis*, reflecting the plant's long history of varied uses. Thus over the years it has been called sweet bay, cooking bay, and spice laurel—names that all reflect the leaves' use as a culinary spice—as well as Greek laurel, poet's laurel or victor's laurel—names that reflect the ancient Greek custom of weaving its branches into the wreaths

Greek Laurel (*Laurus nobilis*) (*William C. Welch*)

used to crown a victor.

This beautiful evergreen shrub or small tree is a native of southern Europe. Although grown throughout the world as a container plant, the laurel is cold sensitive and freezes back occasionally even in Zone 9.

Because of their agreeable flavor, the leaves are popular in cooking and in various confections. One source (Peter Henderson, 1890) indicates that in the last century the dried figs imported into this country were usually packed with bay leaves.

In the garden, the bay is valued for its tolerance to shearing. The leathery, evergreen foliage responds well to clipping and the plant is popular as a topiary specimen shaping well into cones, pyramids, standards or hedges. Leaves are typically two to four inches long, dark green with a compact tapering form to the plant. Frances and Milton Parker's beautiful garden in Beaufort, South Carolina, has a bay hedge about eight feet tall that separates their landscape into two "rooms." This planting is reported to be at least 150 years old, and only occasionally suffers damage from cold.

Large old specimens of treelike proportions are supposed to exist in Brenham, Texas, and a very old plant at the Gideon Lincecum homesite at Long Point, Texas (Washington County) may date back to the year of the house's construction, 1843. Though neglected for many years, the Lincecum bay continued to prosper until its recent exposure to a large bulldozer. Even that experience has not caused its demise, for bay trees sprout readily from the roots and form clumps.

Since I have never seen fruit on *L. nobilis*, I surmise that all the plants I have grown and seen were propagated from male stock. The flowers are described as yellowish, and the fruit black or dark purple, the size of a small cherry. References describe the bay's fruit as a source of essential oils from which are made laurin ointment, a remedy useful in human and veterinary medicine. These berries are also used to create sweat-inducing aromatic baths and are distilled to make a liqueur called Fioranvanti.

Probably the best known decorative use of this plant is the one referred to in many of the common names: the weaving of its leaves and branches into wreaths for crowning heroes and scholars. The term "laureate" refers to that tradition. This plant was considered a medicinal cure-all until the eighteenth century, and according to Culpeper's *The English Physician Enlarged, or the Herbal*, 1653, it "resisteth witchcraft very potently."

The bay is not fussy about soil, but does require good drainage. It is quite drought tolerant, but grows best where it receives some afternoon shade during the hot summer months. Propagation is by division of the root parts, cuttings, or seed. Cuttings are not easily rooted, but nurserymen experienced with mist systems and semi-hardwood cuttings during the summer report some success.

Bay plants are available from nurseries specializing in herbs and unusual plants. Although susceptibility to cold limits their use, bays are otherwise easily grown and are an interesting and useful plant for containers.

Southern nurseries often offered bay trees to their customers 75 or 100 years ago. Fruitlands Nursery, Augusta, Georgia in their 1906–07 catalogue describes the plant well:

> "*Laurus nobilis* (Bay tree, Apollo's or Spice Laurel) A beautiful evergreen with long, narrow, glossy green leaves, which are very aromatic…there is a growing demand for these beautiful trees. We offer a nice lot of standard and pyramid bays in tubs."

In their 1881–82 catalogue, Langdon's Nurseries, Mobile, Alabama offered plants of "*Laurus nobilis*, Spice Laurel—Leaves very aromatic."   —WCW

Leucojum aestivum
Summer Snowflake, Snow Drops, Dew Drops
Family: Amaryllidaceae (Amaryllis)
Zones: 6–9

Leucojums are among the most persistent of the spring flowering bulbs that grow in the South. Their ability to naturalize is comparable to the hardiest of the narcissus. The ¾-inch fragrant flowers appear in midspring and are bell-shaped, and marked with a distinctive green spot on the margin of each petal. Beginning in March or April in the South, the leucojums' bloom lasts for several weeks. What is more, the dark green foliage the snowflakes produce is among the most attractive of any spring bulb, and it is outstanding for several months from late fall through winter.

Leucojums—or snowflakes, as they are commonly known—show to best advantage in the landscape when planted in large clumps of bulbs. They also combine well with other spring-flowering bulbs and thrive in sun or shade of deciduous trees. Clumps may be left undivided for many years without sacrificing flowers, but division is an easy means of propagation. Mature clumps may be divided in late spring after the foliage has yellowed. Snowflakes thrive even in heavy clay soils.

I have recently combined snowflakes with blue plumbago (*Plumbago auriculata*) in my garden. After the first hard freeze in fall I cut back the plumbago and enjoy the dark green foliage of the snowflakes all winter. By the time the flowers have faded in spring the blue plumbago is beginning to flower and conceals the dying snowflake foliage. Both plants like some protection from the hottest afternoon sun. 'Gravetye Giant' is a cultivar that has much larger flowers than the species, though locating a commercial source of this particular type may require persistence. It has done equally well as the species form in my garden and the flowers are definitely larger and showier.

One of the nicest landscape uses of *L. aestivum* I have observed is their placement as a one-foot-wide border between the walks and a large panel of turf in the main *parterre* of Robert Smith's garden in Breaux Bridge, Louisiana. Robert has created a beautiful setting for his home and his Au Vieux Paris Antiques business with a garden that features many Southern heirloom plants. Snowflakes are natives of Central and Southern Europe. They are often found along stream banks in southern France. The name is derived from the Greek *leukos*, for white, and *ion* a violet. According to Peter Henderson (1890) snowflakes were first introduced

Summer snowflake (*Leucojum aestivum*) (Greg Grant)

in 1596 and are dedicated to St. Agnes, the patron saint of young virgins, for their loveliness and purity, and hence are sometimes called St. Agnes' Flower. In Parkinson's time they were also known as the Great Early Bulbous Violet.

Leucojum aestivum (the summer snowflake) is often confused in the trade with *L. vernum* (the spring snowflake), a species that is less well adapted to gardens of the lower South. One source of this misidentification may be that the so-called summer snowflake actually blooms in the spring and dies back in the summer, at least for us here in the South. But if in doubt about the identity of your snowflakes, wait until they bloom, for the two species are easily distinguished then: *L. vernum* bears solitary flowers on each of its arching stems, whereas *L. aestivum* bears multiple flowers on each stalk.

In *A Southern Garden*, Elizabeth Lawrence wrote about her experiences with growing both the spring and summer snowflakes. Her North Carolina experiences are similar to those I have had here in Texas. When comparing the two, she says of *L. aestivum* that it is "a much more robust plant, with stems to two feet, larger and broader bells, and longer, thicker leaves. The summer snowflake is much handsomer."

In another of her books, *The Little Bulbs*, Miss Lawrence commented on another source of confusion about the identity of the snowflake: "Nearly everyone in the South calls a snowflake a snow-drop. No matter how often Southerners are told that *Leucojum*

aestivum, found in every dooryard, is a snowflake, they go on calling it snow-drop, just as they go on calling camellias japonicas, and daffodils jonquils."

I have not been able to establish a date for the introduction of snowflakes to Southern gardens, but they are definitely not newcomers. They are frequently found at cemeteries and abandoned homesites at least one hundred years old. I have had reasonably good luck in ordering bulbs from commercial sources, but it is hard to go wrong with those collected from old naturalized plantings.   —WCW

Ligustrum sinense
Privet, Chinese Privet
Family: Oleaceae (Olive)
Zones: 7–11
If you live in the South, you've seen this privet growing in all sorts of shapes, in hedges and along fence rows. You've seen it running loose in the woods, too, as it has a great tendency to chase after

Japanese honeysuckle. Actually, these two plants' combination of fragrance and tenacity make a happy marriage.

Ligustrum sinense was introduced from China in 1852 by none other than Robert Fortune. It was originally listed as *L. fortunei*. The origin of the name privet is somewhat of a mystery, although the suggestion has often been made that the shrub was named this because it was so commonly planted around privies. Smells "funny," but I'll buy it.

Everybody used to grow privet, and practically every early Southern nursery carried some form of it. In his letter to the editor of the *Natchez Daily Courier*, Thomas Affleck wrote: "There are several forms of the Privets which form beautiful ornamental evergreen trees. The handsome evergreen, so generally admired on the top of the mound between the house of our friend Mr. Andrew Brown and the river is the Chinese Privet. It is at all times a

Privet (*Ligustrum sinense*) topiaries in a Navasota, Texas, garden. (Greg Grant)

Privet *parterre* in the New Roads, Louisiana, garden of Dr. and Mrs. Jack Holden. (William C. Welch)

beautiful plant, but more especially when covered with its racemes of white flowers. The Evergreen, the Myrtle-leaved, and Box-leaved, though commonly all used for hedging, may be readily trained into pretty smallish trees."

Affleck's 1851–52 Southern Nurseries catalogue listed all four of the above. Langdon Nurseries, near Mobile, listed *L. vulgaris* (common privet), *L. californicum* (California privet), *L. japonicum* (Japan privet), *L. nepalensis* (Nepal privet), and *L. amurense* (Amoor River privet) in its 1881–82 catalogue. Pearfield Nursery in Frelsburg, Texas listed the California privet in its 1888 catalogue, while Mission Valley Nurseries of Nursery, Texas listed not only that but also privet, and the Japanese ligustrum in its 1898–99 catalog. Prince's Nursery of New York

carried the Japanese ligustrum in its 1835–36 catalogue. Maybe one reason that our ancestors favored privet more than we moderns do is that they had a much better selection of forms at their disposal.

Bailey's 1917 *Standard Cyclopedia of Horticulture* says that "*L. sinense* is used as a hedge plant, particularly in the South." It also describes three different ways of making hedges, including the following: "At Biltmore Nursery, North Carolina, the privet cuttings are run through a stalk-cutter and the pieces sown in a furrow." Sounds like something even an Aggie could handle. Bailey also says: "In some southern nurseries, *L. sinense* has been offered under the name of *L. amurense*."

Another ligustrum sometimes found in the South is *L. lucidum*, the glossy privet, which used to be confused with

L. japonicum, the Japanese ligustrum. Glossy privet actually has less glossy and larger foliage than *L. japonicum*, and the leaves of the glossy privet have a translucent rim around their margins. It also forms a larger plant. I have found very large, treelike specimens of glossy privet all around the San Antonio area.

Today, the variegated Chinese privet is more often planted than the green form, although in rural, poor, and inner city areas the green form is still the common one. Of course, Japanese ligustrum has become the most popular privet of all. Today's horticulturists love to hate privets of all types. I think that must be taught to them at school. I myself can't remember anything from school except the girl who thought potatoes grew on trees. They shouldn't let city folks in ag schools.   —GG

Lonicera spp.
Honeysuckle
Family: Caprifoliceae (Honeysuckle)
Zones: 7–11

The sweet perfume of this flower is an inseparable part of Southern memories, and both the native and introduced honeysuckles are important garden vines and shrubs. Perhaps the most important species horticulturally is the native coral, or trumpet, honeysuckle, *Lonicera sempervirens*. Indigenous from Connecticut to Florida and westward to Nebraska and Texas, trumpet honeysuckle is adapted to a wide variety of soils and growing conditions. It will grow in sun or shade, though it blooms

Coral honeysuckle (*Lonicera sempervirens*) (William C. Welch)

Japanese honeysuckle (*Lonicera japonica*) (Greg Grant)

**Far left:
Winter
honeysuckle
(*Lonicera
fragrantissima*)
(*William C.
Welch*)
Left: Winter
honeysuckle
(*Lonicera
fragrantissima*)**

better in a brighter site.

Trumpet honeysuckle flowers vary in color from a beautiful pure yellow—in the cultivar 'Sulphurea'—to bicolored blossoms that are orange-red or red on the outside of the tubular corolla and yellow to yellow-orange inside. The twining vines are vigorous but not invasive, and the foliage is red-purple, turning bluish green at maturity.

Since this attractive vine is native to much of the South, it found use on trellises and arbors early on. It is propagated easily from cuttings or seed from the ¼-inch fruit that ripens in fall. Fruit production is unpredictable, but cuttings may be taken from April on throughout the growing season.

Lonicera japonica, the Japanese honeysuckle, was introduced from East Asia and has become a serious weed in the South—it can be found invading woodlands throughout the region. The creamy white flowers are highly fragrant—the perfume is noticeable even from a passing car—and this vine has, over the years, covered many trellises, arbors, and fences. *Lonicera japonica* 'Halliana', better known as Hall's honeysuckle, is the best known form in cultivation and may be used as an aggressive groundcover or vine. *Lonicera japonica* 'Purpurea' has purplish foliage and is a shrubby vine that may be used as a low-maintenance shrub or groundcover.

Winter honeysuckle, *Lonicera fragrantissima*, is another of the many plants brought back from China in 1845 by Scottish plantsman Robert Fortune.

This species, curiously, has never been found in the wild. It is another very easily grown plant, forming a deciduous shrub rather than a vine. The small, creamy white flowers open in mid- to late winter and are extremely fragrant, although not very showy. The lemonlike scent permeates the air in the vicinity of the plant, and on warm winter days, the result is almost shocking, since that is not a season when one looks for flowers. Small bright red fruits sometimes form during May and June but they remain hidden beneath the foliage and are not conspicuous.

Winter honeysuckle is one of the toughest and easiest grown shrubs imaginable. I have seen it thriving from Amarillo to Beaumont in Texas and throughout the South. It can reach six to ten feet tall and almost as wide, and is useful as a specimen planting, or as a background shrub or hedge. Every garden should have at least one!

Best of all, this shrub requires very little maintenance, though it keeps a neater appearance if some of the old canes are removed at ground level each winter. This can be done when the branches are in flower, so that the prunings may be enjoyed as cut material inside the home. I have also seen old specimens trimmed up and effectively used as small, multitrunk trees.

Many old-time nurseries listed winter honeysuckles; for example, W.A. Yates of Brenham Texas advertised this plant in their 1906–08 catalogue. Some of the finest old specimens I have seen are located in the Mt. Holly Cemetery in Little Rock Arkansas. Personally, I have fond memories of a large old specimen that grew by my grandmother's gate in Yoakum, Texas.

Although its origins are a bit obscure, *Lonicera* x *heckrottii*, better known as goldflame honeysuckle, is thought to be a hybrid of *L. sempervirens* and *L. americana*. Whatever its parentage, the plant is a genuine antique, for it is known to have been introduced onto the market prior to 1895—Fruitlands Nursery, in Augusta, Georgia listed *L.* x *heckrottii* along with four other honeysuckles in their 1906–07 catalogue.

Goldflame honeysuckle is a vine and remains evergreen except in severe winters. The flowers start opening early and recur during spring, summer, and fall. With its carmine buds that open to blossoms yellow on the outside and gradually change to pink, it is surely one of the most handsome of the climbing honeysuckles. Flowers occur simultaneously with new growth all season, and the fragrance is pleasant, though slight.

**Goldflame
honeysuckle
(*Lonicera* x
heckrottii)
(*Greg Grant*)**

Red spider lily
(*Lycoris radiata*)
(*Greg Grant*)

Although fairly vigorous in growth I describe the goldflame honeysuckle as a "mannerly" vine. Cuttings root readily and new plants often begin flowering the second year. I have noticed that this vine is susceptible to powdery mildew in some areas and it appears to me that this honeysuckle's vigor and flowering is better a hundred or more miles inland from the Gulf of Mexico.

Several years ago I observed a strikingly beautiful blue-green foliaged honeysuckle in Rachel's Garden at "The Hermitage" near Nashville. Jane Symmes identified it as *L. prolifera* and grew it at her nursery, Cedar Lane Farms, near Madisonville, Georgia. *Hortus Third* describes the flowers as pale yellow marked with purple. It is a summer bloomer and native from Ohio to Tennessee. Plant form is a shrubby vine.   —WCW

Lycoris radiata
Spider Lily, Guernsey Lily, British Soldiers, Naked Ladies
Family: Amaryllidaceae (Amaryllis)
Zones: 7–9
Among the flowers that I first cherished as a child was what I knew as the spider lily. There's something about flowers that magically spring forth after long hot dry periods that still mesmerizes me. If there is any true magic in horticulture, this seems to be it.

Of course, determining the true identity of my spider lilies proved to be no child's play. To begin with, there is the usual confusion that comes with common names. In the South, "spider lily" always seems to apply to members of the Amaryllis family, but depending

on where you live, which genus you tag with that name changes. Had I grown up near the Gulf Coast, I would have cultivated *Hymenocallis* as spider lilies. But since I grew up inland I, like other gardeners of the mid- and upper South, used the name to describe the bulb that botanists today call *Lycoris radiata*.

Not that botanists don't make mistakes, too. By now, it has been determined that *Lycoris radiata*, which is naturalized widely in the South, is a native of Japan. Yet from the day this bulb arrived in the United States, botanists insisted that it had come from South Africa (can't they read a packing slip?), and for decades thereafter, they misidentified it as *Nerine sarniensis*, the Guernsey Lily. How this mixup occurred is anyone's guess, but it wasn't until 1936 that anyone noticed.

In that year, W.M. James of Califor-

nia and Wyndham Hayward of Florida contributed an article to the bulletin of the American Amaryllis Society, pointing out that the Japanese bulb was different from the South African one. But it was up to Elizabeth Lawrence to trace the real history of spider lily (the mid- and upper South kind), which she did in *A Southern Garden* (1942):

> In North Carolina we might have wondered before, if we thought at all about the flowers that grow in our gardens, about the name nerine. For the nerine is a South African genus, and the first red spider-lilies in North Carolina (and probably in this country) came directly from Japan to a garden in New Bern. They were brought to that garden nearly a hundred years ago by Captain William Roberts who was with Commodore Perry when he opened the port of Japan. The Captain brought three bulbs which were, his niece Mrs. Simmons says, in such a dry condition that they did not show signs of life until the War between the States. The original bulbs have increased and been passed on until they have spread across the state.

Dr. Henry Nehrling also helps to clear up the matter. He writes in *My Garden in Florida* (1944):

Left: Surprise lily (*Lycoris squamigera*) (*William C. Welch*)
Above: Golden spider lily (*Lycoris africana*) (*Greg Grant*)

Red spider lilies
(*Lycoris radiata*)
in the Grace
Episcopal
Cemetery, St.
Francisville,
Louisiana.
(**Greg Grant**)

[I]n 1888 Mrs. Thompson of Spartanburg, South Carolina, an ardent flower lover, sent me about 50 fine bulbs of another species, *L. radiata*.

L. *radiata*, often called *Nerine japonica*, is an old garden plant, for it was noted by Kaempfer in 1712, and cultivated in England around 1750. It is a native of China and Japan, where it is commonly cultivated in gardens, and offered by nurserymen at about 75 cents/100. It is very like a nerine. Thunberg mistook it for the Guernsey Lily (*Nerine samiensis*), which it resembles.

In addition to a huge population of *L. radiata*, there are other less common species of *Lycoris* blooming across the South as well. *L. squamigera*, the real naked lady, or surprise lily, is common only in the upper South, as it apparently needs a period of winter chilling to bloom. *L. africana* (*L. aurea*), the yellow spider lily or hurricane lily, is only common in the lower South as it does not tolerate frost well. This flourishes in large numbers in Florida, and had the distinction of being included (under the name *Amaryllis aurea*) in *Les Liliacees*, the famous collection of watercolors that the French floral artist Pierre Joseph Redouté finished in 1816. Finally, a white form of *L. radiata* is occasionally met with by the observant gardener.

All of these are available commercially, although Scott Ogden of New Braunfels tells me that the bulb sold as red spider lily is different genetically than the form found naturalized in old gardens. The naturalized form is a sterile triploid—that is, it has three sets of chromosomes rather than the usual two and so cannot reproduce by seed. But if slower to propagate, it is stronger growing, so if you can get the naturalized form, plant that.

Gardening friends are often a good source of unusual spider lilies. Cleo Barnwell of Shreveport gave me the bulbs of *L. incarnata* and *L. caldwellii* that I grow. Sam Caldwell of Tennessee is probably the most famous collector and breeder of spider lilies in the United States.

Spider lilies are very easy to grow in sun or shade. They thrive and multiply best in a somewhat acidic, loose, and well drained soil. Propagation is by division. Although summer is the preferred time for division they will survive transplanting at any time of the year.

One of the most beautiful sights that I have ever seen was the Grace Episcopal Church cemetery in St. Francisville, Louisiana. It was covered with red spider lilies—what Virginians call British soldiers—in full bloom. Knowing that Martha Turnbull, the mother of the beautiful gardens at Rosedown Plantation, lay buried there, I couldn't help but think that she would approve of resting in a beautiful moss-draped Southern garden with hundreds of British soldiers standing at attention.

—GG

Magnolia grandiflora
Southern Magnolia, Bull Bay, Big Laurel, Laurel Tree of Carolina
Family: Magnoliaceae (Magnolia)
Zones: 7–11

The finest and most superb evergreen-tree that the earth produced.
Dr. Alexander Garden, Charleston, South Carolina, 1757

The monarque of the Southern forest, and needs no description.
Gilbert Onderdonk's Mission Valley Nurseries, Nursery, Texas, 1898–1899

Magnolia grandiflora! The most beautiful tree in the world; no picture and no painting can do thee justice; no description, and be it ever so glowing, can give an idea of thy natural and noble beauty.
Henry Nehrling, *My Garden in Florida*, 1944

No other flower, perhaps no other plant, evokes images of the South the way the magnolia does. It is the emblem of the Southern Garden History Society, and the state flower of both Louisiana and Mississippi. This stateliest of the evergreen trees is native from Texas to North Carolina and can reach an immense size (up to 100 feet!) on deep soils in the wild. For the early naturalists and gardeners, to see this tree, with its large glossy leaves and huge fragrant flowers, was to fall in love. William

Southern magnolia (*Magnolia grandiflora*) (**Greg Grant**)

Left: Southern magnolia (*Magnolia grandiflora*) (*Atlanta History Center*)
Above: Southern magnolia bloom (*Magnolia grandiflora*) (*Greg Grant*)

day as common as the lilac." I think he stayed in the bedroom sniffing it a little too long.

Other magnolias cultivated in the early South included three more southeastern natives: the cucumbertree magnolia (*M. acuminata*), the umbrella magnolia (*M. tripetala*), and the bigleaf magnolia (*M. macrophylla*). In fact, an amazing selection of these trees were available to our ancestors. Bartram and Sons' Nursery carried *M. acuminata* and *tripetala*, while Prince's Nursery of Flushing, New York listed Thompson's magnolia, a cross between the sweet bay and the umbrella magnolia, in their 1823 catalog. In *Breck's Book of Flowers* (1851), Joseph Breck, a Boston nursery-man, listed *M. glauca*, *M. acuminata*, *M. auriculata*, *M. fuscata*, *M. conspicua*, *M. Soulangiana*, *M. purpurea*, and *M. gracilis*.

By mid- to late nineteenth century, magnolias from the orient were arriving in the South to further enrich our native selection. Two Chinese species—*M. heptapeta* (formerly *M. denudada* and *M. conspicua*), the yulan magnolia; and *M. quinquapeta* (formerly *M. liliflora* and *M. purpurea*)—crossed to produce the

Bartram made numerous references to the "glorious magnolia" in the chronicles of his travels through the Southeast in the 1780s.

According to Alice Coates in *Garden Shrubs and their Histories* (1964), huge native specimens were regarded by Frenchman Andre Michaux, early American explorer and botanist, as some of the finest productions of the vegetable kingdom. Coates adds: "It is said that the Indians would not sleep under such a tree when in bloom, because of the overpowering scent of its flowers—one of which, if kept in a bedroom, could cause death in a single night." I never realized that Indians *had* bedrooms! All early Southern nurseries carried this tree, and almost everybody in the South grew it.

The genus is named for Pierre Magnol (1638–1715), professor of medicine and director of the botanic gardens in Montpelier, France. Of course, *grandiflora* refers to the huge flowers. Southern gardeners soon added to this species a number of fine varieties, including *gloriosa*, which bears larger flowers; *angustifolia* and *lanceolata*, which have narrow leaves; *rotundifolia*, a rounded-leaf form; and *praecox*, which is early flowering.

The Southern magnolia was introduced into England around 1734

but never thrived there as in its home. This fits a rule that I have developed over the years: if it thrives in England, it won't grow in the South, and if it sulks in England, send her home to Dixie!

Actually some magnolias from our region did succeed reasonably well in European gardens. The first American magnolia to make the trip to the Old World (and the plant from which the genus was named) was *Magnolia virginiana*, the sweet bay, or swamp magnolia, a native of the Southeast. Formerly known as *M. glauca*, it was listed as such in John Bartram and Son's 1792 catalogue with the description "charming—the neat white rosette blossom possesses an animating fragrance." According to Coates, this species was introduced into England as early as 1688.

William Cobett, who wrote *The English Gardener* in 1833, was obviously a fan of *M. virginiana*. He said that its fragrance was "the most delightful that can be conceived, far exceeding that of the rose; in strength equaling the jasmine or tuberose, but more delightful....None of the other magno-lias are nearly so odiferous as this; all but this are somewhat tender; this might be in every shrubbery in England with the greatest of ease, and I cannot help expressing my hope that it may be one

Saucer magnolia (*Magnolia x soulangiana*) with flowering quince (*Chaenomeles speciosa*) and assorted *Narcissus* cultivars. (*William C. Welch*)

early-blooming, deciduous M. x *soulangiana*, the saucer magnolia. A mainstay now of our Southern gardens, this plant—which I knew as the "tulip tree"—was another of my childhood favorites. Anyone passing by the Louisiana State University campus in Baton Rouge should pause to see the beautiful specimens there.

Prince's catalogue was listing M. x *soulangiana* by 1832, and since that nursery had many Southern customers, we can assume this tree was current in our region by then. In the case of many other oriental magnolias, it is difficult to establish exactly when they arrived in the South, though the date of introduction into England provides a clue. So, the white-flowered yulan magnolia was introduced into England from China by Sir Joseph Banks around 1879; there are also very nice specimens of this tree scattered around Baton Rouge. The purple-flowered M. *quinquapeta* was introduced into England from Japan by Thunberg in 1790. Samuel Parson (another New York nurseryman who shipped to the South) listed M. x *soulangiana* 'Lennei' and M. *stellata*, the star magnolia in his 1876–77 catalogue.

Magnolias require deep, acidic, well-drained soils. Otherwise they are easy to grow. Propagation is from stratified seed, by cuttings (which are somewhat difficult to root), or by grafting. Even if it's just for the fragrance, everybody in the South should have a magnolia. I think it's a law.   —GG

Melia azedarach
Chinaberry, Pride of China, China Tree, Bead Tree, Umbrella China, Texas Umbrella, Pride of India, Syrian Bead Tree, Japanese Bead Tree
Family: Meliaceae (Mahogany)
Zones: 7–11
In her book *Gardening for Love* the late Elizabeth Lawrence wrote of chinaberries:

Before the Civil War [chinaberries] had become as typical of the South as lilacs are of New England. Longfellow wrote in "Evangeline" of the houses of planters shaded by China trees, and Harriet Beecher Stowe described them in detail. When

Texas umbrella chinaberry (*Melia azedarach umbraculiformis*) (Greg Grant)

Uncle Tom arrived at Simon Legree's plantation, "The wagon rolled up a weedy gravel walk, under a noble avenue of China trees, whose graceful forms and ever-springing foliage seemed to be the only things that neglect could not daunt or alter—like noble spirits, so deeply rooted in goodness, as to flourish and grow stronger amid discouragement and decay…"

Today's horticulturists frown on the chinaberry because its wood is weak and because the tree is relatively short-lived. But this stately member of the mahogany family used to be a universal fixture in Southern landscapes. In his diary, George Washington mentions planting the pride of China tree at Mount Vernon and Thomas Jefferson makes numerous references in his garden journal to the pride of China trees cultivated at Monticello.

The English, of course, grew it first. According to the 1993 *Hillier Manual of Trees and Shrubs*, the chinaberry has been cultivated in England since the sixteenth century. It was frequently used on that island, as in our South, as a street tree. So, an early Victorian classic, *Loudon's Encyclopedia of Gardening* (London, 1830) remarks that "the village of Riceborough…is very picturesque. Most of the houses have verandas; and it is observed, both by Captain Hall and Mr. Stuart, that the pride of India [Chinaberry], the Melia Azedarach, is planted along the streets, as well as in those of most of the southern towns, particularly Charleston

and Savannah."

In his letter to the editor of the *Natchez Daily Courier*, Thomas Affleck was among the first horticulturists to bash the ever-so-common chinaberry with the written word. "The perpetually recurring Pride of China tree, beautiful though it be, to the exclusion of the scores of magnificent trees, native and introduced, is, to say the least of it, in very bad taste. It is a filthy tree, too, about a yard, when compared with many others." He goes on to chastise the city of Natchez, saying "Suppose that, instead of the China tree, your streets and pleasant Bluff promenade, had been lined and shaded with…oaks!"

Still, Southerners persisted in their affection for the chinaberry, especially the choice form known as Texas umbrella china (M. *azedarach umbraculiformis*). Bailey's 1916 *Standard Cyclopedia of Horticulture* describes it this way: "Leaflets are less broad than in M. *azedarach*, and the branches erect, and, in a manner, radiating from the trunk, the drooping foliage giving the tree the appearance of a giant umbrella.…The first tree that came to notice is said to have been found near the battlefield of San Jacinto, Texas, but no record of its introduction there [sic]. If the flowers are cross-pollinated with the common sort, the percentage of seedlings which reproduce the exact umbrella shape seldom varies; hence it is supposed by some to be a distinct species."

I'm not sure when the umbrella form was introduced. Langdon Nurseries of Alabama lists it in the 1881–82 catalogue, mentioning that it originated

Chinaberry (*Melia azedarach*)
(Greg Grant)

in Texas, and by 1888 the catalogue of Mission Valley Nursery near Victoria, Texas, says it is "Too well known to require description…" However, this form was not listed in Thomas Affleck's 1851–52 Southern Nurseries Catalogue from Washington, Mississippi. So perhaps it is safe to say that it gained currency sometime in the third quarter of the nineteenth century.

The umbrella China was eventually offered by most Southern nurseries, and probably every early Texas nursery, including F.T. Ramsey's Austin Nursery at Austin, R.B. Halley's Alvin Fruit and Nursery Co. at Algoa, G.A. Shattenberg's Waldheim Nursery at Boerne, William Watson's Rosedale Nurseries at Brenham, W.A. Yates' Nursery at Brenham, D.G. Gregory's Val Verde Nurseries at Alleyton, T.V. Munson's Denison Nurseries at Denison, J.F. Leyendecker's Pearfield Nursery at Frelsburg, Anna Nickels' Arcadia Garden at Laredo, and Gilbert Onderdonk's Mission Valley Nurseries at Nursery. The 1905 Alvin Nursery catalogue describes the Texas umbrella as the "finest shade tree known. With care the tree will make a spread of fifteen feet in one year. A most beautiful shaped tree, making a very compact head without pruning."

I remember as a child the umbrella chinas at my grandparents' home in Shelby County, Texas. In particular, there was a huge one in the back yard where the corn shucking always took place. This specimen had an open spot in the center where the chickens nested and I would perch in hiding. I also remember my grandad, Eloy Emanis, topping the young trees to make the umbrella shape even more pronounced. This severe topping, or pollarding, was and still is a common practice on chinaberries in the rural South.

Before he died, my grandad planted some chinaberries that turned out not to be umbrella chinas, and he was *not* pleased. I got my own young umbrella chinaberry last year, from Clyde Ikins, the waterlily expert from Bandera, Texas. I'll use it to replace my grandad's bastard ones.

Recently John Fanick of the famous Fanick's Nursery in San Antonio showed me photos of a spectacularly gaudy variegated chinaberry he found in the Rio Grande Valley of Texas. Amazingly, the brilliant blotches of white on that tree's leaves don't burn in the hot South Texas sun. He and I recently visited the tree, and after babbling helplessly in my private version of Spanish and by trading a collection of brightly colored new plants, I obtained graft wood of this treasure from the tree's owner, Francisca Medina of Harlingen. As near as I could tell, she did not know the origin of the tree—apparently it sprang up as a seedling. Her neighbor called the tree "Lila." I wonder if it is a corruption of *Melia*?

While going through the Lyendecker family papers recently at the Barker Texas History Center on the University of Texas campus at Austin, I ran across an 1888 catalogue from Hill Side Nursery of Marksville, Louisiana, featuring an "Albino Umbrella China Tree." Although I have never seen one, I can easily select all white branches of Ms. Medina's to reproduce it. Maybe the North Carolina State Arboretum would like one for their white garden. Imagine the sight of it with a characteristic whitewashed trunk! I would like to plant an *allée* of white, or at least variegated, chinaberries at my grandparents' old homeplace. How about that, a French twist to a truly white-trash-tree? Scott Ogden, garden writer and expert horticulturist from New Braunfels, Texas has located several other variegated forms to enhance my demented garden antics.

Chinaberries are very easy to grow in all areas of the South. Propagation is by seed, cuttings, or grafting.   —GG

Michelia figo
Banana Shrub, Magnolia Fuscata
Family: Magnoliaceae (Magnolia)
Zones: 8–11

Originally known as *Magnolia fuscata* and still called that by many today, the evergreen banana shrub provides one of the most distinctive fragrances in our Southern gardens. The pale, creamy-yellow blossoms it bears in the spring are not showy—but when you smell like ripe bananas, you don't have to be.

The banana shrub is a native of China and according to *The Hillier Manual of Trees and Shrubs*, was introduced into Europe in 1789 as a greenhouse plant. Like many European greenhouse plants, it found itself right at home in gardens of the Deep South. I couldn't locate a date of introduction

Variegated chinaberry (*Melia azedarach*) in the Harlingen, Texas, garden of Francisca Medina.
(John Fanick)

Banana shrub (*Michelia figo*) (*Greg Grant*)

Banana shrub (*Michelia figo*) (*Neil Odenwald*)

into American gardens, although Philadelphia nurseryman Robert Buist listed it among the greenhouse plants in his *American Flower-Garden Directory* in 1860. Early nursery catalogues in which I found advertisements of "Magnolia fuscata" included Affleck's Central Nurseries near Brenham, Texas (1860), Mission Valley Nurseries near Victoria, Texas (1898–99), Rosedale Nurseries, Brenham, Texas (1901), Fruitland Nurseries, Augusta, Georgia (1906–07), and W.A. Yates' Nursery, Brenham, Texas (1906–08).

I'm sure there were many other sources of this plant in the southeastern states. It was apparently, a popular plant. In this regard, it's worth noting that the 1917 edition of Liberty Hyde Bailey's *Standard Cyclopedia*—the foremost American garden reference of the time—calls *Michelia fuscata* "one of the most popular garden shrubs in the southern states." Bailey also lists *Michelia champaca* as being cultivated in the Southern states—a species I'm not familiar with.

Whatever degree of popularity the banana shrub enjoyed a century ago, it is a good shrub for today. It grows best in an acidic, deep sandy loam soil and is basically pest-free. It may occasionally suffer freeze damage, especially in or near zone 7, but is otherwise trouble-free. Banana shrub may be grown as a medium-sized shrub or pruned up to make a small tree. I have one at my parents' home in East Texas that I've trained as a small tree to shelter a cedar bench—the effect is quite nice.

—GG

Mirabilis jalapa
Four–O'Clock, Marvel of Peru
Family: Nyctaginaceae (Four–O'Clock)
Zones: 7–11

Felder Rushing, co-author of *Passalong Plants*, calls four-o'clocks a "can't fail perennial." Actually, gardeners in colder climates must grow them as annuals, but in most of the South they develop fleshy tubers that not only persist from year to year, they seem to last forever. *Hortus Third* says that these tubers may eventually grow to a weight of forty pounds in warm climate regions.

Dr. Alice Le Duc, now at Kansas State University, wrote her doctoral thesis on four-o'clocks and found that the Aztecs had grown them and even developed strains with different flower colors many years before the Spanish conquest of the Southwest. The conquistadors were struck by this achievement, apparently, for they sent four-o'clocks back to Spain sometime during the sixteenth century. Within seventy-five years, this plant had turned up in English gardens, and it had been in cultivation in Europe for about 200 years before Linnaeus first described the species in 1753.

The specimens described by Linnaeus were those of cultivated plants. Curiously, although four-o'clocks are often found on old garden sites in Mexico (and the Southern United States), they are no longer found in the wild there.

Plants are lush and bushy to three feet. The tubular flowers come in colors ranging from iridescent purple, white, red, yellow, and striped. Their name derives from the fact that their flowers open in the late afternoon, staying open until the next morning—on cloudy days, four-o'clocks may open somewhat earlier. The fragrance of the flowers is a strong plus and a major reason for their

Four-o'clock
(*Mirabilis jalapa*)
(*Greg Grant*)

Four-o'clock (*Mirabilis jalapa*) (William C. Welch)

popularity. Four-o'clocks attract hummingbirds and moths to the garden.

This is a very heat- and drought-tolerant plant, and one which blooms well in sun or fairly dense shade. I remember visiting a cemetery on a ranch near Yoakum, Texas, where four-o'clocks were the only reminder of a once well-tended plot. They had escaped the small fenced area under a great live oak tree and were happily flowering in profusion during the hottest time of our summer.

Thomas Jefferson grew what he referred to as the "fragrant Marvel of Peru" at his home, Monticello; he also cultivated M. *longiflora*, a creamy-white flowering species native to West Texas and Mexico. A few years ago we secured seed of this plant and sent it to Peggy Newcomb, Director of the Historic Plant Collection at Monticello, so that M. *longiflora* is again blooming in that garden. Currently, seed is available through the Monticello mail order catalogue.

Four-o'clocks may be easily started from seed or tubers. In colder parts of the country the tubers may be dug in the fall and stored until spring. This plant tends to produce a great deal of seed and it can become a garden pest, although the young seedlings are easily pulled or hoed. One year I planted a number of magenta-colored four-o'clocks at our farm and they reseeded prolifically by early fall, covering an area of about 120 square feet. It was an unusually dry year and the young plants received no irrigation. They remained wilted and stunted until the first good fall rain, whereupon they miraculously freshened, covering themselves with flowers in just a few days. They were as showy as azaleas that autumn, and I developed a new appreciation that year for this plant's old name: "Marvel of Peru."
—WCW

Myrtus communis
Myrtle, Sweet Myrtle, Bride's Myrtle
Family: Myrtaceae (Myrtle)
Zones: 9–11

If your garden should lie on the Gulf Coast, then this densely foliaged, aromatic evergreen is the plant for you, for myrtles thrive in seaside locations. They also tolerate alkaline soils and intense heat, and when planted outdoors may make a shrub fifteen feet tall. They do not tolerate cold well, however, which means that through most of the South, *Myrtus communis* must be grown in a pot and moved indoors in wintertime. But such plants make fine specimens for setting out on a terrace or lawn in summertime, and because myrtle tolerates clipping well, potted specimens lend themselves to topiary. In midsummer, too, they bear white flowers that give way to purple-black berries.

Myrtle was a prized plant in ancient Roman gardens, and provided the material for the garlands worn by generals who had won bloodless victories. Later on this shrub featured prominently in Spanish gardens, and by 1562 it had been introduced into England, where it ranked with such highly esteemed imports as lemons and pomegranates.

In classical mythology, the myrtle was the plant of Venus, the goddess of love, who is said to have worn a garland of myrtle when she rose from the sea. Small wonder, then, that the distilled water of myrtle flowers was regarded as a beautifier and aphrodisiac. The berries have been used as an ingredient for sauces to accompany meat. At one time myrtle was a common component of bridal bouquets. The flowers were very popular for cutting in Europe, especially in the 1700s.

Dwarf forms such as 'Microphylla' have smaller leaves and are more compact in form. Various common names include German, Greek, and Roman myrtle. In coastal areas of the south myrtles were sometimes used as a substitute boxwood because they were better adapted to salty and sometimes alkaline conditions. They root readily from semi-hardwood cuttings and have few insect and disease problems.

Langdon Nurseries, Mobile, Alabama, described and offered myrtles in their 1881–82 catalogue:

> *Myrtus communis*, Sweet myrtle, Pretty shrub, very desirable for ornamental hedges. 50 cents. *Myrtus angustifolia*, Narrow leafed, a pretty variety of myrtle with smaller leaves than the above. 50 cents.

Myrtle (*Myrtus communis*) (Atlanta History Center)

Myrtle (*Myrtus communis*)
(Greg Grant)

Myrtus communis compacta
(William C. Welch)

The leaves, which remain purple-tinged all year, may actually intensify in color with the onset of cold weather, turning bright red or purple in winter. This seasonal coloring is most dramatic on plants growing in sunny, exposed areas. Complementing this dormant-season foliar show is the nandinas' colorful fruits. Pea-sized and typically bright red (there is a yellow-berried form), these are borne in bold clusters in the fall, but commonly last all winter, right through to spring. Nandinas are attractive when in bloom, too; plumes of small white flowers open at the stem tips in summertime. Whether in flower or fruit, however, nandinas are hard to miss, for the typical height is four to six feet, with an occasional specimen reaching seven or eight feet.

As their appearance suggests, the nandina is of exotic origin. It is native to China and Japan, but was well established in the American South by 1890. In that year, Peter Henderson wrote in *Henderson's Handbook of Plants* that this was "also a favorite ornamental plant in the Southern States where it is now thoroughly domesticated." In part this popularity may have been due to the ease with which nandinas are propagated. New plants may be started from semi-hardwood cuttings or from seeds, but the method most often practiced by rural homeowners in search of a house-warming present is division. A many-stemmed clump of nandina is dug from the ground with a sharp spade and split into two clumps, each of which, if replanted promptly, provides the start of a new clump.

Because of their vigorous growth,

Fruitlands Nurseries, describes and offers two forms in their 1906–07 catalogue:

> *Myrtus communis*, double, A dwarf evergreen, with small, glossy green leaves. Flowers double, pure white and very fragrant.
> *Myrtus communis*, single, A very desirable evergreen. bright glossy green leaves larger than those of the double myrtle. Flowers single: very fragrant.

—WCW

Nandina domestica
Nandina, Heavenly Bamboo
Family: Berberidaceae (Barberry)
Zones: 6–11

Sometimes when a plant becomes a cliche, there's good reason. Or many reasons, as in the case of nandina.

This is an exotic-looking plant with a down-home toughness. As the common names suggest, nandinas have the look of a bamboo—where they are happy, nandinas form clumps of long, erect, unbranched stems topped with feathery, compound green leaves. And nandinas seem to be happy just about everywhere. They adapt easily to a range of soil types, and shrug off all but the most extreme heat and drought. Nandinas thrive in full sun or partial

shade, and they are troubled by few insects or diseases.

Small wonder that this plant was perhaps the most popular landscape plant in the South during the first half of the twentieth century. In fact, nandinas used to be a common housewarming gift in rural regions—when a couple built a new home, neighbors, friends, or family divided their mature clumps to start a foundation planting that often consisted of little else.

Even if they weren't so tough and adaptable, nandinas would still deserve their popularity, for they provide an unusual amount of garden color, and at a time of year when it is most precious.

Nandina
(*Nandina domestica*)
(Greg Grant)

Nandina berries (*Greg Grant*)

nandinas require periodic pruning, and this can be a puzzling process for the uninitiated. If the gardener follows the common impulse, and uses his or her hedge clippers to shave off the top foot or so of a clump's stems, the result will be a woody, awkward, and generally unattractive plant. A more pleasing, natural look is achieved by removing whole stems: cut out at ground level about one third of each clump's oldest canes each year. New sprouts and plants will soon emerge, to make a denser, more compact plant.

Nandinas make good material for container planting, especially in the dwarf forms that have begun to appear in recent years. These, of course, also lend themselves to planting in smaller gardens. My favorite of the dwarf nandinas is one that I acquired sometime around 1970. The late Mrs. U.B. Evans of Ferriday, Louisiana, a well-known and respected horticulturist, gave me a nice, one-gallon-size plant of *N. domestica* 'Nana Purpurea', a cultivar that was then new to the nursery trade. 'Nana Purpurea' has since proven to be a great popular success, and I certainly treasure my plant. It thrives in a difficult location where it receives little water and much radiated heat. Each winter the foliage turns a magnificent red-purple and the clump has slowly spread to cover an area about two feet in diameter. Yet this plant doesn't exceed a

height of eighteen inches.

Unfortunately, this particular dwarf, 'Nana Purpurea', has proven to be rather finicky about soil type, and requires good drainage. But other dwarf forms, such as 'Harbor Dwarf', appear to adapt well to a broader range of growing conditions. They, however, lack the spectacular fall color of 'Nana Purpurea'. None of the dwarf nandinas, I should add, has ever flowered or set fruit in my garden. Which is why I will continue to grow the larger, heirloom type as well. It offers not only history, but berries. —*WCW*

Narcissus spp.
Daffodils, Narcissus, Jonquils
Family: Amaryllidaceae (Amaryllis)
Zones: 5–11

> But now, regarding the Daffodil from an artistic standpoint rather than as a mathematical problem, or as an achievement, have they not gone far enough with its development? Should not there be a halt called in this race for bigger and better Daffodils? It is essentially a simple and friendly flower, gay, graceful, appealing, and when it is made bold, and huge, and brazen, it has been called out of character, degraded not improved.
> Louise Beebe Wilder, *Adventures with Hardy Bulbs*, 1936

Ethereal, springtime displays of yellow and white narcissus are synonymous with abandoned homesites throughout the South, serving as annual reminders of this flower's popularity and tenacity. Because they are so long-lived, daffodils and jonquils can be an invaluable tool for garden restorers—for enduring patterns of these flowers often provide excellent evidence of garden designs and site orientations that have otherwise vanished.

According to *Hortus Third*, there are some twenty-five to thirty species of *Narcissus*, and most hail from Central Europe and the Mediterranean region.

Because narcissus have been cultivated for a thousand years in this homeland, distinguishing between stands of truly wild, native bulbs and those that were once cultivated but naturalized perhaps centuries ago is a difficult or impossible task.

To confuse the matter still further, gardeners from a very early date were tinkering with every wild narcissus they could get hold of. A number of these early plants often proved to be natural hybrids from the wild. In 1629 John Parkinson described ninety-four distinct kinds of narcissus in his *A Garden of Pleasant Flowers*—and interestingly, his list includes many of the forms commonly found naturalized in the South today. These and many other types of *Narcissus* were introduced into Southern gardens by the earliest settlers. Thomas Jefferson was among the colonial admirers of this flower, bringing what he called simply "Narcissus" into bloom at Shadwell in 1766. Entries from his diary reveals that later he cultivated "daffodils, jonquils, and narcissus" at Monticello.

Narcissus proliferated in America's first gardening books. Bernard M'Mahon's *American Gardener's Calendar* mentioned jonquils, double jonquils, narcissi of sorts, double-narcissus (daffodils), and polyanthus-narcissus in 1806. By 1833, H. Bourne's

Assorted *Narcissus* cultivars in a Louisiana garden. (*William C. Welch*)

Lent lily (*Narcissus pseudonarcissus*) (*Greg Grant*)

Jonquil (*Narcissus jonquilla*) (*Greg Grant*)

Florist's Manual was citing the daffodil, jonquil, poetic or poet's narcissus, primrose daffodil, fragrant narcissus or great jonquil, and polyanthus narcissus.

Although there are many species and cultivars of *Narcissus*, historically the most commonly cultivated ones in the South were *N. pseudonarcissus* and its somewhat grotesque double form, *N. jonquilla*, *N.* x *odorus*, *N. tazetta*, *N.* x *intermedius*, *N.* x *medioluteus*, and double forms of *N.* x *incomparabilis*.

Little *N. pseudonarcissus* is known as the lent lily in Europe, but more frequently as the "early daffodil" here, as it blooms around February. It is the forerunner of today's large flowered daffodils such as 'King Alfred'. It is small, very early blooming, and has typical wide, bluish gray-green foliage. The petals of the early daffodil are pale yellow while its trumpet is golden yellow. It's odd-looking double form—commonly known as *N. telamonius plenus* or 'Van Scion'—is often encountered, although not near as frequently as the species type. Many consider the double form's ragged combinations of yellow and green petals downright homely.

Sweetly scented *N. jonquilla* is the true jonquil, occasionally referred to as the "johnny-quill." The gracious and enduring Cleo Barnwell of Shreveport calls them "sweeties." She's really the sweetie! *N. jonquilla* bears clusters of small, yellow, fragrant flowers held above deep green, rushlike foliage. Jonquils also bloom around February. It naturalizes quite prolifically and even spreads by seed.

N. x *odorus* is a natural hybrid, a cross between *N. pseudonarcissus* and *N. jonquilla*. It is known as the campernelle jonquil and occasionally as the giant or great jonquil. It's probably my favorite of all the narcissus. It is exactly intermediate—in foliage and bloom characteristics—between the two parents, as all good little hybrids should be. It has two to three "giant," fragrant, yellow, jonquil flowers held above foliage which looks like jonquil foliage on steroids. The large rushlike leaves are somewhat concave, and they have inherited a touch of the daffodil's bluish gray tint. It blooms alongside the early daffodils and jonquils. Typical of many first generation hybrids, it is very strong growing and appears to be sterile, setting no seed.

N. tazetta is considered the oldest cultivated narcissus. It was known in ancient Egypt and Greece, and cultivated in Britain before 1597. In 1851, Boston nurseryman Joseph Breck proclaimed this species the most desirable of all the narcissus. Its many forms and offspring, which are officially classed together as tazetta narcissus, are also known as polyanthus narcissus, and are often what gardeners mean when they refer simply to "narcissus."

The often forced paperwhite (*N. tazetta papyraceous*) belongs in this group. Except for a few yellow types like 'Grand Soliel d'Or', tazettas are mostly white with white, cream, or yellow cups. They bear clusters of many small flowers, which are intoxicatingly fragrant. As a matter of fact, my Grandmother Emanis, with her rural East Texas tact, frequently

told me to "get those stinking things out of the house!"

Because they bloom so early in the season, tazettas often suffer from frost damage. Many a bouquet has been picked the day the "norther" blew in. As a rule, the true paperwhites are very, very early blooming (opening at Christmas or New Year's even), bearing pure white, delicate flowers with a scent somewhere between cotton candy and fresh manure. You either love it or run for fresh air. True paperwhite foliage is wide and grayish green. They naturalize most readily along the Gulf Coast where the winters are mild.

Another tazetta frequently found along the Gulf Coast is *N. tazetta orientalis*, the Chinese sacred lily. This plant has very wide, robust foliage and is also very early blooming. There is a double form of it that goes by the name of 'Grand Emperor'. Paperwhites and Chinese sacred lilies are frequently sold for indoor forcing. It appears, however, that most of the bulbs available from commercial sources are infected with virus.

As you move farther in from the coast, you begin encountering later-blooming types of tazetta narcissus. The earliest blooming of these is the delicate but somewhat "rag-tag" *N. tazetta italicus*. It has narrow, twisting petals and small, pale yellow cups. Because it is early-flowering (usually in January), it often blooms above stunted, freeze nipped foliage.

The most often found tazetta narcissus in the South are several hard to distinguish variants each of the later

Campernelle jonquils (*Narcissus* x *odorus*) in a Louisiana garden. (*William C. Welch*)

Campernelle jonquil (*Narcissus* x *odorus*) (*Greg Grant*)

blooming cultivars 'Pearl' and 'Grand Primo'. The "Pearls" seem to be whiter and earlier, while 'Grand Primo' is the latest and initially upon opening has a citron-yellow cup. It appears that 'Grand Primo' was sold and passed around for years under the name of 'Grand Monarque'. Bloom time is February to early March.

N. x *intermedius* is a natural hybrid between *N. jonquilla* and *N. tazetta*. I've never heard this form referred to as anything but jonquils, although the ever-cheerful Celia Jones of Gibsland, Louisiana, says her grandmother called them "Texas star" jonquils.* This is the lowest growing of the commonly found narcissus. As a matter of fact it usually looks like somebody stepped on them.

* Celia and I recently found out that we were related. That explains her cheerfulness and good taste in plants.

The foliage is dark green and flattened, and the clusters of flowers are pale yellow and fragrant. The short-stemmed flowers occur right amongst the foliage. Bulb expert and good friend Scott Ogden of New Braunfels, Texas says they're "homely," but most "normal" people mistake them for regular jonquils. Bloom time is around February, along with its kin.

The late-blooming *N.* x *medioluteus* formerly *N. biflorus* goes by the names of primrose peerless, April beauty, and twin sisters. It is supposedly a natural hybrid between *N. tazetta* and *N. poeticus*. It bears two flowers per stem, and each has white petals and yellow cups. I don't see this one that often but Celia Jones has a great many and Flora Ann Bynum says it's frequently found around North Carolina. My only problem with this particular narcissus is that I'm partial to the early blooming

types. If I stick to them, I can mow the meadow in the spring whenever I get "yard-man" fever, without mowing flowers or maturing foliage.

The double flowering forms of *N.* x *incomparabilis* give us the best names of the group. Cultivars of this hybrid have been cultivated through the years under such names as butter and eggs, eggs and bacon, codlins and cream, milk and honey, orange phoenix, golden phoenix, and primrose phoenix. Some have considered these flowers abominations, while others consider them charming. *Narcissus* x *incomparabilis* is supposedly a hybrid of *N. pseudonarcissus* and *N. poeticus*. It is found quite commonly throughout the South, blooming in February or early March.

Most of the old-fashioned, "early" blooming narcissus are of very easy culture. As a rule, those that bloom in clusters and those with smaller flowers tend to be the best performers in the South. Even these well-adapted types grow and multiply best, however, in situations with at least half to full sun and well-drained, sandy loam soils. Propagation is by division. Although the best time to divide narcissus is after the foliage has died down, I have found that just about anytime works as long as you are dealing with the old-fashioned, tougher types. I do most of my naturalizing in December as the foliage is just emerging and the plants still bloom normally. I have also been known to move plants while in full bloom with minimal consequence.

Narcissus tazetta **'Grand Primo'** (*Greg Grant*)

Oleander (*Nerium oleander* 'Hardy Red') (*Greg Grant*)

Oleander (*Nerium oleander*) (*William C. Welch*)

If I had my way, all the highways of the South would be lined with natural-ized plantings of our historic, easy to grow narcissus. They're much easier than wildflowers, they finish blooming before it's time to mow, they never die, and they get better every year. Even the highway departments couldn't mess this up! There would be no need to wait for seeds to ripen or to have those hideous "no mow" or "wildflower area" signs. Garden clubs, civic groups, students, and the like, could add some each year until the effect was truly arcadian. What a great idea! My Mamma didn't send me to college for nothing.   —GG

Nerium oleander
Oleander, Rose Bay, Rose Laurel
Family: Apocynaceae (Dogbane)
Zones: 8–10

The genial kindness of our climate assimilates the most precious plants of other countries to itself, and exotics like the Camellia, the Oleander, the Gardenia, the Tea Roses, are rapidly becoming indigenous in the milder portion of our State. When these beautiful genera were first introduced among us, they were treated in Carolina and Georgia as they were treated in England and the Northern States, nursed and protected into feebleness and ugliness. By and now the Gardenias and the Tea Roses are as much at home in all lower and middle Georgia as in

any portion of the world, and the Oleander and Camellias are rapidly becoming weeds in the Eastern counties of the State… Rev. Stephen Elliot, Jr., first Episcopal Bishop of Georgia, addressing the Southern Central Agricultural Society, 1851

Maybe oleanders aren't true weeds, but if the Texas Highway Department can grow them, anybody can! No other flowering shrub that I know of can tolerate as much abuse as the oleander and still flourish. I was surprised to find out that in its native Mediterranean habitat, the oleander is a water-loving plant found in wet sites only. I have always thought of it as a drought-tolerant, xeriphitic plant. I guess it's like bald cypress, crinums, and hymenocallis—they'll all grow in standing water or in the middle of a unirrigated parking lot. We (especially Bill!) need more of these "death proof" plants.

I became a fan of oleanders after moving to San Antonio, where they flourish in the heat, drought, and rocky limestone soils. After a recent tour of Galveston, "The Oleander City," with Kewpie Gaido, Elizabeth Head, Sherry Brahm, and Dr. Jerry Parsons, I'm an even bigger fan.

The following information is taken from *Oleanders, Guide to Culture and Selected Varieties on Galveston Island* published by the International Oleander Society in 1991.

"Oleanders grow in the wild in Asia and countries of the Mediterranean area and have been in cultivation since ancient times. Holy forests of oleanders were maintained by the ancient Greeks and altars were decorated with their blossoms to honor the sea-god Nereus and his fifty daughters, the Nereides. Chinese literary men grew them as a hobby. They liked them for their fragrance and recognized them as an emblem of grace and beauty. The oleander was planted in Roman gardens during the time of Cicero, 106–103 B.C. In mural paintings excavated from homes in Pompeii, the oleander was the flower most often pictured in 79 A.D.

"Plants with single odorless pink or white flowers were the only known varieties in Europe until about 1683. At this time, a cultivated plant with a strong, sweet scent was introduced from India. Subsequently a French nursery developed many new cultivars in the late 1800s. Today, oleanders are a favorite for planting in gardens of tropical and subtropical countries.

"The first oleanders came to subtropical Galveston in 1841. Joseph Osterman, a prominent merchant, brought them aboard his sailing ship to his wife and to his sister-in-law, Mrs. Isadore Dyer. Mrs. Dyer found them easy to cultivate and gave them to her friends and neighbors. The familiar double-pink variety that she grew has been named for her. Soon these plants were growing throughout the city.

"As early as 1846, note was taken of

Oleander (*Nerium oleander* 'Mrs. Isadore Dyer') (*Greg Grant*)

the yards in Galveston with oleanders and roses in full bloom and the contribution they made to the beauty of the city. Oleanders flourished in these early days of the city and were able to withstand the subtropical weather, alkaline soil, and the salt spray. Therefore, it was logical for oleanders to be chosen as one of the predominant plants to be used in the replanting of the city following the destruction of the 1900 hurricane and grade raising that covered the existing vegetation with sand. Concerned ladies of the city soon organized the Woman's Health Protective Association (WHPA) with the mission to beautify the island and improve the health conditions of the city. They planted along Broadway, the entrance to the city, and on 25th street, the path to the beach front, and in a few years oleanders made a spectacular display of blooms for citizens and visitors. Although the name of the WHPA was changed to the Woman's Civic League, planting continued for many years up and down city streets, in parks, in yards, around public buildings and schools and soon the whole city became a garden of oleanders. As early as 1908, an editorial in the *Galveston Tribune* observed that the oleander was emblematic of Galveston and that

people came from all over to see them. In 1910, *The Galveston Daily News* also reported that Galveston was known throughout the world as "The Oleander City" and in 1916 an article named it one of the most beautiful cities in the South."

In 1806 Bernard M'Mahon gave instructions for cultivating oleanders in the greenhouse section of his book. Early nursery references to the oleander include Langdon Nurseries 1881–82 catalogue listing of "*Nerium splendens*, the double rose oleander," and "*Nerium alba*, the white oleander." The 1904 catalogue of Alvin Fruit and Nursery (Algoa, Texas) listed "Oleander—One of the South's favorite flowers," while the 1904 Royal Palms Nurseries (Oneco, Florida) catalogue offered "14 sorts of this old favorite," including 'Single Pink', 'Double Pink', 'Lilian Henderson', 'Single Cream', 'M. Leon Brun', and 'Carneum'. In 1906–07, Fruitland Nurseries (Augusta, Georgia) listed in its catalogue 'Carneum', 'Mme. Peyre', 'Savort', and 'Single White'.

Oleanders are very easy to cultivate in all types of soils. They grow and bloom best in areas with full sun. They are easy to propagate from seeds and cuttings, and will even root in water, a trick I learned from the good folks in Galveston. Oleanders make great low-maintenance landscape plants, and the new dwarf, everblooming types are superb when grown as container plants. Grow what you like, but if you can't grow oleanders, wish that you could.   —GG

Opuntia spp.
Prickly Pear, Indian Fig
Family: Cactaceae (Cactus)
Zones: 8–11
Of all the plants they discovered in the New World, the Spanish considered the prickly pear one of the most valuable. This cactus was valued for its fruit, of course, but even more for an insect parasite that infested the plant. Called the cochineal insect, *Coccus cacti* was the source of a rich scarlet dye. This is extracted from

the female insect, which the dye-makers scraped from the plant and dried in ovens.

Franciscan missionaries learned of this process from the Aztecs, and sent specimens of the prickly pear back to Spain as part of the loot seized after Cortez conquest of Mexico. Soon the processed bugs were selling for the equivalent of $2,000 per ton, and the Spanish were establishing prickly pear plantations not only in Mexico but also in New Granada and the Canary Islands. Today, though cochineal is no longer a commercially important crop, the prickly pear still features in the coat of arms of the Mexican Republic.

Modern gardeners are more likely to value the prickly pear for its flowers, which appear from midspring to early summer on the outermost parts of the plant. Vigorously growing plants may continue to bloom over several weeks and are very showy with their bright yellow, orange, or red, tulip-shaped flowers. The fruit that follows the flowers ripens from mid- to late summer and is variable in size and shape, but often does resemble an elongated pear. Its color changes from green to red as it ripens, with a final change to purple announcing maturity. Although often covered with spines, the fruit is edible and considered a delicacy by some.

Prickly pear (*Opuntia* spp.)
(*William C. Welch*)

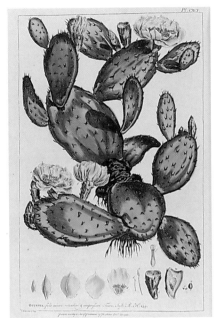

Prickly pear (*Opuntia* spp.) (*Atlanta History Center*)

Prickly pear fruit (*Opuntia* spp.) (*Greg Grant*)

The bold texture of the stems, the attractive flowers and fruit, and its ability to withstand very hot and dry conditions makes prickly pear useful as a landscape plant. Some forms of the plant are more shrublike and may reach ten or twelve feet tall while others are in the two to three feet range. Spiny forms may be useful where vandalism or traffic control are wanted but spineless types are available and much more "user friendly."

More than 250 species of prickly pear have been identified, and this plant ranges naturally from the tropics to the northernmost parts of the continental United States. There are forms of prickly pear native as far north as New England, but the most attractive and useful ones come from Mexico and Texas.

Both the fruit and pads of prickly

pear are often found in the produce sections of Southwestern grocery stores, or in areas with large Latin American populations. The pads (which are actually stems) are eaten as a green vegetable, somewhat like green beans, and various cultivars are considered superior for the quality of pads they produce. The flesh of the fruit is very sweet and may be eaten fresh or preserved.

Propagation is from seed or by cuttings. To root a cutting, cut a whole pad from an existing plant and, setting it in a sunny, relatively dry area, partially cover it with soil. Roots soon sprout from the pad's base, and the plant which grows from it will usually bloom the second year.

Prickly pears flourish in containers since they require little, if any, irrigation and add interesting color and texture to the garden. In ranching areas of the Southwest where prickly pear is plentiful it has sometimes performed a role as cattle feed during times of drought. Flame throwers have been used to burn off the spines and the pads are eagerly consumed by cattle. In addition to their long spines, prickly pear also have numerous small hairlike structures called glochids that are arranged in clusters on the pads. Although not as dangerous as the spines they can be quite irritating. —WCW

Osmanthus fragrans
Sweet Olive, Tea Olive, Fragrant Olive
Family: Oleaceae (Olive)
Zones: 8–11

The flowers of the sweet olive, which are borne in early spring and sometimes fall and winter, are small and a colorless white, but their perfume is powerful, one of the most distinctive of garden fragrances. Originally from China, the sweet olive has been cultivated in temple and home gardens there for so long that its origins are uncertain. Following the usual route west, sweet olives were brought to England in 1771, and from there to America. This plant forms a shrub or small tree, and can reach a height of twelve to fifteen feet in coastal areas of the South, where hard freezes have cut it back. Its foliage is evergreen, and a fairly dense form make this plant valuable as a specimen, hedge, or mass. In areas where winters are too severe to grow them as landscape plants sweet olives are sometimes grown as container specimens.

Propagation is usually by cuttings, although Peter Henderson in his 1890 *Henderson's Handbook of Plants and General Horticulture* suggests that grafting them onto privet is quicker. Sweet olives prefer moist, deep, acid soils but they adapt fairly well to less favorable growing conditions. An orange flowering form, known as

Left: Sweet olive (*Osmanthus fragrans*) (*William C. Welch*)
Below: Sweet olive (*Osmanthus fragrans*) (*William C. Welch*)

aurantiacus, is sometimes found in Southern gardens.

Records from Rosedown Plantation in St. Francisville, Louisiana show that its owners, the Turnbulls, purchased three "Chinese fragrant olives (used to scent their tea)" from the New York nursery William Prince and Son in 1836. Today the scent of huge descendants from those plants permeates the entire garden.

Most of the older catalogues list sweet olive as *Olea fragrans*. Affleck's Central Nurseries, near Brenham, Texas, offered it in the 1860 price list. Fruitlands Nurseries, Augusta, Georgia in their 1906–07 catalogue offers the following: "Olea fragrans (Tea, or Sweet Olive). One of the most desirable flowering shrubs of southern gardens. The white flowers, although small, are produced in clusters and emit the most pleasing fragrance. It is well said that 'each individual bloom has more sweetness than the most fragrant lily.' As a conservatory shrub for northern florists it will be found invaluable and of ready sale. The blooming period begins in the fall and lasts for several months. It is of easy culture and especially desirable as a window plant."

W.A. Yates, in his Brenham, Texas, catalogue of 1906–08 lists the holly leaf tea olive: "Osmanthus (Holly-leaved Tea Olive) A beautiful evergreen shrub with dark green spiny-toothed leaves resembling the holly. Delightfully fragrant flowers produced in the fall in great profusion. These trees attain a height of 25–30 feet, very attractive, Hardy to New York."

—WCW

Paeonia spp.
Peony
Family: Paeoniaceae (Peony)
Zones: 8 and North

One of the best-loved (and most beautiful) of cultivated flowers, peonies have played an important role in American gardens for more than a century. Unfortunately, they are not adapted to the climate of the Deep South. But a number of the older cultivars flourish in the Upper South, and peonies are an important element of historical gardens in that region.

I remember clearly my own intro-

Peony (*Paeonia*) (*William C. Welch*)

duction to peonies, which came when I left my boyhood home in Houston to enroll at Southwestern University in Georgetown, Texas in the fall of 1957. When assigned the task of buying floral decorations for a fraternity function, I went to a German-American lady who operated a small florist and greenhouse business from her home. From her garden she gathered bouquets of double pink blossoms that amazed me with their size and richness; they were peonies, which she was growing in a spot where the plants were protected from the hot, afternoon sun.

Those peonies have remained in my mind as a beautiful memory, but I didn't try to grow this flower myself until recently. In 1991, though, Bertie Ferris of Dallas, knowing of my interest in heirloom plants, graciously offered me roots of peonies that had been in her family's possession for more than seventy-five years. Bertie's gift has been growing in my College Station garden for three years now, but I am still anxiously awaiting the first blooms. I have some hopes of success, since I have seen a few successfull plantings in the Texas Hill Country. Still, the fact is that peonies are generally better adapted to the region north and east of a line drawn from Dallas, Texas to Shreveport, Louisiana and Jackson, Mississippi.

This flower is well rooted in classical mythology, and the name *Paeonia* (the botanical name for the genus) was given to peony by the ancient Greeks because of the plant's supposed connection with a youth named Paeon. He was the pupil of Aesculapius, the first doctor, and Paeon's fame comes from the fact that

he was so rash as to outshine his master. For according to legend, when the god of the underworld, Pluto, was wounded by the hero Hercules, Paeon used a peony root to heal the injured god. This aroused Aesculapius' jealousy, and the healer killed the too-successful pupil. Even the god of the underworld could not restore Paeon to life, but as a gesture of gratitude, he changed him into a flower, the peony.

Actually, there was a certain basis for this story, because peony roots contain an alkaloid with a sedative effect, and an infusion of the seeds acts as an emetic and purgative. Indeed, peonies originally found their way into gardens as a source of medicines rather than as a source of flowers. But by the seventeenth century, John Parkinson was extolling the aesthetic virtues of peonies in his pioneering gardening book, *Paradisi in Sole*. Today, all parts of the peony are considered poisonous to some degree, and the plant is cultivated only for its visual appeal.

The older peonies found in Southern gardens are usually varieties of either *P. officinalis* or *P. lactiflora*. *Paeonia officinalis* in particular is a venerable garden plant. First described around 300 B.C. by the Greek scientist Theophrastus in his *Enquiry into Plants*, *P. officinalis* had traveled as far as England before the beginning of the sixteenth century, when a double-flowered form was cultivated. These flowers were greatly admired because of the luminescent quality of the blossoms. Closer to home, it is known that *P. officinalis rubra* grew in the gardens of Old Salem, North Carolina from the early days of that settlement, where it has been handed down as an heirloom in the Winkler family. White and pink forms are also said to be still growing in many American gardens.

Paeonia lactiflora came into the garden from Siberia near the end of the eighteenth century. It was known earlier as *P. albiflora* and was widely used by peony hybridists of the 1800s who admired this species for the creamy color of its flowers and their outstanding perfume. Probably the most frequently found peony in old Southern gardens is a variety of this species, 'Festiva Maxima', which was introduced by the French grower Miellez in 1851. This cultivar blooms early, producing fragrant, double white flowers that are streaked with crimson at the center.

Paeonia suffruticosa, better known as the tree peony, is not a common Southern heirloom plant, but it has a rich history in the Orient and is highly prized by modern gardeners. Tree peonis were described in Chinese literature over 1,500 years ago, and the first varieties date back at least to the T'ang dynasty in 6,400 A.D. The Japanese created forms with enormous semi-double blooms and thick stems to better hold the weight of the flowers. In 1804 William Kerr successfully sent tree peonies from Canton to England and live plants also arrived in France, where they created a "peonie mania" in 1814. When the Royal Horticultural Society sent Robert Fortune to China in 1843, he found that each district boasted its own varieties, and he succeeded in bringing home some thirty to forty different kinds. These were introduced into the United States about the turn of this century, and the American Peony Society was formed soon afterwards.

Southern nurseries have been offering peonies to their customers from early days. Thomas Affleck's Southern Nurseries of Washington, Mississippi stated in its 1851–1852 catalogue that it had for sale "a few of the finest phloxes, paeonies, amaryllis, hyacinths, etc." Fruitland Nursery, Augusta, Georgia was more specific in its 1906–07 catalogue: "Peonies, Herbaceous—After trying many varieties we have at last succeeded in securing a collection of these beautiful plants which succeed admira-

bly in this section. We offer 12 best sorts."

The cultivation of peonies in the South was specifically addressed by Mrs. K.M. Colby, of Monroe, Louisiana, in an October 1966 article in the *Peony Quarterly*. There, Mrs. Colby stated that there is no magic to growing peonies in the South, but the culture is different from that in colder climates. She noted that at one time she had been growing over a hundred different peonies, and she had found that the early and mid-season blooming varieties were best in the South since they flower before our weather becomes too hot. The peak flower season in her garden in Monroe ran from April 15 through mid-May. In her article Mrs. Colby also mentioned having found thirty-year-old plants of 'Festive Maxima' in a nearby garden.

Her recommendations for peony cultivation called for planting in a site away from competing roots of heavily feeding trees, shrubs, and hedges, where the peonies would receive a half to a full day's sun. According to Mrs. Colby, it is important to purchase good quality plants and to plant them in the fall. The plants should be spaced about two feet apart in very well-prepared holes—as she noted, it is the digging process that separates the coffee drinkers from the serious gardeners! She called for holes about three feet in diameter and two feet deep. Any good topsoil excavated from the hole should be saved, but any hardpan or subsoil should be replaced with good, loamy soil. Before replacing soil in the hole, it should be mixed with about a pound of bone meal. Then the

hole should be refilled to within eight inches of its top, and the soil fill tamped down thoroughly—if necessary, more soil should be added and packed in sufficiently so that you are satisfied winter rains will not cause settling.

The next step is to mound soil in the center of the hole so that when the dormant peony is set on the mound's top, the peony's "eyes"—its crown—rests an inch or two above ground level. Fill the remainder of the planting hole, gently shaking the peony from time to time to make sure that the soil settles in around the roots and fills any air pockets. When the planting is completed, the peony's eyes should be covered with about three-fourths inch of soil. Water well, and after the water has drained away, add soil if necessary to recover the peony's eyes.

Do not mulch at this time, since in the South peonies relish exposure to winter cold. In summertime, however, a mulch of pine straw or bark helps to conserve moisture and prevent weeds. Remove the mulch in the fall and the dead stalks to the ground when the plant goes dormant. Otherwise, the only care necessary is to water occasionally during dry spells and to administer an annual feeding of one cup of bone meal per plant.*
—WCW

* Special thanks to Greta Kessenich, Secretary of the American Peony Society, for providing information for this profile. The Society was formed in 1904 and is active in collecting and distributing educational information about peonies to the membership.

Paeonia 'Festiva Maxima' (*William C. Welch*)

Far left: *Petunia violacea* (Greg Grant)

Left: *Petunia axillaris* (Greg Grant)

Petunia x *hybrida*
Old–fashioned Petunia
Family: Solanaceae (Nightshade)
Zones: 7–11 as an annual or short–lived perennial

If you travel around any rural area of the South you are sure to see bouquets of small-flowered petunias poking out of everything from old dishpans to crown tire planters. They're everywhere—they even naturalize in the grass—and nobody pays them any mind. Called a "hybrid swarm" by the botanists, this unruly crew with its pastel shades of purple, pink, and white represents the parents of our large-flowered, brightly colored modern petunias. Although the old fashioned petunias are rarely sold in the nursery trade they are still very common in gardens. Partially because they're pretty and fragrant, and partially because they keep coming back whether you want them to or not.

The two parents of these old-fashioned petunias are the white-flowered and night-fragrant *Petunia axillaris* (formerly *P. nyctaginiflora* and *Nicotiana axillaris*) and the purple-flowered *P. violacea* (formerly *Salpiglossis integrifolia*), both perennials from southern South America. The large white petunia was introduced from Brazil in 1823 while the violet petunia was introduced in 1831 from Argentina.

I noticed last year that the Atlanta Botanic Garden was growing a cute little small-flowered petunia labeled *P. integrifolia*. I had never heard of this species, and Bill was later able to obtain a plant for us to observe and propagate from. Later in the season I made a trip to Germany and saw a large bed of *P. violacea* growing beneath a wisteria at the horticulture exposition in Stuttgart. I brought back seeds, and, after growing the German petunia beside the Georgian one, I realized that the two were the same species. The German clone, however, has darker, slightly larger flowers and is more floriferous. I think this species' refined nature and pretty little purple flowers are going to make it very popular in our gardens again.

Once breeders get started on "improving" a plant, they often go too far, and that's just what they have done, in my opinion, with the petunia. Despite all the hoopla we hear each spring about new and vigorous, heat-tolerant "miracle petunias," "perennial petunias," and "super petunias," it's time that people realize we already have such flowers—and we've had them for a long time.
—GG

Philadelphus spp.
Mock Orange
Family: Saxifragaceae (Saxifrage)
Zones: 7–9

Mock orange is found in many Southern gardens but its use there is primarily a twentieth-century phenomena. These multistemmed shrubs bear bright white, single or double, dogwoodlike blossoms in April and May, after the foliage emerges from the bare stems. At maturity, the height of mock oranges can be eight to ten feet, and some bear

Right: Mock orange (*Philadelphus* spp.) (William C. Welch)

Far right: Mock orange (*Philadelphus* spp.) (Barry Fugatt)

flowers that are extremely fragrant, while others bear blossoms with no scent at all.

Philadelphus coronarius appears to have been the most important species in the South. This species came to Europe from Turkey in 1562, when Ogier Ghiselin de Busbecq, ambassador from Emperor Ferdinand to Soleiman the Magnificent, brought it back to Vienna. Another Middle Eastern flowering shrub that was introduced into the West around the same time was the lilac, and though this belongs to an entirely different genus than the mock orange, the two plants were lumped together under the name of *syringa*. This mislabelling seems to have originated not in the shrubs' appearances (the flowers and foliages are quite different) but in a practical application; both mock oranges and lilacs produce hollow stems, which were used by the Turks to make pipes.

The genus *Philadelphus* includes many species, and the different species hybridize easily, which makes the plant breeder's work easier, but the mock oranges' promiscuity makes the identification and maintenance of distinct cultivars difficult. Complicating the task of distinguishing the different mock oranges is their sheer numbers, for the Lemoine Nursery of Nice, France crossed *P. coronarius* with *P. micropohyllus* and *P. coulteri*, and introduced a host of hybrids and named selections in the years from 1894 to 1927. There is also one native American species in cultivation: *P. inodorus*, whose name reflects the flowers' lack of scent. This species was discovered and described by Mark Catesby in South Carolina in 1726.

In addition to the cascades of white flowers they produce, a major reason for the mock oranges' popularity is their ease of culture. Though they prefer slightly acid soils, they thrive in a wide variety of soils both moist and dry, and in sun or partial shade. Pruning should be done after spring bloom and new plants may be started from cuttings, division of mature plants, or seedlings that often sprout in the garden. They are sometimes known as "English Dogwood," and although they are quite different from the flowering dogwood,

Arborvitae (*Platycladus orientalis*) (*Greg Grant*)

the mock oranges are valuable for their comparatively easy culture, for their tolerance to cold, heat and drought, for their late spring flowering, and for the powerful scent of some cultivars.

—*WCW*

Platycladus orientalis
Oriental Arborvitae, Chinese Arborvitae, Arbor Vitae
Family: Cupressaceae (Cypress)
Zones: 6–9

I know everybody is conditioned to hate arborvitae these days, but we can't hide from its historical use in Southern gardens. And of course there's hardly a cemetery in the South that doesn't have this common evergreen in it. According to my Grandmother Ruth and Great Aunt Ruby Dee, arborvitaes lined the "walk" up to my great grandmother's house. "Big-Momma," as we all called her, had a number of pretty things in the yard.

I recently polled my collection of old Southern nursery catalogues to see what plants were the most popular. In a stack of nineteen catalogues from 1851–1906, arborvitae was offered by fifteen of them! Still don't like it do you?

Platycladus orientalis was formerly known as *Thuja orientalis* and *Biota orientalis*. According to *The Hillier Manual of Trees and Shrubs*, this China native was introduced into Europe around 1690. In America, John Bartram and Sons' Nursery carried it in 1792. By 1854 it was standard feature of Southern gardens: in the letter he wrote to the *Natchez Daily Courier* on October 28 of that year, nurseryman Thomas Affleck said: "The Arbor Vitae is well known—

that is, the Chinese, (orientalis), the sort common here. And to form a pretty screen hedge, I know of nothing more beautiful."

The Chinese arborvitae was listed in Affleck's 1851–52 Southern Nurseries catalogue as *Thuja orientalis*. Langdon Nurseries of Alabama listed this shrub as *Biota orientalis* in its 1881–1882 catalogue, and included the related species *B. aurera*, *B. hybrida*, *B. meldensis*, and *B. Filiformis Pendula*. The Mission Valley (Texas) catalogue of 1898–99 offered *B. Aurea*, *B. Aurea Nana*, *B. Orientalis*, *B. Pyramidalis*, Arbor Vitae Compacta, and the Rosedale Arbor Vitae. This last is a dwarf juvenile-foliaged type that was

Arborvitae (*Platycladus orientalis*) (*William C. Welch*)

Dwarf golden arborvitae
(*Platycladus orientalis* 'Aureus
Nanus') (*Greg Grant*)

introduced by Rosedale Nursery of
Brenham, Texas and afterwards carried
by many early nurseries across the
South.

The 1906–07 Fruitlands Nurseries
(Georgia) catalogue listed three
introductions of their own—*Biota
orientalis Aurea conspicua, Aurea nana*
(Berkman's Golden Arborvitae), and
Aurea pyramidalis—together with the
varieties *Japonica filiformis*, Intermedia
Green, and the Rosedale arborvitae.

Though these shrubs have moved in
and out of fashion, their toughness has
ensured that many old established
plantings have survived in Southern
gardens, even if often in an overgrown
and neglected condition. According to
Bill, an effective way of utilizing such
survivors is to limb them up into
attractive multi-trunked small trees. I've
had others tell me they make good
kindling!

In honor of the arborvitae's
popularity in early Southern nurseries, I
have planted three dwarf golden ones in
the yellow section of my rainbow border,
next to the also maligned variegated
Arundo donax. Some plants don't
deserve all the grief we give them. Like I
tell my mamma about our "occasional"

undesirable relatives and ancestors; you
can't hide from your true heritage. And
if you didn't know who they were, you
might even like them. She doesn't buy
that, though.   —GG

Polianthes tuberosa
Mexican Tuberose
Family: Agavaceae (Agave)
Zones: 8–9 (Late Summer)
Spanish invaders found tuberoses
growing in Aztec gardens; presumably
the plant is a Central American native,
but no botanist has ever found tuberoses
growing wild and this flower's origin
remains a mystery. But if the origin of
the tuberose is obscure, its appeal as a
garden flower is obvious. The foliage is
long, slender, and grasslike, with little
landscape value, but the flowers, which
appear in three- to four-foot tall spikes
in late summer through early fall, are
spectacular. Tubular and white, the
blossoms breathe a sweet and powerful
perfume—indeed, tuberoses are among
the most fragrant of all garden flowers.

Tuberoses were among the first
plants taken back to the Old World, and
Spanish gardeners adopted them eagerly,
making them a common feature of their
landscapes. They are known to have
perfumed the garden of the sixteenth-
century Sevillian physician, Simon
Tovar. Tuberoses also proved well
adapted to the Spanish colonies along
the Gulf Coast of Morth America, and
they were mentioned in an early

Tuberose (*Polianthes tuberosa*)
(*William C. Welch*)

account of horticulture in the Gulf
states written by William Bartram. He
noted them as being among the many
useful and interesting exotics growing
on a plantation along the Mississippi
near Baton Rouge in 1777. There,
according to Bartram, tuberoses "grew
from five to seven feet high in the open
ground, the flowers being very large and
abundant."

Tuberoses are as easily cultivated in
the South now as then. Midspring is the
best time to set out new tubers. Tuberoses prefer a sunny location with well-
drained soil. For mass effect in the
border, space the tubers four to six
inches apart and two inches deep.

In the fall, the elongated tubers are
best dug and stored like gladiolus in all
zones except 9 and 10, where they may
be left in the ground year round. Of the
varieties commonly available, 'Mexican
Single' performs better in the garden
than does the double-flowering 'Pearl'.

One interesting footnote to the
history of the tuberose is that this flower
is still popular among Mexican gardeners, who call it "Nardo" or "Azucena."
Cultivated worldwide as a source of cut
flowers and perfumes, tuberoses have
been a commercial crop for many years
in the San Antonio area, where the
tubers are propagated to supply the
needs of florists and bulb distributors.
                    —WCW

Prunus caroliniana
**Carolina Cherry Laurel, Wild Peach,
Mock Orange**
Family: Rosaceae (Rose)
Zones: 7–11
I'm willing to bet that most people don't
realize what an important role our
native cherry laurel has played in our
Southern gardening history. Found wild
from Texas to North Carolina, this
shrub was traditionally used as an
evergreen hedging material in the
gardens of the early South. But it often
played a more important role, helping
farmers and planters choose the site for
their operations. For the old description
of first-class arable land in the old South
was that a tract was "peach and cane."
"Peach" referred to the cherry laurel or
"wild peach" while cane referred to our
native bamboo or "switch cane"; the
presence of these two plants on a virgin

Cherry laurel (*Prunus caroliana*) hedge in Ryan Gainey's garden, Atlanta, Georgia. (*Greg Grant*)

site indicated excellent soil.

(Of course, I always thought those old timers were saying "peachy-keen," whatever that is! Another interesting bit-o-trivia is that when crushed, the new growth of the cherry laurel smells like maraschino cherries. Some say almonds, but I don't. Pay attention, you may need to know this for a surprise appearance on "Jeopardy" one day.)

At one time cherry laurel was such a standard part of Southern horticulture that its presence on a site today as a naturalized tree—it will form a small to medium-sized tree with time—is a good indication that the land was once developed as a garden. We find evidence of this popularity in the incredible garden diary of Martha Turnbull. The mistress of Rosedown Plantation in St. Francisville, Louisiana, she made numerous references to her cherry laurel hedges. In her entry for June 14, 1837, for example, she noted that she had that day "trimmed wild peach and rose hedge"; on January 22, 1849 she "trimmed down the wild peach hedge to 14 inches." Sounds like she needed the compact selection available today.

To sidetrack for a moment, I'd like put in a word here for Martha's Turnbull's diary, which is preserved in the special collection of the Hill Memorial Library at Louisiana State University. It is a fabulous source of information, as well as a heart-touching story. It tells a fascinating tale of a woman going from a position of wealth to that of a pauper, while never losing her overwhelming and undying love of gardening. Unfortunately, it hasn't been used—as it could be—to accurately restore the grounds of Martha's former home or toward furthering the cause of historic garden preservation in the South. As far as I'm concerned, this diary is the most important and complete source of historic garden documentation in the South. Martha was an incredible gardener and plant lover. I wish she was alive today. I'd have an affair!

But to return to cherry laurel. Martha Turnbull wasn't this plant's only admirer. In his letter to the *Natchez Daily Courier*, Mississippi nurseryman Thomas Affleck wrote, "Nothing can be more beautiful than the Laurier Amandier, (Cerasus Caroliniensis), Cape Jessamine, Arbor Vitae, some of the Viburnums, Pittosporums, Euonymus, and Myrtles; yet, there is a sameness in our lawns and dooryards, from the general and almost exclusive use of these."

Langdon Nurseries near Mobile, Alabama, listed *Cerasus caroliniensis* in the 1881–82 catalogue and called it mock orange, carolina cherry, and lauramundi. The description noted that it was "beautiful for hedges, screens, or single specimens."

Fruitlands Nurseries listed it among their ornamental hedge plants in a 1906–07 catalogue. They called it "wild orange" and "mock orange of the South." And in a 1901 catalogue from Rosedale Nurseries in Brenham, Texas it is listed as *Cerasus caroliniana* or "wild peach."

Today the cherry laurel is underused in Southern gardens, particularly as a hedge—an indication of what it can do in that line may be found in the Georgia garden of the talented Ryan Gainey. The compact selection on the market today is particularly suited for this purpose. The old-fashioned, wild-type cherry laurel will make an excellent small evergreen tree as well.

This plant is very easy to grow, particularly in acid, well-drained soils. Propagation is by seed or rather difficult to root cuttings under high humidity. The compact variety is available from many nurseries and garden centers, while the standard type is a frequent volunteer in many Southern gardens.

—GG

Compact cherry laurel (*Prunus caroliana* 'Compacta'), Texas A&M University, College Station, Texas. (*Greg Grant*)

Prunus glandulosa
Flowering Almond
Family: Rosaceae (Rose)
Zones: 4–9

Flowering almond is a welcome ornament in early spring, when the bare branches burst into bloom even before the leaves open. The plant's form is that of a multistemmed, deciduous shrub which reaches a height of four feet, spreading to a width of about three feet. Single-flowered forms exist and may produce ½-inch dark pink-red fruit, but double-flowered strains are most commonly found in Southern gardens.

Flowering almond (*Prunus glandulosa*)
(**William C. Welch**)

Flowering almond (*Prunus glandulosa*) (**Greg Grant**)

The cultivar 'Sinensis' has ¼ -inch blossoms that are bright pink, very double, and tightly spaced in the stems. 'Alboplena' bears double flowers of the purest white. S. Millar Gault in his *The Dictionary of Shrubs in Colour* lists 1774 as the date of introduction for 'Sinensis' and 1852 for 'Alboplena'. Native to China and North China, flowering almonds have long been cultivated in Japan.

Its early-flowering habit also makes this shrub a valuable source of cut flowers, for its branches can fill a vase most gracefully at a time of year when

White flowering almond (*Prunus glandulosa* 'Alboplena')
(**William C. Welch**)

little else is in bloom. Indeed, in Europe flowering almond is commonly grown and forced for the floral trade.

For healthy, compact growth and the heaviest crop of flowers, prune the plants back severely during or just after bloom. Landscape uses range from single planting as specimens, or in groups as masses, or even in hedges. New plants are started from cuttings or from the suckers that spring up around the mature plants.

Flowering almond was popular in Edwardian and Victorian gardens, and is easily grown and long-lived. A characteristic which makes it especially valuable for Southern gardeners is that this shrub requires only a very short period of chilling to induce flowering. I grew up admiring flowering almond in a neighbor's garden in Houston and have enjoyed growing both the white and pink forms at our home in Washington County, Texas. My plant of 'Alboplena' came from the Childress garden in Mangham, Louisiana, and has grown and bloomed beautifully for the past three years.

A century ago, many nurseries listed flowering almonds in their catalogues. For example, Langdon Nurseries of Mobile, Alabama, listed both the double white and pink forms in their 1881–82 catalogue; Rosedale Nurseries of Brenham, Texas advertised both forms in 1901, as did Fruitlands Nurseries of Augusta, Georgia in 1906–07.

This plant is less generally available today. You may wish to check the

bargain counter of packaged deciduous shrubs at local discount stores, since the flowering almond often finds itself there. The white form is more difficult to locate than the pink.   —WCW

Punica granatum
Pomegranate
Family: Punicaceae (Pomegranate)
Zones: 8–11
Native to Arabia, Persia, Bengal, China, and Japan, pomegranates may prove hardy in favored spots as far north as Washington, D.C., but are best adapted to the Deep South. They have a long history there, for the plant was introduced into North America by Jesuit missionaries following in the footsteps of Cortez. From Mexico, pomegranates were carried northward to missions in California and possibly east to Texas. They were also thought to have been planted by Spanish settlers in St. Augustine, Florida. At any event, they thrive along the Gulf Coast, and long ago escaped from gardens there to establish themselves in the wild. The plant form is that of a small deciduous tree or large shrub to twenty-five feet tall, and pomegranates typically are multistemmed unless pruned to a single trunk. This makes them good material for hedges—the foliage is dark green and the stems are somewhat thorny. Though most commonly grown for their fruit, pomegranates are also remarkable for the beauty of their flowers, which are borne over a period of several months in spring and early

Pomegranate (*Punica granatum*)
(*Atlanta History Center*)

summer. Most commonly these blossoms are red-orange, but white, pink and variegated flowers may also be found.

Pomegranates appear very early on in the history of western gardens. The ancient Roman encyclopaedist Pliny considered pomegranates to be among the most valuable of ornamental and medicinal plants. Theophrastus provided an early description about 300 years before the Christian era. Many legends concerning the pomegranate have been handed down by Asian people. The many seeds are supposed to be a symbol of fertility and in Turkey there is a custom that a bride throw a ripe pomegranate to the ground. Then

by counting the number of seeds that fall out of the fruit, she can divine the number of children she will bear. Legend also says that the pomegranate was the "tree of life" in the Garden of Eden, and from this belief it became the symbol of hope and eternal life in early Christian art. The erect calyx-lobes of the fruit were the inspiration for Solomon's crown, and so for all subsequent crowns.

In Peter Henderson's *Handbook of Plants and General Horticulture*, published in 1890, the dwarf form is recommended. Henderson says that this plant, *P. nana*, although naturalized in the southern United States is native to the East Indies and was introduced into England in 1723. I recall seeing beautiful three- to five-foot specimens of *P. nana* in flower and fruit in August as a part of the foundation planting near the main house at Filoli Gardens near San Francisco.

In a monograph titled "The Pomegranate: A Southern Tradition," Jack E. Rice of Laurinburg, North Carolina states: "The pomegranate (*Punica granatum*) was once a proud tradition in the South and graced many gardens with their beautiful flowers and fruit. I fondly remember the fall ripening fruit as a young boy [in the 40s] and the wide variety of sizes, colors, and tastes. Most of these have vanished along with the traditional farming communities. I have never lost my taste or affection for the pomegranate and it remains one of my favorite fruits.

For a period in the early 1900s pomegranates were grown in commer-

cial quantities in California, Arizona, Georgia, Alabama, Nevada, and even Utah. American consumers have, however, really never developed much appreciation for the pomegranate fruit, though in Mexico they are very popular.

Jack Rice blames the lack of popularity of the pomegranate fruit in this country on the prevalence of one cultivar, 'Wonderful'. This is an old clone, which was discovered by a Mr. Bears of Porterville, California in 1896 as one of a group of cuttings he received from Florida. Jack Rice insists that despite the name, 'Wonderful' bears poor-quality fruit, though if aged at room temperature for a month or two after picking the 'Wonderful' pomegranates do develop the rich, sweet taste characteristic of better-quality cultivars.

Although of very easy culture, pomegranates prefer a sunny location and deep soil. They thrive in acid or alkaline soils and tolerate heavy clay as long as there is sufficient drainage. Many forms exist and not all fruit well. Generally, double-flowering types provide little, if any, fruit. Mature specimens withstand drought well, but fruit often splits after rainy spells following extended dryness. Plants are often long-lived with some trees in France recorded as having fruited for over two hundred years.

Double-flowering types have flowers that are carnation-like. Propagation is by seed or cuttings, with cuttings being necessary to perpetuate specific cultivars. Dormant hardwood cuttings root well, as do softwood cuttings kept under mist in the summer.

Pomegranate (*Punica granatum*) (*Greg Grant*)

Pomegranate (*Punica granatum*) (*William C. Welch*)

Pomegranate (*Punica granatum*) (*Greg Grant*)

Though most commonly eaten fresh, pomegranate fruits may also be processed into syrups, such as grenadine, fermented into alcoholic beverages, or cooked into jellies. Plants of the dwarf and large growing forms are sometimes available in the southern half of Texas. In all but the warmest zones, plants may freeze back to the ground. Interesting trials with pomegranates from Iran and Russia are being conducted in the Houston area by fruit specialists who believe that some of these plants may have superior fruiting, growth, and hardiness characteristics.

Pomegranates were often found in nineteenth-century Southern gardens and nurseries. In his *Southern Rural Almanac, and Plantation and Garden Calendar* for 1860, Thomas Affleck listed them as grown in his Washington County, Texas nursery and said, "The pomegranate grows, thrives and bears most admirably."

By the late 1800s pomegranates were available from a number of Southern nurseries, as is illustrated in these catalogue quotes: Langdon Nurseries (Mobile, Alabama, 1881–82): "Pomegranate—Dwarf/ Pomegranate—Alba flore plena—Double White/ Pomegranate—variegata—Variegated double." Mission Valley Nursery (Victoria County, Texas, 1898–99): "Fruiting Pomegranates…Spanish Ruby—Sweet/ Sour—for making beverages/ also double flowering."

—WCW

Quercus virginiana
Southern Live Oak
Family: Fagaceae (Beech)
Zones: 8–11

As a shade and ornamental tree, there is none will compare with our magnificent Water oak, and Live oak. The latter is more beautiful and permanent… Suppose that, instead of the China tree, your streets and pleasant Bluff promenade, had been lined and shaded with these oaks! By this time, you would have had ornamental trees such as few cities can boast of. The Mobilians were alive to the beauty of the Live Oak as a shade tree for their streets and squares, and see the results now! Thomas Affleck, Mississippi nurseryman, in a letter to the editor of the *Natchez Daily Courier*, October 28, 1854.

It's impossible to discuss the gardens of the Deep South and ignore the "evergreen" live oak. Almost every early visitor to the Gulf Coast sent home a marvelling description of the great, spreading live oaks with their Spanish moss-bedecked limbs.

This tree, *Quercus virginiana*, is widely adapted to Southern conditions, for it is native from Texas all the way to the Carolinas. Throughout this region, the live oak's broad-reaching form and dense, persisting foliage made it the shade tree of choice, the premier material for lining the streets and *allees* of early Southern towns and gardens. It's not hard to understand the appeal—all it takes is one visit to an old plantation home with an *allée* of live oaks to be smitten. Two of my favorite examples are Oak Alley and Rosedown Plantations in South Louisiana. In that state there is actually a live oak society, which has named and recorded the most cherished specimens.

Live oaks are easy to grow in most types of soil. They are, however, prone to ice and freeze damage in the upper South. Nor does *Q. virginiana* thrive in the drier, alkaline soils of the Texas Hill Country—but there you can substitute

Live oak (*Quercus virginiana*) *allée*, Rosedown Plantation, St. Francisville, Louisiana. (*Greg Grant*)

Live oak (*Quercus virginiana*) in Independence, Texas. (*Greg Grant*)

"Wild honeysuckle" (*Rhododendron canescens*)
(*Greg Grant*)

'Fisher Pink' azaleas (*Rhododendron indicum*)
(*Tom Pope*)

the smaller live oak species native to that region, *Quercus fusiformis*. Unfortunately, the live oaks there are battling a crippling vascular disease known as oak wilt. Let's hope that oak wilt never gets to the Deep South. It'll make chestnut blight and Dutch elm disease seem like a mild case of aphids.   —GG

Rhododendron spp.
Azalea, Wild Honeysuckle
Family: Ericaceae (Heath)
Zones: 6–9

Whereas the magnolia blossom once served as the floral symbol of the South, today that honor most likely belongs to the evergreen azaleas. Historically, though, it was the members of the other major group of azaleas, the deciduous azaleas, that were important in the early gardens of the South.

That was because the first azaleas to be cultivated in America were our own native species, and these are deciduous. In early days, the selection of azaleas available to American gardeners was slim. In a letter to James Madison in 1791, Thomas Jefferson noted that "I find but two kinds, the *nudiflora* and *viscosa* acknowledged to grow with us." This situation had changed dramatically, however by the middle of the nineteenth century, as exotic species were crossed with the American species to create a host of hybrids suited to Southern conditions. The 1851–52 catalogue of Thomas Affleck's Mississippi nursery, for instance, offered "fifty named varieties of the new Ghent

Azaleas, hardy hybrids, between *Rhododendron Ponticum* and *Azalea Nitida*, the latter the beautiful, fragrant Wood Honeysuckle of the South." Affleck was also offering at this time "*Azalea Ponticum*, very much like the Wood Honeysuckle, but with larger corymbs of bright yellow, highly fragrant blossoms."

Although their parentage was half American, the Ghent hybrids originated with the nurserymen of the Belgian city of Ghent. This was a substantial contribution that these growers made to Southern gardening, for as Alice Coates noted in her book, *Garden Shrubs and their Histories* (1964), there were by 1850 were some five hundred types of these deciduous "Ghent Azaleas" in commerce. Later, these same growers were to present the South with another gift, when they developed the evergreen "Belgian Indicas."

However, the real story of the evergreen azaleas belongs to the orient, mainly China and Japan. In Japan especially the cultivation and breeding of evergreen types had been a fashionable hobby for hundreds of years. Evidence of the azaleas' popularity can be found in the fact that as early as 1692, a Japanese expert named Ito Ihei had published a monograph on these plants, discussing in it every major azalea species of Japan, plus those introduced from China and Korea.

The appearance of evergreen azaleas in Southern gardens, by contrast, is a relatively modern occurrence. George

Stritikus, Extension Horticulturist for the Alabama Extension Service and the Birmingham Botanical Gardens, came across an article in the May 1859 issue of *American Cotton Planter and Soil* (published in Montgomery), which points this out. Written by Robert Nelson, a horticultural editor and nurseryman from Columbus, Georgia, "Chinese Honeysuckle, (Azalea indica)" begins by remarking, "It is surprising, indeed, that this magnificent shrub— the beauty and glory of the Northern greenhouses in the early spring—is hardly ever to be met with in the South. True, a few specimens in pots may now and then (though seldom) be seen, in a very poor condition. But why keep them in pots? Turn them out of doors, into the open ground; give them but one-tenth of the attention which you bestow on the plant, while in a pot, and you will have the most beautiful blooming shrub in your garden, during March and April, that your eyes ever beheld."

Nelson ended his article with an exhortation: "Two of the most brilliant varieties, I ever had were the two old, well known kinds, *A. phoenicea* and *A. Hibbertia purpurea*; but in fact all the *Azalea indica* will thrive well in this latitude."

Actually, a few perceptive Southerners were already experimenting with the evergreen Asian species. Martha Turnbull of Rosedown Plantation in St. Francisville, Louisiana had been investing in Chinese azaleas for more than twenty years when Nelson's article

'Pride of Mobile' azalea (*Rhododendron indicum*) (Tom Pope)

hit the press. In the Hill Memorial Library of Louisiana State University there is an invoice dated February 8, 1836 from the New York nursery firm William Prince and Son, billing Turnbull for four "Chinese scarlet flowering azaleas," four "Chinese white flowering azaleas," four "Chinese superb cerulean azaleas," one "Chinese blue flowering azalea," and one "Chinese Young's splendid new flowering azalea." Another bill dated February 27, 1837 records Turnbull's purchase of one "blue or cerulea azalea," one "splendid hybrid or cerulean azalea," and one "scarlet or Indica azalea."

Martha Turnbull's garden diary tells another part of the story: on February 15, 1847, she noted, "Azaleas put in ground." There's no mention of the variety she was planting, however. And whatever she may have used to enrich the Turnbull plantation, Southern gardeners as a whole didn't follow suit until this century.

The tender "Indian azaleas" (a group which includes the Belgian Indicas) were the first evergreen azaleas to gain wide acceptance in the South. These large-flowered beauties are hybrids derived from *R. indicum*, *R. simsii*, and others. They were developed in Europe, primarily Belgium, Holland, Germany, and England, and were grown there in greenhouses. When the indicas reached the mild climate of the Southern United States, though, they proved well suited to cultivation outdoors.

Subsequently, a race of southern indica hybrids sprang up in the Carolinas in the latter half of the nineteenth century. According to Harold Hume

(*Azaleas and Camellias*, 1936), "[H]ad it not been that many found a place in the gardens of the Lower South and that the old nursery firm of P.J. Berckmans Co. [Fruitland Nurseries, Augusta, Georgia] became interested in them as garden plants, they would have made little impression on the gardens of America." The Southern indicas remained the only evergreen azaleas grown outdoors in the United States until the importation of the Kurumes direct from Japan to California in 1915.

This event occurred when Japanese nurseryman Kojiro Akoshi entered twelve plants in the Panama Pacific Exposition of 1915, held in California, according to Christopher Fairweather in *Azaleas* (1988). A more significant introduction was brought about by Ernest "Chinese" Wilson of the Arnold Arboretum, who had seen some small plants of these azaleas in bloom in Japan in 1914, returned in 1918 to select fifty cultivars for importation to the United States. The "Wilson fifty" reached the Arnold Arboretum April 24, 1919, in time to cause a considerable sensation at the Massachusetts Horticultural Society's annual flower show in the spring of 1920 (Hume, *Azaleas and Camellias*).

From there the evergreen azaleas moved south, inspiring famous displays at Magnolia Gardens, Middleton Place, and The Oaks, near Charleston, South Carolina; Pinehurst at Summerville, South Carolina; Belle Isle at Georgetown, South Carolina; Wormsloe Plantation near Savannah, Georgia; the Whitney Estate at Thomasville, Georgia; the Brewer Garden, Winter

Park Florida; Airlie at Wilmington, North Carolina; and Rosedown Plantation at St. Francisville, Louisiana.

The evergreen azalea craze spread eventually to Houston, at the western edge of azalea country. According to information from Sadie Gwin Blackburn and her garden club's archives, the River Oaks Garden Club in Houston held their first Azalea Trail in 1936 with an attendance of over 3,000. A 1937 *Houston Chronicle* editorial explains the evolution of this event:

> In the past several years thousands of Houstonians have made pilgrimages to Southern Louisiana and Mississippi, and some gone farther eastward in the South, following the Azalea Trail. Only in the past few years have any great number of these plants been set out here, but already it has become evident there is no need of leaving Houston to enjoy the sight of these exquisite blossoms. Doubtless the day will come when people from all over the country will come to Houston to see the azaleas and camellias, just as they now go to Natchez and Charleston.

Great numbers indeed. A March 1937 article in the *Houston Chronicle* mentioned "the marvelous garden of Mrs. H.R. Cullen, which has over eight thousand Camellias and Azaleas—the largest known planting outside the famous Bellingrath Gardens of Mobile, Alabama."

Although the azalea did not reach commonplace status in the South until the era of the Azalea Trail, one couple had obviously started planting much earlier. A 1937 *Houston Press* article, headlined "Hanszen Garden Has Four Acres: 2000 Tulips: Rare Azaleas," states: "Mr. Hanszen has collected some of the finest azaleas to be found in Louisiana. Among these, his Rosedown Orchid, over 60 years old, and the Salmon Pink, over 40 years of age, dominate the planting."

Azaleas require acidic, well-drained, organic soils for successful cultivation. They generally need at least some shade to protect them from burning in summertime. Most gardeners prefer to grow them directly under trees, although this may increase the need for watering, which is considerable, anyway; azaleas have very shallow roots and require frequent irrigation during dry periods. Although not considered easy to propagate, they can be layered or rooted with cuttings kept in conditions of high humidity.   —GG

Rosa spp.

Rose
Family: Roseaceae (Rose)
Zones vary with varieties
The most aristocratic of flowers, roses also rank among the most democratic, at least in the South. Roses have been a fixture in the gardens of the rich and mighty throughout our history, and a century ago no plantation was complete without its beds of tea roses or noisettes. Because of their popularity with the well-to-do, roses are the best documented of heirloom flowers, and the titled names of the more fashionable roses—the types named for European aristocrats that came to us from nurseries in France and England—appear constantly in old diaries and historic garden plans.

Yet if roses have been the flowers of elegance in the South, they have also been just as much a fixture of our rural cottage gardens. Indeed, it was often the more modest gardeners who kept alive the splendid heirloom varieties. Whereas wealthy gardeners might follow fashion by rooting out old favorites and replacing them with the

latest introductions, poorer gardeners couldn't afford such extravagant gestures. Not only did cottage gardeners keep their old roses, they commonly helped to keep them in circulation after they had dropped out of nursery catalogues. Roses are, for the most part, easy to propagate by cuttings, and cottage gardeners used to pass along starts of their favorite types to friends and family members. As a result, modern rose collectors commonly find the finest specimens of eighteenth and nineteenth century roses in the humbler neighborhoods. The owners of these glorious antiques may not know the name of what they have been preserving, but they know a special beauty when they see it.

For the collector, part of the appeal of the heirloom roses lies in their authenticity. As with other plants grown from cuttings, grafting or tissue culture roses are not re-creations of past artifacts but are in fact a piece of the original plant, a part of the original creation. But if the old-fashioned roses are a Southern tradition, they are also very timely plants. For the old roses have all the virtues we cherish in heirloom plants.

They offer a special and very different kind of beauty. There is tremendous variation in the form and size of the flowers, and the perfumes are, typically, richer and more varied than those of modern roses. The colors of the heirloom roses tend toward pastels of pink, purple, yellow, white, and rose, and they tend to blend more easily into garden and interior settings than the eye-catching bright reds, oranges, and

'Mermaid' shows the landscape versatility of antique roses.
(*William C. Welch*)

yellows of the modern hybrids. Old roses often bear handsome foliage and attractive hips (fruit) that help round out their seasonal interest. And finally, these floral antiques are tough. Often these roses are found flourishing on the site of abandoned homesteads and cemeteries, where they carry on without pruning, spraying, fertilization, or irrigation. These roses are beautiful, but they are survivors, too, survivors from an era when garden plants had to thrive without the help of sprinkler systems, pesticides, and all the other aids of modern horticulture.

Some idea of the role that these heirloom roses played in yesterday's landscape can be gained from an observation of a nineteenth-century tourist named Harriet Martineau. In *Retrospect of Western Travel*, while describing a visit in 1837 to the site of the battle of New Orleans, Martineau noted, "Gardens of roses bewildered my imagination. I really believed at the time that I saw more roses that morning than during the whole course of my life before."

Today, the same roses that charmed Harriet Martineau are beginning to play an important part in the Southern landscape once again. Modern gardeners

(*William C. Welch*)

Yellow Lady Banks' rose (*Rosa banksia* 'Lutea') (*William C. Welch*)

are rediscovering their charms and strengths, and organizations and nurseries are forming to provide educational information and sources of plants. Nostalgia has a part in this "old rose revival," but practicality is more of a spur to those bent on recovering the forgotten treasures of the flower's fame.

More complete information on the classes and varieties as well as culture and landscape use of these fascinating plants is available in my book *Antique Roses for the South*. In this present volume, we will concentrate on the best classes of old roses for the South along with photographs of those most often found marking old homesites, cemeteries, and other historic sites. Varieties from each class that have shown the best adaptability and potential as assets in the landscape will be listed along with their dates of introduction, if known, so these living antiques can be used authentically in garden restorations.

LANDSCAPING WITH HEIRLOOM ROSES

Using old rose authentically—and effectively—is easy. All that is necessary is that you combine a touch of imagination with patient reflection on how roses were used in our ancestor's gardens. Trellises, espaliers, arches, pillars, pergolas, are all appropriate means of displaying old roses, and you may also introduce them (as our ancestors did) into mixed borders, or plant them as specimens or in hedges. When designing with old roses, keep in mind that these shrubs make their most spectacular display during spring in the

South. Many, however, repeat during summer and fall, and Tea roses, in particular, seem to reach their peak in the fall.

When I first fell in love with antique roses, I strongly favored those that rebloomed, the types usually known as "everblooming" in the South. However, after observing some of the "spring only" bloomers in Europe and in old gardens of the South, I came to the realization that although these varieties may only flower for three to eight weeks each spring, they often produced more flowers during that period than their everblooming cousins do in a whole year. For lavish effect I consider some of these spring bloomers—roses such as 'Lady Banks', 'Vielchenblau', 'Tausendschon', 'Carnea', *Rosa* x Fortuniana, "Cherokee", 'Cl. American Beauty', "Swamp Rose," and "Seven Sisters"—to be indispensable for my garden. In addition to their exuberant spring display, these roses commonly prove more disease and drought tolerant

than the everbloomers. Besides, there is enjoyment in expectation: I look forward to the spring bloomers' season of display and the flowering ends before I can grow satiated.

Still, in researching old roses, it is important to recognize how exciting the everbloomers were when they first made an appearance in our gardens. Few events in horticultural history equal the importance of the arrival of the first everblooming rose from China in the eighteenth and nineteenth centuries. Until that time only two fairly minor types of roses, the musk rose and the autumn damask, had ever bloomed after springtime in the West, and even those two rebloomed only sparingly. When the first truly everblooming roses did arrive from China, rose breeders (especially those in France) immediately began crossing them with Western roses to produce a flurry of new types and classes.

Though spectacular as flowers, many of the new roses proved too frost-sensitive to thrive in northern Europe, or the northern half of North America, for the Chinese everbloomers were natives of warm weather regions. But experience has shown these old timers to be ideally suited to the climate of the Southern states. The classes we know today as Tea and China roses are especially well adapted to the South and were cherished by our gardening ancestors. They are just as welcome and appropriate in a modern garden as a restoration and, thanks to the renewed interest in antique roses they are widely available from mail order sources, if not at most local garden centers.

Swamp rose (*Rosa palustris scandens*) (*William C. Welch*)

Chestnut rose (*Rosa roxburghii*) (William C. Welch)

ANTIQUE ROSES BY CLASS

It has been estimated that more than ten thousand rose varieties were introduced in the period between 1804 and 1935. This, coupled with the fact that roses can, and frequently do, mutate spontaneously (this is called "sporting"), helps us to understand why it is difficult to identify the roses we find growing in old cemeteries and gardens. Of all the thousands of roses that were introduced (and which may still be growing unrecognized on some abandoned homestead), only a small fraction are commercially available today. Further limiting the average gardener's choice of roses is the fact that of the choice band of old roses still offered in nursery catalogues, many prefer the cooler temperatures of the North.

We have chosen to concentrate on the old roses that will perform well in modern Southern gardens. That's why the photographs in the following pages represent those types of roses most commonly found enduring benign neglect in our Southern cemeteries and gardens. We list many other roses here as well, but we believe that when nature chooses to send a message, the gardener ought to listen. If a rose commonly flourishes on its own, then it is, truly "time tested" and is a good choice for new or restored gardens.

As you look through our recommendations, you will find the roses listed together in "classes." Developed originally by rose nurserymen and refined by generations of rose growers, the class system is simply a convenient way to organize roses into groups of plants that are similar in appearance and in need. Members of the various classes commonly share a similar parentage—they descend from similar crosses of species or types—and so have many characteristics in common. In my coverage of each class I have included a list of varieties with which I have been successful and, therefore, recommend to other Southern gardeners.

Following the name of each rose is the approximate date of its introduction (the date it first appeared on the market), if known. Knowing the date of introduction is important when you are planning a garden that you want to reflect a specific period of time. You would not want, for example, to plant a rose that was introduced in 1870 in a colonial-era garden. In addition, I have included in the description of each rose variety the approximate size the plant will attain when mature.

SPECIES AND RELATED HYBRIDS

Species roses may be defined as those of types found growing in wild populations in nature. Most of the roses listed here are species, but I have included a number of hybrids as well, hybrids that retain many species characteristics. All the roses in this section, both species and species-like hybrids, tend to be of excellent vigor and are for the most part disease resistant. They are good choices for naturalizing and will often grow well without regular maintenance if planted properly and given some care during the first year or so. Species roses work particularly well with plantings of native shrubs, perennials, and wildflowers since they all tend to thrive with minimal attention.

Besides their carefree quality, species roses are desirable for the natural elegance they impart to the landscape and fit well into a wide range of settings. Most bloom only in the spring and spend the rest of their energy producing healthy, abundant foliage. Some species roses also produce handsome fruit (hips) that add to their attractiveness in the landscape and have value as food for wildlife. Most grow to a large size and look their best when given ample room in which to expand. Although many are climbers, with a minimum of training and pruning, these too can be grown as large shrubs.

Though we tend to think of an interest in native plants as a new trend, in fact the enthusiasm for species roses is well rooted in Southern garden history. So, for example, in 1858 a visitor to Natchez extolled the beauty of Laurel Hill, owned by Dr. Mercer, a man considered to be of great culture and wealth. The gardens at Laurel Hill included a hedge, "miles upon miles of Cherokee Rose," described as having a breadth of ten feet. Natchez at this time, according to this correspondent, was the "Persia of roses. In no other part of the Union have we ever seen them attain such perfection and beauty." The rose in question, *Rosa laevigata*, is a species rose (Hedrick).

White Lady Banks' rose (*Rosa banksia* 'Alba Plena') (Greg Grant)

Yellow Lady Banks' rose (*Rosa banksia* 'Lutea') (*William C. Welch*)

Recommended species and varieties:

Rosa moschata, Musk Rose, 1540, 6–10 feet

Rosa eglanteria, Sweetbrier, prior to 1551, 8–10 feet

Rosa palustris scandens, Swamp Rose, 1726, 6–8 feet

Rosa laevigata, Cherokee, 1759, 5–15 feet

Rosa virginiana, Virginiana, before 1807, 3–6 feet

Rosa multiflora 'Carnea', 1804, 15–20 feet

Rosa banksia 'Lutea' (yellow), 1824, and 'Alba Plena' (white), 1807, Lady Banks' Rose, 10–20 feet

Rosa setigera, Prairie Rose, 1810, 4–6 feet

Rosa roxburghii, Chestnut Rose, prior to 1814, 5–7 feet

Rosa multiflora 'Platyphylla', Seven Sisters, 1817, 15–17 feet

Rosa multiflora 'Russelliana', Russell's Cottage Rose, prior to 1837, 5–7 feet

Rosa anemoneflora, White Carolina Rambler, 1844, 10–15 feet

Rosa x odorata pseudindica, Fortune's Double Yellow, 1845, 6–10 feet

Rosa x fortuniana, Fortuniana, 1850, 8–10 feet

Rosa multiflora 'Vielchenblau', 1909, 10–15 feet

Rosa multiflora 'Tausendschon', 1906, 10–15 feet

CHINA ROSES

A thousand years before the birth of Christ, the Chinese had bred a single-flowering native rose (*Rosa chinensis*) into true garden types. These new garden plants had a revolutionary characteristic: they bloomed not just in the spring, but repeatedly, through the growing season. The impact of this ancient innovation persists even today, for all the modern everblooming roses descend from those first Chinese shrubs.

The influence of *Rosa chinensis* has been especially strong in the American South. One testimony to this is the inspirational book, *Everblooming Roses*, that Georgia Torrey Drennen wrote in 1912. Mrs. Drennen was a Southerner, born in 1843 at her parent's plantation, Round Hill in Holmes County, Mississippi, and her book, in its wealth of firsthand experience, reveals that she was a knowledgeable horticulturist as well. "Turn where I may," she wrote, "I cannot find, nor remember, any roses that are more hardy, healthy, long-lived and everblooming than these old Bengals [Chinas]."

Individual blossoms of the China roses are not likely to win "Best of Show," but their profusion of flowers, their disease resistance, and the long,

healthy life they typically live more than compensate. Undoubtedly the best testimony to the China roses' hardiness and vigor is the fact that they are the roses most commonly found surviving without care in Texas and the South.

Chinas serve well as material for hedges, specimen plants, or borders. If pruned severely, most of them can be easily maintained as small, rounded plants. They respond well to heavy pruning in winter but seem to resent it in summer. If pruning is limited to the removal of dead or weak wood, these shrubs will slowly attain a large size.

My own interest in old roses began when I was a child, back in the mid-1940s as I watched my Aunt Edna carefully planting a hedge of the China rose 'Old Blush' with plants she had grown from cuttings at her home in Rosenberg, Texas. In this hedge she alternated 'Old Blush' (which she called "The Fisher Rose," in honor of the dear friends and neighbors who had given it to her) with bridal wreath spiraea, to create a living wall that enclosed two sides of her garden. The effect was memorable.

Actually, though Aunt Edna had gotten her start of 'Old Blush' from a neighbor, she was familiar with the rose from her grandmother's garden, and including it in her own garden was like welcoming an old friend. When Aunt Edna moved back to her hometown of Yoakum, Texas in 1951, she took starts of her bridal wreath and "Fisher Rose" with her and repeated the display at her new home. Although Aunt Edna is gone both the plantings in Rosenberg and Yoakum bloom and make a cheerful

'Cl. Old Blush', Nimitz Hotel, Fredericksburg, Texas. (*William C. Welch*)

spectacle each spring.

Another experience of mine associated with 'Old Blush' has to do with the way in which I acquired its climbing form. Cleo Barnwell of Shreveport, Louisiana, is one of the most expert horticulturists it has been my privilege to know; when she became aware of my interest in old roses, she said that I must have a cutting from the 'Climbing Old Blush' she had obtained many years ago from her friend Elizabeth Lawrence of Charlotte, North Carolina. I eagerly accepted the cuttings and shared them with the newly established Antique Rose Emporium near Brenham, Texas.

A few years later I noticed beautiful specimens blooming on trellises in front of the Nimitz Hotel in Fredericksburg, Texas and was pleased to know that they were descendents of the cuttings I had been given by Mrs. Barnwell. These large trellised specimens were literally stopping traffic when I photographed them.

The story doesn't end at the Nimitz Hotel. In the spring of 1993 I was pleased to participate as a speaker in the "Winghaven Symposium," an annual event sponsored by friends of Winghaven Gardens in Charlotte, which is a private foundation dedicated to educational endeavors centered around birds and gardens. Attached to the foundation are the beautiful gardens that Mr. and Mrs. Clarkson developed and left in trust. These gardens are found on the same street, just a few houses down, from the Elizabeth Lawrence home and garden. Apparently the Clarksons and Ms. Lawrence enjoyed sharing gardening experiences and, of course, plants.

This is how what was originally a Texan rose found its way into the Lawrence garden. For during my stay in Charlotte I learned that Mrs. Clarkson was actually a native of Uvalde, Texas. The 'Climbing Old Blush' she had planted at her home in Charlotte was a cutting she had taken from a rose at her childhood home in Uvalde, a rose that she knew as "Mama's Rose." The cutting Mrs. Clarkson planted in Charlotte is thriving still, as is the cutting from it that she gave to Elizabeth Lawrence (that grows by a tree near the entrance

to her home). It was a treat to know that in setting out my plant of 'Climbing Old Blush' (a cutting that came from Elizabeth Lawrence's bush via Cleo Barnwell) I was merely returning a Texan rose to its native soil.

Another instance of the China rose's durability came to me during an unscheduled visit I made with several Southern Garden History Society members who (like myself) were attending the May 1994 annual meeting in Colonial Williamsburg. Our stop was at the Dora Armistead garden on Duke of Gloucester Street. According to the present owner, Judge Robert T. Armistead, the home was built in 1890 on the foundations of a 1715 home where, it is said, George Washington once slept. Dora Armistead was a noted gardener in her day and her nephew a botanist. Today, this late Victorian structure, one of only a handful remaining in the historic district, has lost much of its original splendor, but the remnants of the garden included some true gems.

Several roses throughout the property were in full bloom; one of these I considered to be a major find. For years I had searched for the climbing form of 'Cramoisi Supérieur', a robust dark red China rose. The bush form is frequently found on old homesites, cemeteries, and similar locations throughout the South. Although I had seen references to the climbing form, it had always eluded me—until now.

Quite often the old roses found at abandoned sites survive in less than ideal conditions. The magnificent specimen I found in the Armistead garden, however, had been carefully trained to shade the large front porch of the house. Judge Armistead testified that this rose is so vigorous, it sometimes climbs well on to the roof of the porch, although a freeze several years ago had cut it back. He speculated that Dora Armistead planted this particular specimen in the 1890s.

Although I had never encountered this rose in the flesh before, I had come across it in print, in an article published in *The San Antonio Express* (September 2, 1934) and *The Dallas Morning News* (December 16, 1934) by Adina de Zavala. Miss de Zavala was chair of the

'Cl. Cramoisi Supérieur'
(*William C. Welch*)

Texas Centennial Commission and was encouraging Texans to plant roses to celebrate the state's upcoming centennial celebration in 1936. In the article she related her memories of conversations with her grandmother, Emily West de Zavala, and visits to her garden, which dated to the early 1830s.

Grandmother Emily had begun her garden shortly after her husband Lorenzo returned to Texas from a stint as ambassador to France—he had also served as vice-president for the newly formed Republic of Texas. While in France, Lorenzo reported receiving gifts of new China roses to take back to this home in Texas.

Of the roses Adina remembered seeing in the garden, she specifically mentioned a climbing form of 'Cramoisi Supérieur' that wreathed one of the columns of the plantation house. The curious thing is that her recollections precede the actual introduction of this rose. Greg Grant's files on red China roses include two climbing forms of 'Cramoisi Supérieur': 'Rev. James Sprunt', which was introduced by Sprunt in 1858, and 'Climbing Cramoisi Supérieur', which was introduced by the Coutourier nursery of France in 1885.

Peter Henderson, a well-known horticultural author and plantsman of the period introduced, both roses

'Sombreuil' (*William C. Welch*)

'Old Blush', 1752, 5–6 feet
'Cl. Old Blush', date unknown, 15–20 feet
'Cramoisi Supérieur', 1832, 4–6 feet
'Louis Philippe', 1834, 3–5 feet
'Archduke Charles', prior to 1837, 3–5 feet
'Hermosa', 1840, 3–4 feet
Rosa chinensis 'Viridiflora', The Green Rose, prior to 1845, 3–4 feet
R. chinensis 'Mutabilis', The Butterfly Rose, prior to 1896, 4–7 feet
'Ducher', 1869, 3–4 feet

through his nursery in New York, and they were also listed by two early Texas nurseries: Gilbert Onderdonk's Mission Valley Nurseries in 1888 and William Watson's Rosedale Nurseries of Brenham in 1899. These two forms may be the same, both being climbing sports of the same well-known shrub ('Cramoisi Supérieur'). How either climber found its way so early into Emily de Zavala's garden remains a mystery, unless it was that she had a plant of the original shrub form of 'Cramoisi Supérieur' which sported for her.

In his book *Shrub Roses of Today*, Graham Stuart Thomas wrote, "The climbing form 'Cramoisi Supérieur Grimpante' is a magnificent plant for a sunny wall." And in his catalogue of 1912, nurseryman Tom Smith noted that he had "seen the whole front of a two-story house completely covered with the Climbing Cramoisi," whose flowers "are continually produced all the season through."

But my enthusiasm for this rose goes beyond its unique beauty. There are few truly red heirloom roses and even fewer climbers. Because China roses usually rebloom profusely, it could be a very useful plant for period or modern gardens. Certainly, it was not difficult to infect Southern Garden History Society members Steve Wheaton, Peggy Newcomb, and Peter Schaar with my enthusiasm for this rose. Rumor has it that a few carefully selected cuttings may have left Colonial Williamsburg in their luggage. (Rumor also has it that a few snippings might have made it back to Texas.) As I write this it is mid-July, 1994 and a few cuttings appear to be

taking root. With luck, this interesting rose may be available to Southern gardeners again in a couple of years.

There are many useful roses in the China class, most of them being red or pink. Red Chinas are probably the most commonly found old rose in the South. Most appear to be either to belong to the varieties 'Louis Philippe' or 'Cramoisi Supérieur'. 'Louis Philippe' is common in Louisiana, particularly in the New Orleans area, where it is sometimes referred to as the "Creole Rose." Also of special interest is the China rose known as "The Green Rose," which some describe as beautiful, while at least one rose authority has dismissed it as "an engaging monstrosity." Flower arrangers find the bronzy green flowers useful and long-lasting subjects. It is easily grown and often found in old gardens. An old specimen survives at Grace Episcopal Church, St. Francisville, Louisiana.

TEA ROSES

Tea roses are exceptionally well suited to Southern climates and are often found as large bushes marking old homesites where they have thrived with no care whatsoever for decades. The blossoms themselves are large and memorable roses, the kind people speak of with nostalgia. Tea roses inherited their fragrance and large blossoms from the wild Tea rose, *Rosa gigantea*, a native of the eastern Himalayan foothills. Their everblooming character comes from *R. chinensis*, their other parent.

Many old Tea roses resemble in form the typical high-centered Hybrid Teas of today, and so are generally admired as cut flowers as well as garden plants. This class was very popular from the 1830s until its own more cold-hardy descendants, the Hybrid Teas, superseded it at the turn of the century. As a rule, Teas have an upright habit, forming tall and sometimes narrow bushes with bronzy red new foliage. In the Southern states, they bloom profusely in the spring and

'Mrs. B.R. Cant' (*William C. Welch*)

'Mrs. Dudley Cross' (*Greg Grant*)

fall, with scattered summer flowers. Blossoms are spectacular and large in pastel pinks and yellows, with some reds and a few whites. Fragrance is distinctive, cool, and somewhat similar to that of dried tea leaves.

In *Everblooming Roses*, Georgia Torrey Drennan extolled the virtues of Tea roses above all others: "Nothing in the history of the rose has been of greater importance than the creation of the Tea. Its introduction to the Occident ranks with the bountiful best gifts of the nineteenth century."

Most Teas have good resistance to black spot and seem to thrive in the heat of the South, although they are occasionally damaged by cold in northerly areas of our region. Though susceptible to frost, Tea roses bloom until the arrival of very cold weather. Accounts of early Southerners gathering bouquets for Christmas and other midwinter events indicate that Tea roses were considered an essential part of the garden at that time. The flower stems are weak and often bow gracefully with the weight of the large flowers, and though this might be seen as a defect today, it was considered an elegant trait during Victorian times. It is still admired by those who enjoy the many distinctive and easily grown roses that comprise the Tea class.

Recommended varieties:
'Bon Silenè', prior to 1837, 4–6 feet
'Devoniensis', 1838, 8–10 feet
'Safrano', 1839, 5–7 feet
'Sombreuil', 1850, 6–10 feet
'Duchesse de Brabant', 1857, 3–5 feet
'Perle des Jardins', 1874, 3–5 feet

'Maman Cochet', 1893, 3–4 feet
'Monsieur Tillier', 1891, 3–6 feet
'Souvenir de Mme. Leonie Viennot', 1898, 15–20 feet
'Mrs. B.R. Cant', 1901, 5–7 feet
'Mrs. Dudley Cross', 1907, 4–6 feet

NOISETTE ROSES

The Noisettes are of special interest historically because they are the first class of garden roses to have originated in the United States. John Champneys, a rice planter from Charleston, South Carolina, raised the first of the class by crossing the Musk rose (an old garden rose that reblooms in the fall and so has been popular since Shakespeare's day) with 'Old Blush'. Champneys named the result for himself: 'Champneys' Pink Cluster.' A few years later, a friend of Champneys, a florist from Charleston named Philippe Noisette, raised a seedling from Champneys's rose. In 1817, Noisette sent his rose to his brother Louis in Paris, who named it 'Blush Noisette.' The French eagerly received and expanded the new rose class because of its heavy clustering bloom, musky scent, and strong, healthy growth. The roses which they produced, the early Noisettes, bear flowers in small clusters; later varieties, those which resulted from crosses with Tea roses, have larger blossoms with fewer flowers per cluster.

Although considered more susceptible to cold than most classes, the Noisettes are well adapted to the Southern states and found immense popularity here. Their Musk rose ancestry ensures a good floral display in the fall as well as in the spring. As a rule, however, Noisettes are not as resistant to black spot and mildew as are the Teas and Chinas.

Many of the Noisettes have the ability to create a landscape effect unique among roses. Whether grown on walls, fences, arbors, or even trees, the climbing varieties are valuable to a garden in which a period effect is desired. Noisettes are not found as frequently as Teas and Chinas on abandoned homesites and cemeteries, but many of them are easily grown and long-lived garden plants.

Recommended varieties:
'Champneys' Pink Cluster', circa 1811, 4–8 feet
'Aimée Vibert', 1828, 6–10 feet
'Lamarque', 1830, 8–10 feet
'Jaune Desprez', 1830, 15–20 feet
'Chromatella', 1843, 12–20 feet
'Jeanne D'Arc', 1848, 5–8 feet
'Céline Forestier', 1858, 10–15 feet
'Maréchal Niel', 1864, 10–15 feet
'Rêve D'Or', 1869, 10–12 feet

'Champneys' Pink Cluster' (*William C. Welch*)

Far left: 'Maréchal Niel' (*William C. Welch*)
Left: 'Mme. Alfred Carrière' (*William C. Welch*)

'William Allen Richardson', 1878, 10–15 feet
'Mme. Alfred Carrière', 1879, 15–20 feet
'Nastarana', 1879, 3–4 feet
'Claire Jacquier', 1888, 15–20 feet
'Mary Washington', 1891, 6–8 feet

OLD EUROPEAN ROSES

Included in this section are roses from a variety of classes that are sometimes found in old Southern gardens and which deserve the heirloom gardener's consideration. Since the European roses were developed primarily for shorter growing seasons and colder winters, in the South they may lack the vigor and disease resistance of roses from areas more like our own. However, they are significant historically because of their long association with major events of Western history. Moreover, their beauty and fragrance have inspired great art and literature.

Recommended varieties:
Rosa gallica officinalis, The Apothecary Rose, Very Old, 3–4 feet
Rosa gallica versicolor 'Rosa Mundi', prior to 1581, 3–4 feet
'Celsiana', prior to 1750, 3–5 feet
'Autumn Damask', prior to 1819, 4–6 feet
'Madame Plantier', probably an Alba?Moschata cross, 1835, 4–6 feet
'Banshee', date and origin unknown, 4–5 feet
'Salet', a Moss Rose, 1854, 3–4 feet

BOURBON ROSES

Bourbon roses resulted from a natural cross between 'Old Blush' and 'Autumm Damask', both of which had been planted as hedges on the French island then called Bourbon and now called Reunion. An alert resident noticed this spontaneous hybrid and sent the plant to France, where breeders further perfected the class. The first cultivar was painted by Redouté in 1817. There are about forty varieties still in commerce today.

Bourbons produce some of the most beautiful flowers ever developed. They often have old-fashioned, cupped or quartered blossoms, generally in pastel pinks, on large, robust plants. Due to their Damask influence, Bourbons tend to be more cold hardy than Chinas or Teas. Only a few varieties reliably repeat-flower in summer and fall in the South. These roses also tend to be more susceptible to black spot and mildew than Chinas or Teas. Bourbon flowers are, in general, highly fragrant and beautifully formed, which accounts for their popularity in spite of their sometimes sparse and short bloom period and lack of disease resistance.

In all my hunting, I have found and identified only three Bourbons on old Southern homesites. These are 'Souvenir de la Malmaison', 'Kronprinzessin Viktoria', and 'Zépherine Drouhin', and all are excellent and fairly tough garden plants. Actually, though, I may have found a fourth Bourbon, and that is the rose I call "Maggie," which was the first old garden rose I found and propagated. Judging by various characteristics, this is very possibly a Bourbon.

I had noticed this rose during several visits to my wife's grandmother's farm near Mangham, Louisiana. The plant always seemed to be in bloom and the flowers were very full and highly fragrant—they left an intriguing scent of black pepper lingering on the hand that picks them or handled a stem. Finally, during the Christmas season of 1980, I decided to take cuttings. I took cuttings

'Rosa Mundi' (*William C. Welch*)

'Souvenir de la Malmaison' (*William C. Welch*)

"Maggie" (*William C. Welch*)

of "Maggie" and another rose growing nearby that we later identified as the "Swamp Rose," and wrapped them all in a plastic bag. After several days in the bag, the cuttings were stuck in an east-facing flower bed in our College Station garden.

They rooted and began blooming later that very same spring. They have grown vigorously and were shared with the Antique Rose Emporium, The Huntington Botanical Garden, and Joyce Demits of Heritage Roses in Ft. Bragg, California. Greg obtained his "Maggie," the identical rose, from a different source, a specimen growing on his great-grandmother's garden in East Texas. He noted during a recent plant-collecting trip to Belize that it was the most common dooryard rose in that former British possession. "Maggie" has since been found in numerous other old gardens and cemeteries. It is sometimes

trained as a climber, but most often as a large bush. It seems odd that a rose so fine and popular remains unidentified. There must be a healthy dose of China in its parentage, though, since it reblooms as well as any China Rose I have grown.

Recommended varieties:
'Souvenir de la Malmaison', 1843, 3–4 feet
'Kronprinzessin Victoria', 1888, 3–4 feet
'Zéphirine Drouhin', 1868, 6–15 feet
'Mme. Isaac Pereire', 1881, 6–7 feet
'Variegata di Bologna', 1909, 4–7 feet

HYBRID PERPETUALS

The Hybrid Perpetual class includes some of the most beautiful flowers ever developed. Typically, Hybrid Perpetual blossoms are very large, full, and heavily scented, and some make outstanding cut flowers. The bushes tend to be tall and

sometimes ungainly, but they can be shaped to become usable landscape plants.

Southerners often referred to Hybrid Perpetuals as "Cabbage Roses," although that name more accurately applies to another class of roses. 'Paul Neyron' is among the best known in the class and as such was often described as a cabbage rose. Probably the Hybrid Perpetual most often found in old Southern gardens is 'Climbing American Beauty'. All the members of this class which I have grown bore powerfully fragrant flowers.

An interesting way to grow Hybrid Perpetuals is to "peg" them. This involves fastening the ends of the canes to the ground with stakes or wire pins: the lateral buds along the canes then "break"—that is, they start growing—and the result is a shrub with a beautiful fountain-like effect.

'Zépherine Drouhin' (*William C. Welch*)

'Madame Isaac Periere' (*Greg Grant*)

'Paul Neyron' (*William C. Welch*)

'Baronne Prevost' (*William C. Welch*)

'Perle D'Or', 1884, 3–4 feet
'Marie Pavié', 1888, 2–4 feet
'Clotilde Soupert', 1890, 3–4 feet
'La Marne', 1915, 4–6 feet
'The Fairy', 1932, 3–4 feet

FREQUENTLY FOUND ROSES FROM MISCELLANEOUS CLASSES

There are a number of *Wichuraiana* Ramblers that were introduced around the turn of the century and which have since naturalized throughout the South. 'Excelsa' and 'Dorothy Perkins' are probably the most common of these, although they are usually plagued with powdery mildew.

'Silver Moon' (1910) is a once-blooming climber with healthy foliage that bears semi-double white flowers with good fragrance. 'New Dawn' (1930) claims the distinction of being U.S. Plant Patent No. 1, the first plant ever patented under federal regulations. It is an everblooming sport of the well-known 'Dr. W. Van Fleet' and exceeded the popularity of its parent. Some of the early Hybrid Teas such as 'La France' (1867), 'Radiance' (1908), and 'Red Radiance' (1916) are still found in old gardens and passed on locally as rooted cuttings.

Another interesting plant which has been traditionally viewed as a rose by Southern gardeners is the "Blackberry Rose," which is also known as the "Easter Rose" or "Coronation Rose."

Recommended varieties:
'Rose du Roi', 1815, 3–4 feet
'Rose de Rescht', date or origin unknown, 3 feet
'Marquise Bocella', 1842, 3–5 feet
'Baronne Prevost', 1842, 4–6 feet
'Comte de Chambord', 1860, 3–5 feet
'Reine des Violettes', 1860, 4–5 feet
'Paul Neyron', 1869, 5–6 feet
'Climbing American Beauty', 1909, 12–15 feet
'Ulrich Brünner Fils', 1881, 4–6 feet
'Frau Karl Druschki', 1901, 4–6 feet

POLYANTHA ROSES

Polyantha roses were created by crossing the Chinas with the rambling Japanese Multiflora rose. The goal was to create a group of roses that could be massed together in borders or other, similar, types of landscape displays. In fact, the result of the cross was a group of roses that blooms prolifically, is compact in size, and which bear large clusters of relatively small flowers. The fragrance of the blossoms varies from almost nonexistent to some of the finest ever created. Some of the polyanthas also inherited their China rose parents' everblooming habit.

This class contains several of our favorite roses for Southern gardens. 'Cècile Brunner', better known as the "Sweetheart Rose," is most appreciated for its vigorous climbing form. 'Marie

Pavié' is occasionally found in old gardens and has wonderful fragrance. It is nearly thornless and makes a great three- to four-foot hedge or container specimen. 'La Marne' is often found in cemeteries and is a real survivor. 'Perle D'Or is very similar to 'Cècile Brunner' but with more salmon or orange in its coloration.

Recommended varieties:
'Cècile Brunner', 1881, 3–4 feet
'Cl. Cècile Brunner', 1894, 15–20 feet

'Cl. Cècile Brunner' (*William C. Welch*)

'Marie Pavié' (*William C. Welch*)

**Blackberry rose (*Rubus coronarius*)
(*William C. Welch*)**

Actually it belongs to the genus *Rubus* and is listed in *Hortus Third* as *Rubus coronarius*. Although rarely mentioned in gardening literature it was commonly traded about among Southern gardeners. My plant came from Zada Walker, a long time friend who lives near Kirbyville, Texas. It grows and blooms prolifically in my country garden and suckers freely. This spreading habit has not been a problem since gardening friends have eagerly "rustled" the divisions. Double-white blossoms are less than two inches in diameter and appear around Easter each year. Its foliage looks more like a blackberry than a rose.

Once-blooming roses that appear to belong to the Gallica class are often found in old cemeteries throughout the South. They are spring-only bloomers and tend to sucker, sometimes forming small thickets. Most are very fragrant and occur in interesting shades of dusty purple and pink.

❀

In closing, I would like to repeat that the current renewal of interest in old roses, and their reappearance in nursery catalogues is much more than a symptom of nostalgia. Old garden roses are practical garden plants, and are especially appropriate for the environmental age in which we seem to be entering. Mankind and roses seem to be eternally linked, especially in the South, where climate and soils encourage a flowering of so many beautiful types.
—*WCW*

Rosmarinus officinalis
**Rosemary
Family: Labiatae (Mint)
Zones: 8–11**

As long as the drainage is good, rosemary will thrive even on poor, dry rocky soils. Indeed, in its native range around the Mediterranean Sea, rosemary flourishes in coastal regions so arid that a significant part of the plant's moisture comes from the dew absorbed through the foliage.

But though tolerant of drought, this plant is not cold hardy, and this limits its use as a landscape plant even in the South. However, rosemary is an ideal candidate for container cultivation, in which case the plant can be moved to a protected spot during the coldest parts of winter. It's worth the trouble, for this is a most decorative plant. Rosemary tolerates clipping and responds well to training; it's a good subject for bonsai or topiary, and through these techniques can adopt an endless variety of forms. And whatever the shape, rosemary preserves the same virtue: the needlelike foliage looks good year round—for rosemary is evergreen—and smells even better.

The genus name *Rosmarinus* means "dew of the sea" (a reference to the plant's preference for seaside conditions), while the species name—*officinalis*—indicates that the plant has been used for medicinal purposes. Indeed, early herbals devoted considerable space to the properties (both curative and magical) of this plant. One American authority, Samuel Stearns, noted in his book, *The American Herbal* of 1801, that "It

strengthens the brain, helps the memory."

A comprehensive treatment of rosemary is found in Lady Rosalind Northcote's *The Book of Herbs* (London and New York, 1903), and this identifies it as among the most important of all herbs:

> Rosemary has always been of more importance than any other herb, and more than most of them put together. It has been employed at weddings and funerals, for decking the church and for garnishing the banquet hall, in stage-plays, and in "swelling discontent," of a too great reality; as incense in religious ceremonies, and in spells against magic: "in sickness and in health," eminently as a symbol, and yet for very practical uses.

Reportedly, an aromatic oil used in perfumery and medicine is still distilled from rosemary's fresh needles. And anyone who had the good fortune to participate in the politically incorrect English classes of a generation ago surely remembers Ophelia's speech in Shakespeare's *Hamlet*: "There's rosemary, that's for remembrance; pray, love, remember."

Today, this marvelous, memory-strengthening herb is mostly used for culinary and decorative purposes. This, too, is a matter of tradition. Rosemary was an essential ingredient of earliest herb and kitchen gardens, and is almost always present in English cottage gardens. There it is often planted close

**Rosemary
(*Rosmarinus officinalis*)
(*William C. Welch*)**

Rosemary (*Rosmarinus officinalis*) standard (*Greg Grant*)

to the front door, where people brush against it as they pass, releasing some of the foliage's clean, rich scent. The foliage is popular, fresh or dried, for seasoning various dishes and is particularly good (in this writer's opinion) with meats and potatoes.

An interesting note concerning the landscape use of rosemary comes from Miss Gertrude Jekyll, who recommends in her book *Wood and Garden* (1899),

> ...bushes of Rosemary, some just filling the border, and some trained up the wall. Our Tudor ancestors were fond of Rosemary-covered walls, and I have seen old bushes quite ten feet high on the garden walls of Italian monasteries. Among the Rosemaries I always like, if possible, to "tickle in" a China Rose ('Old Blush') or two, the tender pink of the Rose seems to go so well with the dark but dull-surfaced Rosemary.

Ms. Jekyll's advice, while excellent, represents just one way to use this plant in the landscape. Many distinctive forms of rosemary have been developed by gardeners, and this makes it an exceptionally versatile plant. There are, for example, prostrate rosemaries which furnish an unusual groundcover and

make an attractive detail as they spill over retaining walls. Upright forms, by contrast, provide materials for a compact hedge or elegant container plants, and the mature heights of these may vary from eighteen inches to four feet or more, depending upon the cultivar and the growing conditions. Rosemary flowers, while not spectacular, are attractive, and they vary from lavender-blue to dark blue and white.

Gardeners looking for an upright form of rosemary should consider 'Lockwood deForest', which is also reported to tolerate cold particularly well. This cultivar bears dark blue flowers and tends to rebloom better than most cultivars. Said to be a hybrid of *R. prostratus* and *R.* x 'Tuscan Blue', this, like all rosemaries, thrives in dry, calcareous soils. 'Tuscan Blue' is an upright and rigid rosemary with blue-violet flowers; 'Collingwood Ingram' is a bright, blue-violet flowering cultivar with graceful, curving branches. 'Prostratus' is a low, spreading form that rarely exceeds two feet in height. It is not as cold hardy as the upright forms, but is worth moving or covering for a few nights each winter. For white flowers, try 'Albus'. *R. corsicus* is pine-scented, but similar in its lack of cold hardiness to the prostrate forms.

Mrs. Madelene Hill, a well-known herb authority from Round Top, Texas, found a cold-tolerant rosemary in 1972 in Arp, Texas, that is said to be hardy to Washington, D.C. The National Arboretum has given this plant the name *R. officinalis* 'Arp'. More recently a sport or seedling of 'Arp' has been found

and named "Hill Hardy."

Rosemary is propagated from pencil-size cuttings taken in fall or early winter. Remove the leaves from the bottom half of the stems, and then stick the cuttings in moist garden soil, where they will root by summer. In moist climates where rosemaries often prove short-lived, it is a good idea to root new plants periodically to maintain a supply of replacements.

Rosemary has flourished in Southern gardens ever since the arrival of European colonists on these shores—and in every colony, for this plant was precious to every group that settled here. In *A New Herbal* by D. Rembert Dodoens (London, 1619), in a section titled "Of Rofemary," the author states, "Rofemary groweth naturally and plentifully in divers places of Spaine and France, as in Provence and Languedock: they plant it in this country [England] in gardens and maintaine it with great vigilence." Maintain yours with vigilence, and rosemary will flourish for you, too.*   —WCW

* Special appreciation is extended to Florence P. Griffin of Atlanta for her assistance in researching rosemary. The sharing of her library resources and those of the Cherokee Garden Library in Atlanta have been most helpful.

Ruscus spp., *Danae racemosa*
Butcher's Broom, Ruscus, Box Holly, Jew's Myrtle
Family: Liliaceae (Lily)
Zones: 8–11
Butcher's Broom is a name with an ominous sound to it, yet in truth it is

Butcher's broom (*Ruscus aculeatus*) at Elm's Court Plantation, Natchez, Mississippi. (*Glenn Haltom*)

Ruscus Hypoglossum (Greg Grant)

Danae racemosa (Greg Grant)

only an acknowledgment of this shrub's humblest service to mankind. *Ruscus* is evergreen and the branches flattened, leathery, and oval-shaped—like prickly leaves. A handful of these branches, apparently, was formerly a butcher's standard device for sweeping clean his cutting block.

Quite apart from its utility, this *is* an attractive shrub, albeit one with an odd habit of flowering: because of the form of the branches, the flowers that spring from them seem to be sprouting from leaves. These are followed by red, or sometimes yellow, berries up to half an inch in diameter. The combination of evergreen foliage and bright fruits makes this a popular choice for holiday decoration, and also for florists' winter bouquets.

Though native to Europe, ruscus, especially the species *R. aculeatus*, was often found in old Southern gardens. An old planting of this species exists at Elm's Court Plantation (c. 1835–40) in Natchez, Mississippi, where it was planted in large clumps about twenty feet apart to flank the wide walkway that serves as the axis from the rear entrance of the main house to the garden. Originally the masses of ruscus were alternated with shade trees. Some of the latter, have died, however, and as the garden's owner, Mrs. Douglas H. MacNeil, pointed out, this has exposed the ruscus to a full sun that is burning the foliage—a point to keep in mind when choosing a site for this plant.

My own ruscus came from Felder Rushing's garden in Jackson, Mississippi, and is planted in our herb garden in

Washington County, Texas. I have never seen berries on this plant, but I believe that is because ruscus is dioecious. That is, the male and female flowers are borne on separate plants, and what Felder shared with me is a male (and so fruitless) plant. Watch for this problem—Elizabeth Lawrence wrote in her book, *A Southern Garden*, that she never had fruit on her plants in North Carolina, either.

She gave butcher's broom its due, however, noting that it "is one of the most reliable shrubs for troublesome places. It will grow in the driest places, even under trees, and in all degrees of shade. It does need a good mulch of cow manure in the fall. When the plants are starved some of the new spring shoots become colorless by summer."

I have found that, as Mrs. MacNeil of Elm's Court suggested, butcher's brooms prefer to grow in shady situations under the drip of trees, which is useful since few other plants thrive in such a situation. Propagation is by division of suckers from the root mass that are thrown up in abundance.

Another interesting ruscus is *R. Hypoglossum*. It is not prickly, and bears leaves about four inches long and one and a half inches wide. My plants were given to me by Herb and Betty Langford, who have grown it for many years in their Texas City, Texas, garden, where Betty uses it frequently in her flower arrangements. It is growing well for me under the shade of some giant live oaks.

Danae racemosa* is a native of Asia Minor and Persia that was once

classified as a ruscus, but now is placed in a separate genus. It is similar to the non-spiny forms of ruscus, but has a much glossier foliage, although like ruscus, what appears to be leaves on this plant are in truth leaflike branches. *Danae racemosa* is commonly known as Alexandrian laurel, and it is said by some sources to be the true laurel used to wreathe the brows of poets. This plant's cherrylike berries appear singly on the new shoots and redden in November, hanging on until spring. As with the butcher's broom, the combination of red berries and shiny evergreen foliage make this a popular choice for floral arrangements.

This lovely plant is sometimes found at very old Southern homesites. That's where Steve Wheaton, horticulturist for Barnsley Gardens in Georgia, discovered large plantings of *D. racemosa*—at the old Westover Plantation along the James River in Virginia. The owners shared some of their plants (seedlings) with Steve who in turn provided me with two small transplants. I gave one to my friend Francis Parker in Beaufort, South Carolina, since I knew it was high on her "want list" of plants (that had been all the encouragement I needed to place it on my own).

Fine masses of *D. racemosa* also flank the tree-shaded gates of the Governor's Palace at Colonial Williamsburg. However, I first became interested in this plant when a fellow

* *Hortus Third* gives a useful hint for the pronunciation of the generic name *Danae*: it has three syllables.

A double-flowering form of bouncing bet (*Saponaria officinalis* 'Flora plena') (*William C. Welch*)

faculty member here at Texas A&M brought me pictures of stems and fruit in her mother's garden in Tyler, Texas. No one had been able to identify the plant, which her mother had carried with her for many years as she moved from Virginia to several other states and finally to Texas. It was thriving in her Tyler garden. After identifying the shrub, I learned that it is not a difficult plant to grow, but that it much prefers a good, moist soil and at least partial shade.

Just because the brooms—*Danae* and the two species of *Ruscus*—were once fairly common in Southern gardens, don't expect to find them at your local garden center or discount store. Indeed, these plants are difficult to find in the nursery trade at all. That's unfortunate, for these plants appear to be long-lived with few cultural problems. They deserve more widespread use, especially in heirloom gardens.

—*WCW*

Saponaria officinalis
Bouncing Bet, Soapwort
Family: Caryophyllaceae (Pink)
Zones: 3–9
Upon visiting an historic house in England a few years ago, we noticed that some of the tapestries were being taken down. When we asked why, the attendant informed us that they were to be cleaned with an agent containing *S. officinalis*. I was aware that the plant contained a soaplike substance that was often used in the nineteenth century and earlier to wash new cloth, but did not know that it was still being em-

ployed for this purpose today.

Some say that the name "bouncing bet" originated in England where barmaids, often called "Bets," cleaned ale bottles by filling them with water and a sprig of this plant and then shaking vigorously. Southerners who have grown the plant argue that the name derives from the fact that once planted, *S. officinalis* bounces all about their gardens.

Since bouncing bet tends to outlast the homes around which it was planted and because it has naturalized freely along streams throughout the South, some people think that it is native to North America. Actually, it is indigenous to Europe and Asia and was brought to this country by early settlers.

Certainly this perennial exhibits an immigrant's toughness. But it is also highly ornamental, bearing showy, fragrant pink or white flowers for several months during the summer. Foliage and

stems usually remain at a height of less than a foot until flowering begins, whereupon they may reach two feet or more. Both single- and double-flowering (*S. officinalis* 'Flora plena') forms occur, the double one generally being preferred for ornamental purposes.

Soapwort remains attractive throughout most of the year if it is cut back after it blooms in late summer. I have been known to trim mine with a lawn mower in the fall. This plant spreads by underground rhizomes and is quite aggressive when grown in well-prepared soil, and may become a pest. It flourishes equally in either partial shade or full sun, but in sunny locations plants may suffer some leaf and flower sunburn in midsummer. Propagation is by division of rhizomes preferably in fall, winter, or early spring. I collected my first plants of bouncing bet from the Sam Houston homesite at Independence, Texas. It was surviving there in a partially shaded spot, and it may well have been a survivor of the original 1830s garden. I have also found it on numerous other old homesites in Texas. It tolerates dry or rather wet conditions and is susceptible to few, if any, insect or disease problems. —*WCW*

Spiraea spp.
Bridal Wreath
Family: Rosaceae (Rose)
Zones: 6–9
Although they rank as relative latecomers to the American garden scene, spiraeas have been an important shrub in the South since the mid-1800s. The types most often found in our region are

Bouncing bet (*Saponaria officinalis*) (*Greg Grant*)

Spiraea × *vanhouttei* (Greg Grant)

Reeve's spiraea (*Spiraea cantoniensis*) (Greg Grant)

Spiraea prunifolia 'Plena', *S. thunbergii*, *S. cantoniensis* (*S. reeviesiana*), and *S. × vanhouttei*. All are white-flowering, deciduous shrubs with a graceful fountainlike form.

Reeve's spiraea (*S. cantoniensis*) has an English name and has been grown in that country since 1824, but like most spiraea species it is Asian in origin, having been cultivated since early times in Japan. Although once popular in the United States, it has largely been superseded by *S. × vanhouttei*, which is a hybrid that was produced prior to 1866 by crossing *S. cantoniensis* with another Asian species, *S. trilobata*. Both Reeve's spiraea and its hybrid offspring bear dense umbels of pure white flowers along the branches in April and May, and for this reason they were commonly planted together with spring-blooming azaleas and roses. These two spiraeas were valued not only for their flowers

but also for their ease of cultivation.

The pure white, double flowers that burst open in stalkless clusters along its branches in March and April earned *Spiraea prunifolia* 'Plena' the common name popcorn spiraea in the South. Discovered by the Scottish plant explorer Robert Fortune in a Chinese garden in 1844, popcorn spiraea is a long-lived, low-maintenance plant that can live unattended for many years. When well grown, it makes a graceful shrub of fountainlike branches five to seven feet tall.

Spiraea thunbergii is known as baby's breath spiraea and was introduced into England from the East about 1863. Numerous clusters of small, white flowers appear very early in the season, sometimes in midwinter in the lower South. The overall effect is very airy, providing fine texture in foliage or without. When mature this shrub may

reach a height of six to seven feet with a similar spread. It is often confused with its close relative *S. arbuta*, which differs, however, in having fewer teeth on the margins of its leaves. *S. thunbergii* has been a Southern garden favorite for many years. Like all the spiraeas described here, it is of easy culture, but prefers a neutral to slightly acid soil pH rather than highly alkaline soils, where it tends to develop iron chlorosis.

—WCW

Viola odorata, Viola tricolor
Violet
Family: Violaceae (Violet)
Zones: 6–11

This is an *old* garden flower—it was already in commercial cultivation long before the birth of Christ, not so much for use as an ornament, as for sweetening food and making perfume. Still, the modest beauty of the flower has earned

Popcorn spiraea (*Spiraea prunifolia*) (Greg Grant)

Baby's breath spiraea (*Spiraea thunbergii*)
(William C. Welch)

Violet (*Viola odorata* 'Royal Robe') (*Greg Grant*)

it many admirers along the way; including the warlike Napoleon Bonaparte. Just before his exile, Napoleon is said to have picked a few blooms from the grave of his beloved Josephine and placed them in a locket that he was wearing on his death bed.

During medieval times violets were cultivated in England for culinary and medicinal purposes. Sugar had not yet been imported, and violets were in demand to cover the floors of churches, manor houses, and cottages to mask the dank, musty smell so much a part of those structures at the time.

Violet flowers were also widely used for medicinal purposes. They were considered remedies for a variety of complaints, including headaches, melancholy, and sleeplessness, and were even used in the treatment of cancer (violet leaves were used until fairly recent times in Wales and Ireland as a cure for external cancers). In *The Little Herball*, author Anthony Ascham wrote in 1525: "[F]or they that may not sleep, seep this herb in water and at even let him soak well his feet in the water to the ancles, and when he goeth to bed, bind of this herb to the temples and he shall sleep well by the Grace of God."

Until fairly recent times, chemists still used blue syrup of violets, though for a more mundane purpose. It served as a sort of natural litmus paper, turning red when brought in contact with acids, and green when in contact with alkali.

Violet blooms, both dried and crystallized, have been used for cake decoration and sweetmeats since medieval times and still are utilized today for that purpose as well as to decorate chocolates. Candied violets

may be made by dipping the flowers in a solution of rose water and gum arabic followed by a sprinkle of fine sugar. After drying in a warm oven, the candied violets are ready to serve.

The fragrance of violets is a major factor in their popularity, yet it has often been described as fleeting and of short duration. Actually, it isn't the perfume that is fleeting, but rather the sense of smell when it is exposed to violet fragrance. It contains a substance known as ionine (*ion* is the ancient Greek word for violet) that dulls the olfactory sense after a few sniffs. One's ability to enjoy the violet scent soon returns, but the presence of the ionine, makes sure that the flower fancier never over-indulges, at least in the case of violets.

These flowers were a major florist crop well into the early twentieth century. Their fragrance, rich colors, and relatively easy culture contributed to national and worldwide popularity. They are, however, a very labor-

intensive crop, which is why violets are rarely found in today's florist shops.

Although there are several species of violets native to the South, the violet of choice for most Southern gardens was *Viola odorata*, which is of European, Asian, and African origins. Dark blue or purple is the predominant color of this species' flowers.

Violets prefer a rich, moist, but well-drained soil high in organic content and slightly acid. Partially shaded locations are preferred, but full sun and full shade can also produce good results. Their natural season of bloom is late winter and early spring. Although evergreen, garden violets become semidormant during our long, hot summers. They can, however, endure considerable drought and heat stress, usually resuming lush, healthy growth with the onset of cooler, moister fall and winter conditions.

The landscape uses of violets include borders and groundcovers. Large container shrubs can be enhanced by planting a mass of violets around their bases, for the violets provide attractive foliage, fragrance, and color in winter and early spring, seasons when few other plants are at their peak. The rounded foliage is quite attractive even when the plants are not in bloom. Spider mites are an occasional problem, but may be controlled with insecticidal soaps or chemicals labeled for such use.

Propagation is usually by division of mature clumps during early to midfall. Seeds can also be used to produce new plants, but require considerable attention during the early stages. Borders and masses of garden violets may still be found in many old Southern

Johnny-jump-up (*Viola tricolor*) (*William C. Welch*)

gardens. They can be long-lived and relatively low maintenance perennials. Heirloom hybrids include 'Royal Elk', with long-stemmed dark purple flowers; 'Royal Robe', a dark purple-flowered cultivar that is a garden favorite in the South; and 'Charm', which is a white cultivar.

Violets naturalize well in wooded gardens, and the native species are especially suitable for this use. These include *V. pedata*, the bird-foot violet; *V. primulifolia*, the primrose-leaf violet; *V. affinis*, the Brainard violet; and *V. Walteri*.

One of my favorite violets is the species *V. tricolor*. Known in the nursery trade as violas, these plants are available as seed in a range of forms with flowers of various colors. They perform well as cool season annuals, but the old form, the one known as Johnny-jump-ups, is the only viola to reseed each year in my garden. Its flower is purple and yellow, measuring about one-half to three-quarters of an inch across.

Like miniature pansies, Johnny-jump-ups can cover the ground with their neat foliage and small, fragrant blossoms. Since this plant is very cold tolerant, its bloom often begins in December or January and continues until late May or early June. It is not uncommon for Johnny-jump-ups to move into lawn or other areas adjacent to where they were originally planted. They prefer full sun or partially shaded locations. A good way to introduce Johnny-jump-ups into your garden is to purchase started plants the first year. If conditions are right, they will reseed each year thereafter.

In *A Southern Garden*, Elizabeth Lawrence says of *V. tricolor*: "They will tolerate considerable shade and the meanest conditions. The prune purple of the flowers is the perfect color contrast with spring yellows, and dark, velvet petals are effective with white."
—WCW

Vitex agnus–castus
Chaste Tree, Hemp Tree, Sage Tree, Indian Spice
Family: Verbenaceae (Vervain or Verbena)
Zones: 6–9
This plant thrives so well in Texas and the South that many regard it as a

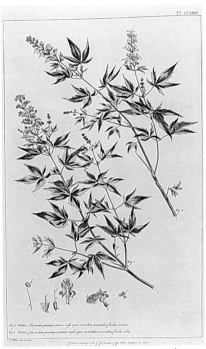

Chaste tree (*Vitex agnus-castus*) (*Atlanta History Center*)

native of that region. In fact, the chaste tree originated in China and India, though it is now naturalized widely in the southern United States. Peter Henderson, writing in 1890, stated that *Vitex* has been in cultivation since 1670.

Preferring sunny sites, it adapts well to a variety of soils, thriving in just about any as long as it is reasonably well-drained. The chaste tree is exceptionally tolerant of drought, which makes it one of the best large shrubs (ten to twenty feet) or small trees for hot, dry sites.

Vitex foliage is palmate, having five to seven aromatic leaflets. The common name "hemp tree" refers to the resemblance of chaste tree leaves to those of marijuana. Steve Bender, co-author of *Passalong Plants*, speculates concerning the "chaste tree" name: "Perhaps the tree was often planted on the grounds of monasteries. This makes sense, because a group of men living celibate lives need all the chastity they can muster." Actually, the chaste tree name originated centuries ago in Europe where the ancient Greeks believed that its aromatic flowers reduced the passions of lust.

The aromatic blossoms of the chaste tree emerge from May to September, and are borne in terminal spikes that range from four to twelve inches long. Flower color ranges from purple to lavender, off-white and pale pink. The fruit ripens in fall and is brown or black and 1/8 to 1/6 inch long. Beekeepers like to plant chaste trees because the flowers are very attractive to their favorite insects. Insect and disease problems are few.

To keep chaste tree neat and attractive, remove all dead wood on a regular basis and prune back in winter-time, cutting back the previous year's growth by several feet. I prefer removing some of the lower branches to expose several feet of trunks near the base. Propagation is from cuttings in summer or winter. Lower branches can easily be ground layered and seed collected in fall will usually germinate the next spring.
—WCW

Chaste tree (*Vitex agnus-castus*) (*William C. Welch*)

Muscadines (*Vitis rotundifolia*) (**William C. Welch**)

Vitis spp.
Muscadines and Grapes
Family: Vitaceae (Grape)
Zones: 6–9

As the Bible and countless other ancient texts bear witness, grapes are among the plants longest cultivated by man. Certainly, they have always been staples in the South. Native Americans were known to preserve wild muscadines as dried fruit (as Bartram noted in 1791), while wine, raisins, and jellies, as well as the fresh fruit of cultivated vines have been important food sources to Southerners since colonial times. Likewise, grape vines and the arbors that support them have also been important components of Southern gardens from early times. This group of plants is also a must for gardeners with an interest in wildlife, since grapevines of cultivated or wild varieties are also important as a food source for numerous species of birds and animals.

Many grapes are native to the South, and it is these that were most important for food and landscape use in our region, since the cultivated grapes of Europe tend to be short lived here. *Vitis rotundifolia*, better known as muscadines or scuppernongs, is by far the most important species in the South. Indigenous populations may be found throughout the southeastern United States, except in mountainous areas. They are most abundant in coastal plains of the Atlantic Ocean and the Gulf of Mexico. Muscadines tend to be insect- and disease-resistant and are easily grown, preferring acid, well-drained soils.

Captain John Hawkins reported in

1565 that Spanish settlements in Florida were making large quantities of muscadine wine (Hedrick, 1908). In fact, wine-making with muscadines continued to be a viable industry in the South until prohibition. The last twenty or so years have seen an increase in muscadine plantings, but today they are grown mostly for juice and jellies.

Though the early harvests were no doubt taken from wild vines, Southern gardeners wasted no time in setting to the task of improving on the native species. Indeed, the very first grape cultivar developed in North America was one selected by Isaac Alexander of Tyrrel County, North Carolina sometime around 1760. Originally this grape was known as "The Big White Grape" or "Hickman's Grape," but it was later was called 'Scuppernong' for the area in which it was found. The naming probably occurred in 1810 and is credited to Dr. Calvin Jones, a noted naturalist and editor of *The Star*, a

Raleigh newspaper. Like many common names, however, this one can be misleading, because over the years all bronze-colored muscadines have come to be known generically as 'Scuppernongs'.

There are also many dark-colored muscadines, sometimes known as bullis, bullace, bullet grapes, or bull grapes. Bartram wrote in 1802 (Hedrick, 1908) that the name "Bull Grape" was an abbreviation of "Bullet Grape," and that it was so-called because the fruit is the size of a musket ball. Other lore suggests that "bull" refers to comparisons of the berries with cow or pig eyes.

Native muscadines and some of the improved cultivars are functionally dioecious (male and female flowers on separate plants), with male vines making up about three-fourth of the populations. This means that a majority of any random planting will be naturally fruitless. However, female vines and self-pollinating types are available from nurseries specializing in muscadines, and the gardener can ensure better harvests simply by ordering from these sources.

Propagation of improved cultivars is done through cuttings or layering. Muscadine grapes do not root easily, though, which accounts for the fact that the relatively primitive technique of ground layering remains a popular method for starting new plants. Muscadines were first transplanted into the garden because of their fruit, but it wasn't long before gardeners came to appreciate the beauty of the vines and use them as landscaping material. As grape arbors became a part of eigh-

Scuppernongs (**John Lipe**)

Mustang grapes (*Vitis candicans*) (William C. Welch)

teenth- and nineteenth-century Southern landscapes, muscadines, with their attractive foliage and ease of culture, became popular for clothing them. Muscadine vines also contribute to the autumn display, for their leaves turn bright yellow just before dropping off in the fall. An additional, and very welcome, virtue of muscadines is their longevity; their vines may live for generations, and individual specimens are a part of the gardening heritage of many Southern families.

In Texas, muscadines are native to the eastern part of the state and are the important grape for that region, but are gradually replaced by other species to the west, as conditions become drier and more alkaline. Most important among these western grapes is *Vitis candicans*, better known as mustang grape. Mustangs are naturally abundant from central Texas westward, and although the fruit is highly acid, are a logical choice within this range for shading arbors, wine and jelly making. Thomas Affleck experimented with making wine from *V. candicans* in the 1850s. This grape is still a popular plant among Texans.

The most important date in Southern viticulture is April 1876: that is when T.V. Munson arrived in Denison, Texas, and settled on a rough piece of timbered land on the bluffs of the Red River. Munson had trained as a chemist at Kentucky State Agricultural College and while doing so had been fascinated by the vineyards of one of his professors, Dr. Robert Peter. Located near Lexington, this planting included nearly all the cultivars of American

grapes then being grown.

Thus, Munson was delighted to discover upon settling in Denison that the ravines and uplands of his Texan home abounded in numerous vines of "Mustang" (*V. candicans*), the "Sour Winter Grape" or "Frost Grape" (*V. cordifolia*), "Post Oak Grape" (*V. lincecumii*), and "Sweet Winter Grape" (*V. cinera*). The area was also the western limit of the "Southern Muscadine" (*V. rotundifolia*). All together, Munson found there at least six or eight good native species, several of which he had never before seen. In his own words, "I had found my grape paradise!"

Munson drew on the experiences of Gilbert Onderdonk of Victoria County, a veteran experimenter with and writer on grapes, and Onderdonk's experiences confirmed his own observation that the traditional grapes of vineyard and table, cultivars of the European species *V. vinifera* and of the northern American native, *V. labrusca*, were prone to disease

in Texas and tended to be short-lived. Thus, he was excited to discover the native Texan species that were perfectly suited to the soils and climate of the region.

Munson began a breeding program, crossing native species with valuable but less hardy exotic grapes. His work first attracted national attention in 1885 when he presented a display of herbarium specimens and live vines grown in pots in the Horticultural Hall of the Cotton Centennial Exposition at New Orleans. He presented a written report on this exhibit to the American Horticultural Society in February of the same year and included a new botanical classification of grape species in that document.

Subsequently, Munson published many further articles on hybridization and varieties of grapes in journals across the United States and France. The exhibit of American and Asiatic grape species he displayed at the Columbian exhibition in 1893 was hailed as the most complete botanical display of the grape genus ever made. In this Munson included not only live plants of every species but also specimens of roots, sections of young and mature vines, pressed leaves in all stages of development, flowers, and clusters of ripe fruit, even life-size photographs—and all were identified according to Munson's own system of nomenclature.

As generous as he was learned, Munson distributed seeds and sets of live plants of American grape species without charge to researchers and grape growers throughout the world. These

'Champanel' (William C. Welch)

'Black Spanish'
(*John Lipe*)

mysterious origin that has been grown for at least two hundred years. The Qualia family's Val Verde Winery of Del Rio, Texas, the oldest continuously operated winery and vineyard in the state, bases its production on the 'Black Spanish' grape, from which they have been producing wines since 1883.

The fruit of this cultivar is small, dark in color, and sweet when ripe. Since about 1900, when Pierce's Disease eliminated all other *V. labrusca* and *V. vinifera* grapes from the South, 'Black Spanish' (together with 'Herbemont') has become the predominant bunch grape for wine-making throughout our region. In particular, 'Black Spanish' is the premium grape for production of port wines because of its unusual acidic strength.

With our abundance of native grapes, and thanks to the inspirational work of T.V. Munson, Southerners can easily grow grapes to shade our arbors and fill our vineyards. Muscadines, 'Champanel', 'Black Spanish' and other heirloom varieties are available for today's gardeners. With minimum care they can produce handsome and prolific vines. Proper pruning is essential for vineyard plantings and helpful for arbors. When planting dormant, bareroot, or container-grown grapes cut the stems back to one or two buds. Pruning of established vines is necessary to prevent overcropping and shading of the fruiting buds. —WCW

activities helped materially in saving the vineyards of France, which in the late nineteenth century were falling prey to a small root insect, the phylloxera, which had been accidentally imported from America. Acting on the belief that native American grapes must be resistant to this native pest, Munson collected fifteen wagons of dormant stem cuttings and shipped them to southern France via three boats. When Munson's gifts were used as rootstocks, and the French wine grapes grafted onto them, they did indeed produce resistant plants. This discovery saved the French wine industry, and the hundreds of villages that depended on it for their economic survival.

By the turn of the century, the T.V. Munson and Son Nursery of Denison, Texas had become the largest fruit nursery in Texas and was one of the largest in the nation. Through it, Munson introduced a series of more than 300 grape cultivars well adapted to growing conditions in the South and Southwestern United States. To accomplish this, Munson traveled over 75,000 miles in forty states, mostly by horse, to collect breeding material and pollinated by hand thousands of grapes in his ten vineyards in Denison. Munson's breeding program focused on natural disease-resistance and adaptation to climate, goals which placed him far ahead of his time and make his grapes of enduring value, even today.

The most famous of Munson's creations is probably 'Champanel', which he released as a Champini-Lambrusca hybrid in 1893. Munson recommend 'Champanel' for its ability

to thrive even in the black, waxy clay soils of the South. In fact, it has proven an unusually vigorous, productive, and useful grape. Long life, great vigor and resistance to Pierce's Disease make them particularly useful for arbors and other landscape uses. 'Champanel' is also used as a rootstock for other cultivars because it has demonstrated a resistance to cotton root rot.

Munson recognized the landscape value of grapes and extolled their use in the home garden. In his book *Foundations of American Grape Culture* (self-published in 1909), he included a chapter titled "The Grapevine for Home Adornment, Shade, Fruit and Health." In this he advised:

> The humblest cottager and the millionaire may engage with pleasure and success in producing handsome clusters, luscious berries, and comforting shade. The plebian is the more likely to succeed best and enjoy the fruits most, for he works with his head and hands in partnership, while the aristocrat depends on his gardener, and has such a multiplicity of other cares that he has few moments to spend in his "pergola" that has cost hundreds of dollars where the simple arbor of the toiler has cost cents.

At least one other grape will be mentioned here because of its long and successful cultivation as a source for wine, juice, and jellies in Texas and other Southern areas. 'Black Spanish' (also known as 'Lenoir') is a cultivar of

Weigela florida
Weigela
Family: Caprifoliaceae (Honeysuckle)
Zones: 5–8

The debt that Southern gardeners owe to the Scottish plant collector Robert Fortune is immense. He had an unexcelled eye for recognizing valuable ornamental plants, and during his journeys to the Orient in the mid-nineteenth century collected many of the plants that are now our most valued garden shrubs, trees, and flowers. Interestingly, because he collected extensively in the warmer regions of China, many of his introductions did not perform well in the gardens of his British employers, but they proved admirably adapted to the American South.

Weigela, which Fortune found in a Shanghai nursery in 1844, proved a success both in British gardens and our own. By 1870, the great British garden pundit William Robinson was writing of the hybrid weigelas that were then appearing on the market, and some of these are still available. These include 'Dame Blanche', 'Candida', and 'Mont Blanc', all of which are white, 'Eva Rathke' (crimson) and 'Conquerant' (deep rose).

In 1890, Peter Henderson (also Scottish by birth, but American by choice) wrote of weigelas, "It is safe to say there is no shrub more deservedly popular, or one that has been more rapidly disseminated. All the species are ornamental, and should be found in every collection."

The weigela makes a spreading shrub with long branches that may eventually arch to the ground to form a mass six to eight feet across. The foliage is rather nondescript, with elliptic, ovate-oblong leaves that are two to four inches long arranged in an opposite manner on gray-brown stems. The flowers are borne in clusters and are funnel-shaped, one to one and one fourth inches long, with rounded, spreading lobes. They appear in April through most of the South, but may recur occasionally at any time during the growing season. The most common flower color is a rosy pink on the outside and a paler pink on the interior.

Weigelas are often used in shrub borders and occasionally as hedges or specimens. They are easily grown, but grow and flower better in zone 8 and north. Propagation is from cuttings

American wisteria (*Wisteria frutescens*) (*Greg Grant*)

taken in winter or summer. Pruning should be done soon after the spring flowering season so that the new flowering stems have plenty of time to mature and set buds before the next spring.　　　　—WCW

Wisteria sinensis
Chinese Wisteria, Wisteria, Wistaria
Family: Fabaceae (Pea)
Zones: 5–10

There's no prettier sight in the spring than wisteria running wild among the pines. Since childhood I've always had a "running" love affair with wisteria. First, I'm partial to purple, and second, I love flowers that bloom before the foliage comes out. It allows the flowers to be the true center of attention.

The genus was named by Thomas Nuttall in memory of Dr. Caspar Wistar, M.D. of the University of Pennsylvania. Although the genus was spelled *Wisteria* by Nuttall, nurserymen spelled it *Wistaria* for many years. The species first introduced to Europe (1724) and the

nameplant of the genus was *Wisteria frutescens*, our own American wisteria, which is native from Texas to Virginia and Florida. Thomas Walter in South Carolina, John Bartram in Pennsylvania, and Lady Skipwith in Virginia all grew it in their colonial gardens. *W. macrostachya* is also an American native growing from Illinois to Arkansas. Both of these are fairly rare in cultivation, although Lone Star Growers in San Antonio produces *W. frutescens* as Texas wisteria.

According to *The Hillier Manual of Trees and Shrubs*, Chinese wisteria was introduced to Europe in 1816 from a garden in Canton. And Julia Morten writes in *America's Garden Heritage* that it reached America via England "after 1825." In *The Flower Garden* (1851), Joseph Breck refers to Chinese wisteria as "one of the most magnificent climbing shrubby plants in cultivation," and mentions that "a new variety, with white flowers, was brought to England from China, by Mr. Fortune." In addition to the purple and the white, there is also a double variety.

An 1860 catalogue from Montgomery Nurseries (Wilson's Nursery) of Montgomery, Alabama offered Chinese glycene (Chinese wisteria). The 1881–82 Langdon Nurseries (near Mobile) catalogue listed both the purple and the white varieties while the 1906–07 Fruitlands Nurseries (Augusta) catalogue listed all three varieties along with *W. frutescens magnifica*.

There is a dependable blooming form in San Antonio referred to as the "Avery Island wisteria" that scatters small dark purple blooms all through the

Weigela (*Weigela florida*) (*Dan Lineberger*)

Chinese wisteria (*Wisteria sinensis*) (*Greg Grant*)

Chinese wisteria (*Wisteria sinensis*) at the San Antonio Botanical Center. (*Greg Grant*)

summer in addition to the big spring display. Avery Island, Louisiana, is the location of E.A. McIlhenny's famous Jungle Gardens, where there is a large wisteria arbor. Although McIlhenny was a remarkable plantsman, today he is recognized only for his famous pepper sauce. The "Avery Island wisteria" is common all over East Texas—my Emanis grandparents had one in their yard.

In addition to the Chinese wisteria cultivated all over the South, the Japanese wisteria (*W. floribunda*) is also

Japanese wisteria (*Wisteria floribunda*) standard (*William C. Welch*)

grown. It has more leaflets and longer bloom racemes. The famous plant explorer, Ernest "Chinese" Wilson, claimed to have seen some in Japan with blooms over five feet long! Wonder if he did any fishing while he was there? The Japanese wisteria has forms with purple, white, pink, double, and longer flowers. Elizabeth Lawrence, in *Through the Garden Gate*, writes: "I was interested to find that the Japanese wisteria was introduced into this country in 1862, about ten years before it was known in Europe, and that it came to the nursery of Samuel Parsons, who wrote *Parsons on the Rose*." *The Hillier Manual of Trees and Shrubs* states that it was introduced to Europe by Philip von Siebold in 1830. Sounded good, didn't it, Elizabeth?

Louisiana Nursery in Opelousas, Louisiana lists a great selection of wisterias, including 'Caroline'; *W. floribunda* and the cultivars 'Alba', 'Macrobotrys', 'Rosea', 'Royal Purple', and 'Violacea Plena'; *W. frutescens* and the white cultivar 'Nivea'; *W. macrostachya* and the cultivars 'Abbeville Blue' and 'Pondside Blue'; the *W. sinensis* cultivars 'Alba', 'Blue', 'Larry's White', and 'Purpurea'; and *W. venusta*, the silky wisteria from Japan.

Wisteria is very easy to grow (it's a relative of kudzu, you know) in almost any kind of soil. It is, however, susceptible to iron chlorosis in alkaline soils. Wisterias need a strong support to be grown as a vine. They eat wooden trellises for snacks. They can also be

pruned as beautiful small trees (my favorite) with at least an annual, preferably more, pruning to remove suckers and runners. A potential (and age-old) problem is with wisterias that don't bloom. Propagating by grafting or cuttings from flowering growth instead of runners avoids this.

When I was a little boy, my Grandmother Ruth had a huge wisteria in her swept yard full of plants that we all called "the bear tree." We built steps up the large trunk so we could climb up into the trees. She told me that my dad and uncle brought her a bouquet of flowers from their grandmother which she had rooted in the ground. It's gone now. I miss my bear tree.   —GG

Zinnia elegans
Common Zinnia, Old–Maids
Family: Asteraceae (Sunflower)
Zones: Warm season annual

I consider zinnias to be the easiest, showiest, and best cut flowers that can be homegrown in Southern gardens. They haven't always been so showy, though. The original wild zinnias from Mexico were red and had just a single circle of petals with a protruding cone in the middle.

According to Peggy Newcomb's *Popular Annuals of Eastern North America 1865–1914* (1985), the zinnia was introduced in 1796; the first double forms appeared in the mid-1800s. Bernard M'Mahon mentioned sowing zinnia seeds in *The American Gardener's Calendar*. In *The Flower Garden* (1851),

Field of zinnias (*Zinnias elegans*) at the Henry Verstuyft farm in Von Ormy, Texas. (*Greg Grant*)

Joseph Breck included *Zinnia elegans*, remarking that the "colors are white, pale to dark yellow, orange to scarlet; shades from rose to crimson, from crimson to light purple, lilac, &c." He went on to say, "The flowers are handsome when it first commences the process of blooming; the central part of it, which contains the florets, as they begin to form seed, assume a conic shape, and a brown husky appearance, which gives a coarse, unsightly look."

In the *American Flower-Garden Directory* (1860), Robert Buist included notes on the varieties *coccinea* (scarlet), *alba* (white), and *pauciflora* (yellow).

Of course, today zinnias come in a multitude of colors, sizes, and flower shapes. Some cultivars have been bred for cut flowers while others were developed as summer bedding plants. All are easily grown from seed during warm weather.

Besides *Z. elegans*, several other species of zinnias are cultivated as well.

Zinnia angustifolia (*Z. linearis*), the narrow-leaved zinnia from Mexico, is commercially available today in both white- and orange-flowered forms. It is a low-growing annual that bears multitudes of small daisylike flowers. It is an excellent summertime bedding plant. *Zinnia haageana*, the Mexican zinnia, is commercially available as well. It is known for its red and yellow bicolored flowers. I have seen the cultivars 'Old Mexico' and 'Persian Carpet' listed in various catalogues.

Whether you're an old maid or not, everybody should have some zinnias to cut in the vegetable garden. Besides, they're prettier than okra and peas.
—GG

Zizyphus jujuba
Chinese Date, Jujubes
Family: Rhamnaceae (Buckthorn)
Zones: 6–9
Chinese dates are among the most persistent and long-lived imported trees

in the South. Some sources indicate they were introduced from Europe by Robert Chisolm in 1837 and first planted in Beaufort, North Carolina. However, they have also been claimed as part of the planting at early Spanish missions in California and so may have been brought to America at an even earlier date.

The Chinese date may be, as its common name suggests, a native of China, but some botanists have proposed Syria as the species' original homeland. What is certain is that they are widely distributed now through the warmer parts of Europe, south Asia, Africa, and Australia. The Chinese have cultivated this plant for hundreds of years, and have developed as many as 400 different cultivars. The Chinese have a great fondness for the fruit, which they sometimes process with honey and sugar and sell as a dessert confection. Most of the Chinese cultivars are not commercially available in the United States, but Roger Meyer of the California Rare Fruit Growers is attempting to identify sources for some of the best jujubes.

Jujubes can reach a height of fifty feet, but are often maintained as much smaller plants through pruning and training. The stems may be thorny and the foliage is shiny, deciduous, and dark green; the flowers are small and inconspicuous, and appear in the axils of the leaves. The fruit ranges from half an inch to two inches long and changes from green to reddish brown as it matures in late summer and early fall.

These fruits were at one time believed to have medicinal properties,

Far left: Zinnias (*Zinnia elegans*) and marigolds (*Tagetes erecta*). (*William C. Welch*)
Left: Bed of yellow and white, narrow-leafed zinnias (*Zinnia angustifolia*). (*Greg Grant*)

Jujube (*Zizyphus jujuba*)
(**William C. Welch**)

and were turned into pastes, tablets, and syrups that were supposed to have demulcent (soothing to mucous membranes) characteristics. Research on the nutritional and culinary uses of jujube fruit was done in the Food Science section of Texas A&M's Horticultural Sciences Department in the 1940s. Dr. Homer Blackhurst, Emeritus Professor of Horticulture, remembers that the vitamin C content of the fruit was found to be very high. He also recalls experiments where the seeds were removed and the fruit cooked with water, sugar, and seasonings. The resulting product was similar in appearance and flavor to apple butter, and in taste tests of the two, the jujube butter was selected as superior.

I have been able to locate numerous recipes for preparing the fruit that appear to be interesting. Following is one recipe taken from USDA publication B-1215, "Methods of Utilizing the Chinese Jujube."

Jujube Butter

6 pints jujube pulp	½ teaspoonful cloves
5 pints sugar	1 lemon
2 teaspoonfuls cinnamon	¼ pint vinegar
1 teaspoon nutmeg	

The fruit should be boiled until tender in sufficient water to cover it. It should then be rubbed through a sieve or colander to remove the skin and seeds. Cook slowly until thick, put in jars, and seal while hot.   —WCW

Appendix

Survey of Plant Listings in Nineteen Southern Nursery Catalogues

These are ranked in order by the number of catalogues they're listed in. Catalogues were from nurseries in Texas (11), Alabama (2), Florida (2), Louisiana (1), Arkansas (1), Mississippi (1), and Georgia (1).

1. Althaea (16)
2. Arborvitae (15)
   Honeysuckles (15)
   Roses (15)
3. Crape Myrtle (14)
   Privets (14)
4. Chinaberry (13)
   Magnolias (13)
5. Gardenias (12)
   Pomegranate (12)
6. Jasmines (11)
   Spiraeas (11)
.7. Red Cedar (10)
8. Desert Willow (9)
   Wisterias (9)

9. Catalpa (8)
   Cherry Laurel (8)
   Euonymous (8)
   Flowering Quinces (8)
   Maples (8)
   Mock Orange (8)
   Ornamental Grasses (8)
10. Boxwood (7)
   Deutzia (7)
   Lilac (7)
   Oleander (7)
   Poplars (7)
11. Camellias (6)
   Cannas (6)
   Carolina Jessamine (6)
   Flowering Almond (6)
   Hydrangeas (6)
   Oaks (6)
   Pines (6)
   Weeping Willow (6)
12. Amaryllis (5)
   Deodar Cedar (5)
   Flowering Peach (5)
   Hackberry (5)
   Italian Cypress (5)
   Pittosporum (5)
   Sweet Olives (5)

Sycamore (5)
Tuberose (5)
Vinca (5)
Yuccas (5)
13. Banana Shrub (4)
   Clerodendron (4)
   Ivy (4)
   Myrtle (4)
   Paulownia (4)
   Sweet Bay (4)
   Trumpet Creepers (4)
   Tulip Tree (4)
   Violet (4)
   Wegelia (4)
14. Azaleas (3)
   Buddleias (3)
   Clematis (3)
   Gladiolus (3)
   Hibiscus (3)
   Hollies (3)
   Hymenocallis (3)
   Locust (3)
   Palms (3)
   Purple Plum (3)
   Varnish Tree (3)
   Viburnums (3)
   Vitex (3)

The Nineteen Nursery Catalogues Surveyed

Alabama: Langdon Nurseries (D.W. Langdon, 1873–1874, near Mobile), Montgomery Nurseries (Wilson's Nursery, 1860, Montgomery). **Arkansas:** Frank Vestal (1896, Little Rock). **Florida:** "The Lily Nursery" (Arnold Puetz, 1881, Jacksonville) Royal Palms Nurseries (Reasoner Brothers, 1904, Oneco). **Georgia:** Fruitlands Nurseries (P.J. Berkmans, 1906–1907; Augusta). **Louisiana:** Hill Side Nursery (J.L. Normand, 1888, Marksville). **Mississippi:** The Southern Nurseries (Thomas Affleck, 1851–1852, Washington). **Texas:** Alvin Fruit and Nursery Co. (R.B. Halley, 1904, Algoa), Arcadia Garden (Anna B. Nickels, around 1900, Laredo), The Austin Nursery (F.T. Ramsey, 1907, Austin), Denison Nurseries (T.V. Munson, 1885–1886, Denison), Mission Valley Nurseries (G. Onderdonk, 1898–1899, Nursery), Pearfield Nursery (J.F. Leyendecker, 1891, Frelsburg), Pilot Point Nurseries (J.W. Austin, 1895–1896, Pilot Point), Rosedale Nurseries (William Watson, 1899, Brenham), Val Verde Nurseries (D.G. Gregory, 1886, Alleyton), W.A. Yates Nursery (W.A. Yates, 1906–1907, Brenham) Waldheim Nursery (G.A. Shattenberg, 1895–1896, Boerne).

* Date listed is catalogue date.

Sources of Southern Heirloom Plants*

Many Southern heirloom plants are still available in the retail nursery trade. Recently, several nurseries have even begun to specialize in old-fashioned plants. If your local nursery can't help you, consider these specialty mail-order sources.

Antique Rose Emporium
Route 5 Box 143
Brenham, Texas 77833
800-441-0002
Beautiful, informative catalogue $5.
Hundreds of varieties of antique roses for the South. Both mail order and retail. Retail facility is beautiful in the spring with restored buildings, display gardens, and wildflowers in surrounding countryside. Retail facility also outside of Atlanta, near Dahlonega. Bill used to be part owner and I used to work there so it has to be good!

Camellia Forest Nursery
125 Carolina Forest Road
Chapel Hill, North Carolina 27516
919-967-5529
Informative catalogue.
Incredible mail order source of camellia species and cultivars, Asian plants, and other hard to find items including magnolias, sweet olives, banana shrub, Chinese quince, and citrus.

Canyon Creek Nursery
3527 Dry Creek Road
Oroville, California 95967
916-533-2166
Informative catalogue $2.
Mail order source of uncommon perennials, including nine cultivars of rosemary and thirty-five different violets and violas.

Carroll Gardens
444 East Main Street
P.O. Box 310
Westminster, Maryland 21158
800-638-6334, FAX: 410-857-4112
Extensive catalogue $3.
Good mail order source of perennials

* These addresses were viable at the time this book was written; the authors are not responsible for changes of address or discontinued firms.

and uncommon plants, including blackberry lilies, daylilies, rose mallows, iris, bouncing bet, rosemary, bay laurel, roses, trumpet creepers, wisterias, honeysuckles, azaleas, boxwood, flowering quinces, deutzias, pearlbush, hydrangeas, crape myrtles, magnolias, mock oranges, spireas, vitex, and weigela.

Daffodil Mart
Route 3 Box 794
Gloucester, Virginia 23061
804-693-3966
Catalogue $1.
Large mail order selection of daffodils and narcissus.

Daisy Fields
12635 SW Brighton lane
Hillsboro, Oregon 97123-9051
503-628-0315
Nice catalogue $1.
Mail order source for "old-fashioned perennials and cottage garden plants."

Daylily Discounters
One Daylily Plaza
Aluchua, Florida 32615
904-462-1539, FAX: 904-462-5111,
800-329-5459 (orders)
Extensive catalogue $2.
Good mail order source of daylilies, including 'Kwanso' and 'Hyperion'.

The Flower and Herb Exchange
3076 North Winn Road
Decorah, Iowa 52101
Annual membership and listing $7.
A unique "seed savers" exchange group with over 250 members offering more than 2,000 rare flowers and herbs that are seldom found in modern catalogues.

Flowerplace Plant Farm
P.O. Box 4865
Meridian, Mississippi 30304
800-482-5686
Informative catalogue $3.
Good mail order and retail source of southeastern perennials and natives, including blackberry lily, *Crinum americanum*, honeysuckle, trumpet creeper, *Gladiolus byzantinus*, rosemary, rose mallow, bigleaf magnolia, mock orange, bouncing bet, and *Zinnia angustifolia*.

Forest Farm
990 Tetherow Road
Williams, Oregon 97544-9599
503-846-7269
Excellent catalogue $3.
Large mail order selection of hard-to-find trees and shrubs, including boxwood, trumpet creeper, catalpas, deutzias, pearlbush, Carolina jessamines, hydrangeas, jasmines, red cedar, flowering quinces, spireas, althaeas, crape myrtles, magnolias, chinaberry, mock oranges, flowering almond, common quince, Chinese quince, live oak, black locust, roses, rosemary, bald cypress, vitex, weigelas, wisterias, iris, violets, mimosa, and honeysuckles.

Fox Hollow Herb and Heirloom Seed Company
P.O. Box 148
McGrann, Pennsylvania 16236
Informative catalogue $1.
Good source of heirloom vegetable, herb, and flower seed, including rosemary and cockscomb.

The Fragrant Path
P.O. Box 328
Fort Calhoun, Nebraska 68023
Informative catalogue $2.
Excellent mail order source for fragrant and heirloom flower seed, including four-o'clocks (including separate colors), petunia, bouncing bet, sweet violet, cockscomb, bachelor button, zinnia, blackberry lily, hibiscus, rosemary, iris, mimosa, boxwood, roses, vitex, jujube, sweet bay, myrtle, pomegranate, trumpet creeper, and Chinese wisterias.

Glasshouse Works
Church Street
P.O. Box 97
Stewart, Ohio 45778-0097
614-662-2142
Extensive catalogue $2.
Long list of rare and hard-to-find mail order plants, mostly tropical and/or victorian, including crinums, amaryllis, jasmines, oleander, pomegranates, boxwoods, hydrangeas, variegated privet, and nandinas. May take a while to receive your order.

Green Hill Nursery, Inc.
5027 Highway 147
Waverly, Alabama 36879
205-864-7500, FAX: 205-864-9400
Free catalogue (wholesale only).
Excellent **wholesale** source of old-fashioned shrubs, including deutzia, pearlbush, althaeas, hydrangeas, crape myrtles, mock orange, honeysuckle, pomegranates, flowering almond, roses, spiraeas, vitex, and weigelas.

Heritage Rose Gardens
16831 Mitchell Creek Drive
Fort Bragg, California 95437
707-964-3748
Catalogue with dates of introduction $1.50.
Good mail order source of antique roses.

Heronswood Nursery
7530 288th Street NE
Kingston, Washington 98346
206-297-4172
Extensive catalogue $3.
Excellent mail order source for rare and hard-to-find plants, including hydrangeas, honeysuckles, privet, sweet olives, mock oranges, rhododendrons, roses, iris, and violets.

Heirloom Old Garden Roses
24062 NE Riverside Drive
St. Paul, Oregon 97137
503-538-1576
Extensive catalogue with color pictures $5.
Very interesting source for all kinds of hard-to-find own-root roses, including many old-fashioned varieties.

Ison's Nursery and Vineyard
Route 1, Box 191
Brooks, Georgia 30205
404-599-6970
Free informative catalogue.
Most complete mail order source of muscadine varieties on earth!

Kelly's Plant World
10266 East Princeton
Sanger, California 93657
209-292-3503
Descriptive list $1.
Fabulous mail order selection of rare and unusual plants for the connoisseur, including crinums, amaryllis, hymenocallis, tuberose, and lycoris (twenty-plus cultivars available!).

Landis Valley Museum
Heirloom Seed Project
2451 Kissel Hill Road
Lancaster, Pennsylvania 17601
717-569-0401
Informative catalogue with approximate dates of introduction $2.50.
Excellent source of limited quantities of Pennsylvania German heirloom vegetable, herb, and flower seed, including cockscomb.

Logee's Greenhouses
141 North Street
Danielson, Connecticut 06239
203-774-8038, FAX: 203-774-9932
Extensive catalogue $3.
Excellent mail order source for mostly showy tropical and semitropical plants, including camellias, gardenias, Carolina jessamine, roses, citrus, boxwood, bay laurel, myrtles, rosemary, violets, oleander, jasmines, and pomegranates.

Louisiana Nursery
Route 7 Box 43
Opelousas, Louisiana 70570
318-948-3696, FAX: 318-942-6404
Magnolia and Other Garden Aristocrats catalogue $6 (deducted from first order). Daylilies and Louisiana Iris catalogue $4 (deducted from first order). Fruiting Trees, Shrubs and Vines catalogue $3. Crinum and Rare Bulb catalogue $3 (deducted form first order). Bamboo and Ornamental Grass catalogue $3.
Mail order and retail. Unequaled source for hard-to-find Southern plants, including amaryllis, boxwood, bay laurel, camellias, flowering quinces, fruiting quinces, citrus, crinums, lycoris, tuberose, hymenocallis, persimmons, figs, grapes, jujubes, gardenias, Carolina jessamines, Confederate roses, hydrangeas, iris, jasmine, crape myrtles, mimosa, privet, althaeas, honeysuckles, magnolias (over 500 varieties!), banana shrubs, sweet olives, mock oranges, oleanders, daylilies, cherry laurel, flowering almond, pomegranates, azaleas, roses, wisterias, and spireas.

Lowe's Own-Root Roses
6 Sheffield Road
Nashua, New Hampshire 03062
603-888-2214
Catalogue with dates of introduction $2.
Good mail order source of antique roses.

McClure and Zimmerman
108 West Winnebago
P.O. Box 368
Friesland, Wisconsin 53935
414-326-4220
Free extensive catalogue.
Extensive mail order listing of rare and hard-to-find bulbs, including daffodils, jonquils, narcissus, spider lilies, snowflakes, byzantine gladiolus, Roman hyacinths, and amaryllis.

Mellinger's
2310 West South Range Road
North Lima, Ohio 44452-9731
216-549-9861, FAX: 216-549-3716,
800-321-7444 (orders)
Free extensive catalogue.
Extensive mail order listing of hard-to-find trees and shrubs including flowering quinces, honeysuckles, trumpet vine, hydrangeas, rosemary, magnolias, mimosa, flowering almond, althaeas, persimmons, and mock oranges.

Old House Gardens
536 Third Street
Ann Arbor, Michigan 48103
313-995-1486
Informative catalogue with dates of introduction $1.
Excellent mail order source of heirloom bulbs for the North and South, including jonquils, daffodils, narcissus, authentic Roman hyacinths, and authentic byzantine gladiolus. Many bulbs offered actually produced in the South instead of Holland. Great move!

Old Sturbridge Village
One Old Sturbridge Village Road
Sturbridge, Massachusetts 01566
508-347-3362 Ext. 270,
FAX: 508-347-5375
Catalogue $1.
Good mail order source of antique flower, herb, and vegetable seed, including bachelor's button, cockscomb, four-o'clock, Johnny-jump-up, and zinnia. Also offers period garden supplies and books.

Park Seed
Cokesbury Road
Greenwood, South Carolina
29647-0001
803-941-4480
Free catalogue.
Dependable mail order source of vegetable and flower seed, including cockscomb, bachelor's buttons, zinnias, Johnny-jump-ups, and four-o'clocks.

Perennial Pleasures Nursery
2 Brickhouse Road
East Harwick, Vermont 05836
802-472-5104 or 802-472-5512
Informative catalogue with plants grouped by century of introduction $2.
Good mail order source of antique annuals, perennials, and herbs, including blackberry lily, daylilies, iris, Johnny-jump-up, four-o'clock, peonies, rosemary, violets, and zinnia.

Pickering Nurseries
670 Kingston Road
Pickering, Ontario L1V 1A6, Canada
416-839-2111, FAX: 905-839-4807
Extensive catalogue with dates of introductions $3.
Excellent mail order source of antique roses.

Plantation Bulb Co.
Box 159
TyTy, Georgia 31795
912-388-9999
Extensive catalogue $1.
Fabulous mail order selection of hard-to-find Southern bulbs and plants, including crinums, amaryllis, sprekelia, hymenocallis, narcissus, lycoris, leucojum, iris, and *Hibiscus mutabilis.* Largest selections of crinums I'm aware of.

Roger and Shirley Meyer
16531 Mt. Shelly Circle
Fountain Valley, California 92708
714-839-0796
Free informative price list.
Most complete mail order source of jujube cultivars on the planet!

Roses of Yesterday and Today
802 Brown's Valley Road
Watsonville, California 95076
408-724-3537
Informative catalogue $2.
Established mail order source for a number of old-fashioned roses.

The Roseraie at Bayfields
P.O. Box R
Waldboro, Maine 04572-1919
Informative catalogue.
Good mail order source of primarily Old European roses.

Seeds Blum
Idaho City Stage
Boise, Idaho 83706
208-324-0858
Informative catalogue $3.
Good mail order source of heirloom vegetable and flower seed, including trumpet creeper, blackberry lily, cockscomb, zinnia, petunia, and Johnny-jump-up.

Select Seeds
180 Stickney Road
Union, Connecticut 06076-4617
203-684-9310
Informative catalogue with reference dates $3.
Good mail order source of antique flower seed, including violas, petunias, blackberry lily, and lemon lily, among many others.

Shepherd's Garden Seeds
30 Irene Street
Torrington, Connecticut 06790
203-482-3638, FAX: 203-482-0532
Informative catalogue.
Good mail order source for hard-to-find vegetable, herb, and flower seeds, including several cultivars of bachelor's buttons, feathered cockscomb, four-o'clocks, zinnia, and Johnny-jump-ups.

Sister's Bulb Farm
Route 2 Box 170
Gibsland, Louisiana
Wholesale or large quantities only.
Outstanding source of heirloom bulbs for the South, including daffodils, jonquils, narcissus, red spider lilies, snowflakes, and authentic byzantine gladiolus. Great for naturalizing! Originally Celia Jones' grandmother's bulb farm.

Southmeadow Fruit Gardens
P.O. Box SM
Lakeside, Michigan 49116
616-469-2865
Free price list. Extensive informative catalogue with pictures and historical data $9.
Mail order source for "choice and unusual fruit varieties for the connoisseur and home gardener," including fruiting quince and a number of Munson hybrid grapes.

Southern Exposure Seed Exchange
P.O. Box 158
North Garden, Virginia 22959
Catalogue $3.
Good mail order source for heirloom vegetable and flower seed.

Stark Brothers Nurseries
Box 10
Louisiana, Missouri 63353-0010
800-325-4180, FAX: 314-754-5290
Free color catalogue.
Established (since 1816) mail order source of fruits, nuts, and ornamentals, including figs, muscadines, persimmons, saucer magnolia, wisteria, mock orange, spiraeas, flowering almond, hydrangeas, and trumpet creeper.

Sunlight Gardens
174 Golden Lane
Andersonville, Tennessee 37705
615-494-8237 or 800-272-7396 (orders)
Informative catalogue $3 (two-year subscription).
Good mail order source of natives and perennials of the eastern United States, including native azaleas, blackberry lily, Carolina jessamines, honeysuckles, rose mallow, and trumpet creeper.

The Thomas Jefferson Center for Historic Plants
Monticello
P.O. Box 316
Charlottesville, Virginia 22902
Very informative newsletter and seedlist $1.
Great mail order and retail source of Jefferson-grown flower and vegetable seed.

Thompson and Morgan
P.O. Box 1308
Jackson, New Jersey 08527-0308
908-363-2225, FAX: 908-363-9356
Free beautiful, extensive color catalogue.
Excellent mail order source for hard-to-find flower and vegetable seed, including cockscomb, bachelor's buttons, rose mallow hibiscus, four-o'clocks, petunias, Johnny-jump-ups, zinnias, violets, mimosa, trumpet creeper, and althaea.

Vintage Gardens
2227 Gravenstein Highway South
Sebastopol, California 95472
707-829-2035
Beautiful, informative catalogue with extensive listings and dates of introductions $4.
Excellent mail order and retail source of many interesting antique roses.

Wayside Gardens
1 Garden Lane
Hodges, South Carolina 29695-0001
800-845-1124
Beautiful color catalogue $1.
Good mail order source of perennials and hard-to-find trees and shrubs, including roses, azaleas, honeysuckles, magnolias, flowering quinces, gardenia, althaeas, hydrangeas, nandinas, mock oranges, spireas, crossvine, trumpet creepers, Carolina jessamines, and wisterias.

William R.P. Welch
Grower of Narcissus Tazettas
P.O. Box 1736
Carmel Valley, California 93924-1736
408-659-3830, 408-645-0816 (pager)
Free informative price list.
World's most diverse selection of old polyanthus (cluster-flowered) narcissus. No orders accepted or sent out after October 1, as these like to be planted in late summer. Be sure to order 'Grand Primo', 'Erlicheer', and 'Golden Dawn'. Will also identify old narcissus samples sent to him at no charge.

Woodlanders
1128 Colleton Avenue
Aiken, South Carolina 29801
803-648-7522
Extensive catalogue $3.
Outstanding mail order listing of hard-to-find trees and shrubs for the South.

Yucca Do Nursery
Peckerwood Gardens
P.O. Box 655
Waller, Texas 77484
409-826-6363
Detailed catalogue $3.
Excellent mail order source of rare and hard-to-find plants, many from Mexico. Includes native magnolias, a number of mock oranges, Chinese quince, crossvines, honeysuckles, desert willow, and prickly pear.

—GG

Organizations

The Dallas Area Historical Rose Group
8636 Sans Souci Drive
Dallas, Texas 75238

The Heritage Rose Foundation
1512 Gorman Street
Raleigh, North Carolina 27606

Heritage Roses Group
810 East 30th Street
Austin, Texas 78705

The Historic Iris Preservation Society
12219 Zilles Road
Blackstone, Virginia 23824

International Oleander Society
P.O. Box 3431
Galveston, Texas 77552-0431

Southern Garden History Society
Old Salem Inc.
Drawer F, Salem Station
Winston-Salem, North Carolina 27108

The Texas Rose Rustlers
9426 Kerrwood
Houston, Texas 77055

The Thomas Jefferson Center for
Historic Plants
Monticello
P.O. Box 316
Charlottesville, Virginia 22902

Bibliography

Affleck, Thomas. *Southern Rural Almanac.* 1860. Louisiana and Lower Mississippi Valley Collections. Louisiana State University Libraries, Louisiana State University, Baton Rouge, Louisiana.

America's Garden Heritage, Handbook on Origins of American Horticulture. Plants and Gardens, Vol. 23, No. 3, Brooklyn Botanic Garden, 1968.

Austin, Max E., Khorsand Bondari, and W. Tom Brightwell. *Effects of Plant Spacing, Trellis System, Irrigation, Fertilizer Rate, and Spur Thinning on the Yield of Muscadine Grapes.* Athens, Georgia: Agricultural Experiment Stations, The University of Georgia, 1988.

Bailey, Liberty Hyde, and Ethel Zoe Bailey. *Hortus Third.* New York: Macmillian Publishing Co., 1976.

Bailey, Liberty Hyde. *The Standard Cyclopedia of Horticulture.* New York: The Macmillan Company, 1917.

Bartram, William. *Travels through North and South Carolina, Georgia, East and West Florida, Etc.* Philadelphia, 1791.

Bender, Steve, and Felder Rushing. *Passalong Plants.* Chapel Hill: University of North Carolina Press, 1993.

Bianchini, Francesco and Franscesco Corbetta. *The Complete Book of Fruits and Vegetables.* New York: Crown Publishers, Inc., 1976.

Bourne, H. *The Florist's Manual.* New York: Munroe and Francis, 1833.

Bowles, E.A. *The Narcissus.* London: Waterstone & Colk Ltd., 1985.

Breck, Joseph. *The Flower Garden, or Breck's Book of Flowers.* Boston: John P. Jewett and Company, 1851.

Britschneider, Emilio. *History of European Botanical Discoveries in China.* Leipzig: Unversandter Nachbuch, Koehler's Antiquorium, 1935.

Bryan, James Perry, ed. *Mary Austin Holley: The Texas Diary, 1835–1838.* Austin, Texas: University of Texas Press, 1965.

Buist, Robert. *American Flower-Garden Directory.* New York: C.M. Saxton, Barker and Co., 1860.

Coats, Alice M. *Garden Shrubs and their Histories.* 1964. New York: Simon and Schuster, 1992.

Condit, Ira J. *The Fig.* Chronica Botanica Co., 1947.

de Zavala, Adina. "In Grandmother's Old Garden Where the Rose Reigned as Queen." *San Antonio Express.* September 2, 1934.

Dirr, Michael A. *Manual of Woody Landscape Plants.* Champaign, Illinois: Stipes Publishing, 1990.

Dorman, Caroline. *Natives Preferred.* Baton Rouge, Louisiana: Claitor's Bookstore, 1965.

Downing, Andrew Jackson. *The Architecture of Country Houses.* New York: Dover Press, 1969.

Downing, Andrew Jackson, ed. *The Horticultural and Journal of Rural Art and Rural Taste.* Vol 4.

Drennan, Georgia Torrey. *Everblooming Roses.* New York: Duffield & Company, 1912.

Earle, Alice Morse. *Old Time Gardens.* New York: Macmillian Company, 1902.

Egolf, Donald R., and Anne O. Andrick. *The Lagerstroemia Handbook/Checklist.* American Association of Botanical Gardens and Arboreta, 1978.

Fairweather, Christopher. *Azaleas.* Chester, Connecticut: Globe Pequot, 1988.

Feathers, David, and Milton H. Brown, Editors. *The Camellia.* Columbia, South Carolina: R.L. Bryan Co., 1978.

Gardner, Jo Ann. *The Heirloom Garden.* Pownal, Vermont: Storey Communications, Inc., 1992.

Genders, Roy. *Pansies, Violas and Violets.* London: The Garden Book Club, 1958.

Gerard, John. *The Herbal.* 1633. Reprint. New York: Dover Publications, 1975.

Goyne, Minetta Altgelt. *A Life Among the Texas Flora: Ferdinand Lindheimer's Letters to George Engelmann.* College Station, Texas: Texas A&M University Press, 1991.

Hannibal, L.S. "Garden Crinums." *Louisiana Society for Horticultural Research,* Volume 3, Number 5, p. 269, 1972.

Hayward, Wyndham. "Nerine Sarniensis and Lycoris Radiata." *Herbertia,* Volume 3, pp. 132–133, 1936.

Hayward, Wyndham. "Nerine-Lycoris Error Disclosed." *Herbertia,* Volume 4, pp. 127–128, 1937.

Hedrick, U.P. *A History of Horticulture in America to 1860.* New York: Oxford University Press, 1950.

Henderson, Peter. *Henderson's Handbook of Plants and General Horticulture.* New York, 1890.

———. *Practical Floriculture: A Guide To The Successful Cultivation of Florists' Plants for the Amateur and Professional Florist.* New York: Orange Judd and Company, 1869.

Hill, Madelene, and Gwen Barclay, with Jean Hardy. *Southern Herb Growing.* Fredericksburg, Texas: Shearer Publishing Co., 1987.

Hillier Nurseries. *The Hillier Manual of Trees and Shrubs.* Sixth Edition. Melksham, Wiltshire: David and Charles Publishers, 1993.

Hume, H. Harold. *Camellias in America.* 1955. Revised Edition. Harrisburg, Pennsylvania: J. Horace McFarland Company, 1978.

———. *Azaleas and Camellias.* New York: Macmillan Publishing Co., 1936.

James, W.M. "Lycoris Radiata." *Herbertia,* Volume 3, p. 132, 1936.

Jekyll, Gertrude. *Wood and Garden.* London: Langmans Green & Co., 1899. Reprint. Salem, H.H.: The Ayer Co, 1983.

Jekyll, Gertrude, and Edward Mawley. *Roses for English Gardens.* London: Country Life, 1922. Reprint. Woodridge, Suffolk: Baron Publishing Co.

Kessenich, Greta M. *The Best of 75 Years.* Second Printing. American Peony Society. 1993.

Lawrence, Elizabeth. *Gardening for Love.* Durham, North Carolina: Duke University Press, 1987.

———. *The Little Bulbs.* Durham, North Carolina: Duke University Press, 1986.

———. *A Southern Garden.* 1942. Chapel Hill, North Carolina: The University of North Carolina Press, 1984.

———. *Through the Garden Gate.* Chapel Hill, North Carolina: The University of North Carolina Press, 1990.

Mallary, Peter, and Frances Mallary. *A Redouté Treasury.* New York: Vendom Press, 1986.

Martineau, Harriet. *Retrospect of Western Travel.* London, 1838.

M'Mahon, Bernard. *The American Gardener's Calendar.* Philadelphia: M'Mahon, 1806.

———. *The American Gardener's Calendar.* Ninth Edition, Greatly Improved. Philadelphia: A. M'Mahon, 1839.

Munson, R.W., Jr. *Hemerocallis, The Daylily.* Portland, Oregon: Timber Press, Inc., 1989.

Munson, T.V., D. Sc. *Foundations of American Grape Culture.* Denison, Texas: T.V. Munson & Son, 1909.

Newcomb, Peggy Cornett. *Popular Annuals of Eastern North America 1865–1914.* Washington, D.C.: Dumbarton Oaks, 1985.

Nottle, Trevor. *Old-Fashioned Gardens.* Kenthurst, New South Wales: Kangaroo Press, 1992.

Oleanders. Galveston, Texas: International Oleander Society, 1991.

Oppenheimer, Evelyn. *Gilbert Onderdonk.* Denton, Texas: University of North Texas Press, 1991.

Owens, Hubert B. *Georgia's Planting Prelate.* Athens, Georgia: University of Georgia Press, 1945.

Parkinson, John. *A Garden of Pleasant Flowers.* 1629. Reprint. New York: Dover Publications, 1976.

Pregill, Philip and Nancy Volkman. *Landscapes in History, Design and Planning in the Western Tradition.* New York: Van Nostrand Reinhold, 1993.

Robinson, William. *The English Flower Garden.* 1933. 15th edition. London: The Amaryllis Press, 1984.

Sargent, Charles Sprague. *The Trees at Mount Vernon.* Annual Report of the Mount Vernon Ladies' Association of the Union, 1926.

Stokes, James. "Notes on Georgia Camelliana." *The American Camellia Yearbook,* pp. 164–186, 1949.

Taylor, Raymond L. *Plants of Colonial Days.* Williamsburg: Colonial Williamsburg, 1952.

Thomas, Graham Stuart. *Shrub Roses of Today.* Revised edition. London: J. M. Dent & Sons, Ltd., 1980.

Thomas Jefferson's Garden Book. Independence Square, Pennsylvania: The American Philosophical Society, 1944.

Turnbull, Martha. *Rosedown Garden Diary, 1836–1895.* Transcription by C.A. Haines, 1958. Shelf #8. Hill Memorial Library, Louisiana State University, Baton Rouge, Louisiana.

Welch, William C. *Antique Roses for the South.* Dallas: Taylor Publishing Company, 1991.

———. *Perennial Garden Color.* Dallas, Texas: Taylor Publishing Company, 1989.

Wolfe, Russel S. "Lycoris Radiata and Nerine Sarniensis." *Herbertia.* Volume 4, pp. 124–127, 1937.

Index

Note: Page numbers in **boldface** indicate illustrations and captions.